Praise for *THE NATURE OF SOUTHEAST ALASKA*

"Unlike the standard nature guides that explain how to recognize common animals, *Nature* stresses the web of interrelationships that link the regional flora and fauna. This affectionate examination of some of North America's most spectacular surviving old-growth forests will delight backpackers and armchair naturalists."

—*Los Angeles Times Book Review*

"This is one book you must have along if you're planning to get marooned on a deserted Southeast Alaskan island. Since the authors—longtime Southeast teachers and biologists—have pondered everything in the Tongass from giant glaciers to the smallest no-see-ums, this book is probably the most comprehensive treatment you can get of the flora, fauna, and habitat of Southeast."

—*Ketchikan Daily News*

"*The Nature of Southeast Alaska* does a good job at weaving together scientific research, personal observations, and down-to-earth writing."

—*Sitka Sentinel*

"The authors write with humor and insight on a range of natural topics—from banana slugs and slime mold to glaciers, old-growth forests, and the reproductive problems of blueberry bushes. . . . This witty reference book goes beyond the traditional field guide, offering in-depth and entertaining insights."

—*Fairbanks Daily News-Miner*

"[This book is] the best Alaska regional nature guide. . . . Unlike some more technical field guides, this one can be read with pleasure by nonspecialists. Without sacrificing their concern for facts, the authors conspire to make their text readable by describing their own field ventures in a lively fashion that conveys their enthusiasm."

—*Anchorage Daily News*

THE NATURE OF SOUTHEAST ALASKA

A Guide to Plants, Animals, and Habitats

Rita M. O'Clair • Robert H. Armstrong
Richard Carstensen

Illustrations by Richard Carstensen

Alaska Northwest Books®
Anchorage • Portland

Second Edition 1997
Fourth printing 2003

Library of Congress Cataloging-in-Publication Data
O'Clair, Rita M., 1945–
    The nature of southeast Alaska: a guide to plants, animals,
  and habitats / Rita M. O'Clair, Robert H. Armstrong, Richard
  Carstensen ; illustrations by Richard Carstensen. — 2nd ed.
       p.   cm.
    Includes bibliographical references and index.
    ISBN 0-88240-488-1
    1. Natural history—Alaska.   I. Armstrong, Robert H., 1936–   .
  II. Carstensen, Richard, 1950–   .   III. Title.
  QH105.A4035   1997
  508.798—dc21   97–7949
                                                                   CIP

Managing Editor: Ellen Harkins Wheat
Editor: Lorna Price
Cover designer: Elizabeth Watson
Interior designer and cartographer: David Berger
Illustrations: Richard Carstensen

All photographs by the authors unless otherwise indicated.
Cover Photos. *Front cover: Mendenhall Lake and Glacier,* Mark Kelley;
Insets: (left) *humpback whale fluke,* Mark Kelley; (center) *shooting stars,*
Karen Jettmar; (right) *bald eagle,* Mark Kelley. **Back cover:** *black
oystercatcher,* Mark Kelley.

Alaska Northwest Books®
An imprint of Graphic Arts Center Publishing Company
P.O. Box 10306, Portland, OR 97296-0306
503/226-2402; www.gacpc.com

Printed in Hong Kong

CONTENTS

. . .

Color Plates, 81–88 and 185–92
Page references in the text indicate color illustrations.

PREFACE

■ ■ ■

Our collective enthusiasm for the natural history of Southeast Alaska precipitated this book. It started with the nature hikes. One of us would collect specimens; another would photograph them or take notes. Identifying things was the most pressing need initially. Then came the questions. How are plants such as yellow skunk-cabbage and early blueberry pollinated, since they often bloom before the snow melts and before we see insects flying about? What do short-eared owls eat? Why do some places support towering spruce forests, while others produce only scrubby pines and sphagnum bogs? Whether emerging together or singly from bog or forest, we came to wonder how each small piece fit into the greater puzzle of Southeast Alaska's natural history.

We pored over the available scientific literature, often collecting all the information we could find on a subject. We interviewed resident experts on tree physiology and pathology, landslides, brown bear denning behavior, and marine plankton. As the capital of Alaska and the headquarters of many state and federal research agencies, Juneau has a pool of professional biologists and geologists perhaps unmatched by any other city its size. And when local knowledge was insufficient, Rita O'Clair prompted the University of Alaska Southeast to bring in authorities on fungi, lichens, mosses, and insects to teach classes so intensive that our heads would swim dizzily for months afterward with new names and new insights. On a few occasions we set up our own research studies, but mostly we just observed and speculated.

We complemented each other well. Rita had a background in invertebrates and plants, Bob Armstrong in fish and birds, Richard Carstensen in mammals and community relationships. Our illustrative skills also dovetailed; Rita and Bob amassed encyclopedic photographic files, while Richard concentrated on ink drawings. We enjoyed teaching each other and dabbling in subjects that were new to us. We resisted the tendency to specialize, feeling that good generalists were sorely needed, we needn't be embarrassed to be dilettantes, and, finally, being generalists was fun! Slowly we realized we had become naturalists.

Eventually our interests and increasing knowledge all evolved into the rewarding task of teaching others. We taught courses and workshops in landforms, general biology, ecology, botany, zoology, habitat mapping, postglacial succession, natural history of Glacier Bay, old-growth forests, alpine and subalpine communities, wetlands, intertidal and marine habitats, bird identification, biology of freshwater fish, migration of Alaska's fishes, nature photography, animal tracks and sign, wild edibles, kayaking, and outdoor survival. We found that teaching others was also the fastest and surest motivation to teach ourselves, and with each class we learned perhaps more than most of our students.

In 1985 we decided to share our expanding insights with other Southeast Alaskans and began writing a monthly column on nature for the *Southeastern Log*, a newspaper published in Ketchikan and distributed free to all residents of Southeast. The *Log* essays provided the seed that grew into this book.

Our strongest motivation in writing *The Nature of Southeast Alaska* was to extend our teaching beyond the classroom to residents and visitors. The study of natural history is the first step in repaying our debt to the earth. We believe that to take our natural inheritance for granted is tantamount to ensuring its destruction. From teaching, we've learned that appreciation awakens a sense of stewardship. Our grandchildren deserve to inherit the sea lion rookeries, cedar groves, sedge flats, and sockeye runs that we are privileged to enjoy today.

ACKNOWLEDGMENTS

• • •

Many people helped us by providing information through interviews, by editing selected articles or chapters, and by the identification of specimens we had collected or photographed. We offer special thanks to the following individuals: Paul Alaback (old-growth forests, plants), Nancy Barr (assistance with field work), Dan Bishop (habitats, hydrology), Sam Bledsoe (mycorrhizae), Richard Bottorff (insects), Terry Brock (peatlands), Fenja Brodo (insects), Irwin Brodo (lichens), Richard Carlson (fish), Joseph Cook (mammals), Richard Gordon (birds, habitats), Tom Hanley (deer, skunk-cabbage), Al Harris (habitats), Lyle Hubbard (small mammals), Mike Jacobson (bald eagles), Jan Janssens (mosses, wetland ecology), Jim King (sea ducks, Vancouver Canada goose), Matt Kirchoff (old-growth forests), Gary Laursen (fungi, mycorrhizae), Donald Lawrence (plant succession), Dave Lubin (plants), Stephen MacDonald (mammals), Tom McCarthy (mammals), Mark Noble (alpine, succession), Chuck O'Clair (marine invertebrates), John Schoen (bears, bunchberry, skunk-cabbage), Mark Schwan (birds), Charles "Terry" Shaw (dwarf mistletoe), Greg Streveler (habitats, mammals), Doug Swanston (surficial geology), Gus Van Vliet (marbled murrelets), and Mary Willson (plant dispersal).

Bonnie Lippitt, Linda Mills, Catherine Pohl, and Graham Sunderland reviewed all or most of the manuscript and offered many useful suggestions.

In the beginning, Nikki Murray Jones provided much encouragement and editorial help when many of our ideas first appeared in the columns "Nature Southeast" and "The Southeast Naturalist" in the *Southeastern Log*. Ellen Campbell first suggested that we write this book.

Ellen Wheat gave us encouragement and helped make the book a reality. Lorna Price's editing always improved our writing, and her tactfulness at dealing with three sometimes-diverging authors kept us on track. To these Alaska Northwest Books editors and others behind the scene, we are especially grateful.

THE WILD SOUTHEAST

Southeast Alaska extends from Icy Bay, just north of the Malaspina Glacier, to the southern end of Prince of Wales Island. Some 525 miles long and 120 miles from east to west, Southeast is composed of a narrow strip of mainland mountains and over a thousand offshore islands of the Alexander Archipelago.

The defining features of "Southeast" are its wetness, its intimate interfingering of land and sea, its isolation from major human thoroughfares, and its *wildness*. Even our village boat harbors are half wild, with sea lions breathing among the slips at night, rich with sea smells and gull cries by day, and only a moment from uncrowded waterways and wild coastal forests, which rise abruptly into even wilder subalpine parkland. To help preserve this wildness, some 21 wilderness areas, encompassing about 43 percent of Southeast Alaska, have been established by Congress. These include the well-known Glacier Bay National Park, Admiralty Island National Monument, and Misty Fiords National Monument wilderness areas (p. 85).

About 77 percent of Southeast Alaska is Tongass National Forest, which, at 16.8 million acres, is the nation's largest. Within this forest lie the biggest tracts of virgin old-growth trees left in the United States. Southeast contains higher densities of both brown bears and bald eagles than any other place in the world.

The wildness of Southeast is further enhanced by its small human population and the relative lack of environmental destruction, a hallmark of thickly settled areas. Today, about 70,000 people are lucky enough to call Southeast Alaska "home," and most live in one of our 33 communities. With some 28,000 residents, Juneau is by far the largest.

The next two largest cities are Ketchikan (14,000) and Sitka (8400).

The climate of Southeast Alaska is moderated by maritime influences. The area is bathed by the Alaska Current, an eddy off the North Pacific Drift, which crosses the ocean from Japan. It buffers the winter sea temperatures, which average 42 degrees F, a full 10 degrees above freezing. On the other hand, the sea cools the area in summer, when sea temperatures average 55 degrees F, and produces a thick blanket of clouds, which obscures the sun for 85 percent of the year.

The same clouds inundate our area with precipitation, which is estimated to reach 400 inches per year in some places, such as the higher elevations on southern Baranof Island. Average precipitation in Skagway is only 27 inches (it lies in the Glacier Bay rainshadow), and at Ketchikan about 160 inches. One important consequence of this high rainfall is that fire has not much influenced our forest communities, as it has the coastal forests south of Vancouver Island, British Columbia.

The abundant precipitation also translates into numerous streams and lakes. Southeast Alaska is drained by over 40,000 miles of streams. We are blessed with over 20,000 lakes and ponds totaling over 260,000 acres (p. 84). Rivers tumble down mountains and out from beneath glaciers, carrying vast quantities of sediments that are deposited in nearshore tideflats. The Stikine Flats near Wrangell and Mendenhall Wetlands at Juneau are good examples of such wetlands supporting the sedge meadows crucial to migrating waterfowl and shorebirds, and also essential as nurseries for commercially important fish.

The structural backdrop of Southeast Alaska is its mountains, and one of the most remarkable features of the area is that you can easily pass from sea level to perpetual ice fields (p. 84) over a distance of only about 8 miles and an elevation gain of just 4000 feet. Summits of islands usually range from 2000 to 4000 feet, but much larger peaks define the Canadian boundary. Kates Needle at 10,023 feet dominates the Stikine Icefield. Mount St. Elias at extreme northern Southeast rises to just over 18,000 feet.

Big mountains spawn big events. In 1986 the Hubbard Glacier, which flows from ice fields near 15,300-foot Mount Hubbard, made world news by advancing to the mouth of Russell Fiord (p. 81), damming it and creating a lake for about 4 months. When this lake finally burst through the ice dam, it produced probably the largest water discharge in North America of the past few centuries.

A major volcanic eruption occurred about 9000 years ago, when Mount Edgecumb, on Kruzof Island west of Sitka, spewed forth ash that covered much of Southeast and can still be found in bog sediments hundreds of miles away. The most recent volcanic activity in Southeast was a lava flow down the Blue River, tributary to the Unuk, about 200 years ago. Several hot springs occur, the most famous of which are at Bell Island and Tenakee.

Incredibly large and beautiful caves have been discovered on Prince of Wales Island. These form by the action of water on soluble limestone and marble. On the surface this landscape, called *karst,* is equally spectacular. Fluted spires and bottomless sinkholes adorn the island summits. Foresters note that the carbonate bedrock supported Alaska's most magnificent forests. Most karst old growth has been logged, not only on Prince of Wales but on the carbonate rocks of Kuiu and Chichagof Islands and Lynn Canal. The search is on for remnant patches of karst old growth worthy of protection. Karst also holds secrets from the deep past. Bones of bear, deer, and marmot which stumbled into the sinkholes have awaited paleontologists for as long as 30,000 years.

Of course, what Southeast Alaska doesn't have is also important; this includes rattlesnakes, poison ivy, and frequent lightning storms!

The Nature of Southeast Alaska is about a place—its glacial history, landforms, natural communities, species interrelationships, and the roles played here by a few key plants and animals. Instead of the dipper, sand lance, and devil's club, we might have chosen the winter wren, the herring, and the salmonberry. Our selection includes those species about which we are most knowledgeable, as well as some that we wanted to learn more about. For the selected species, we offer far more detail than you will find in conventional identification guides. If we have omitted your favorite plant or animal, however, please accept our apologies. Each species offers its own fascinating window into the natural history of this wonderful part of Alaska we call home.

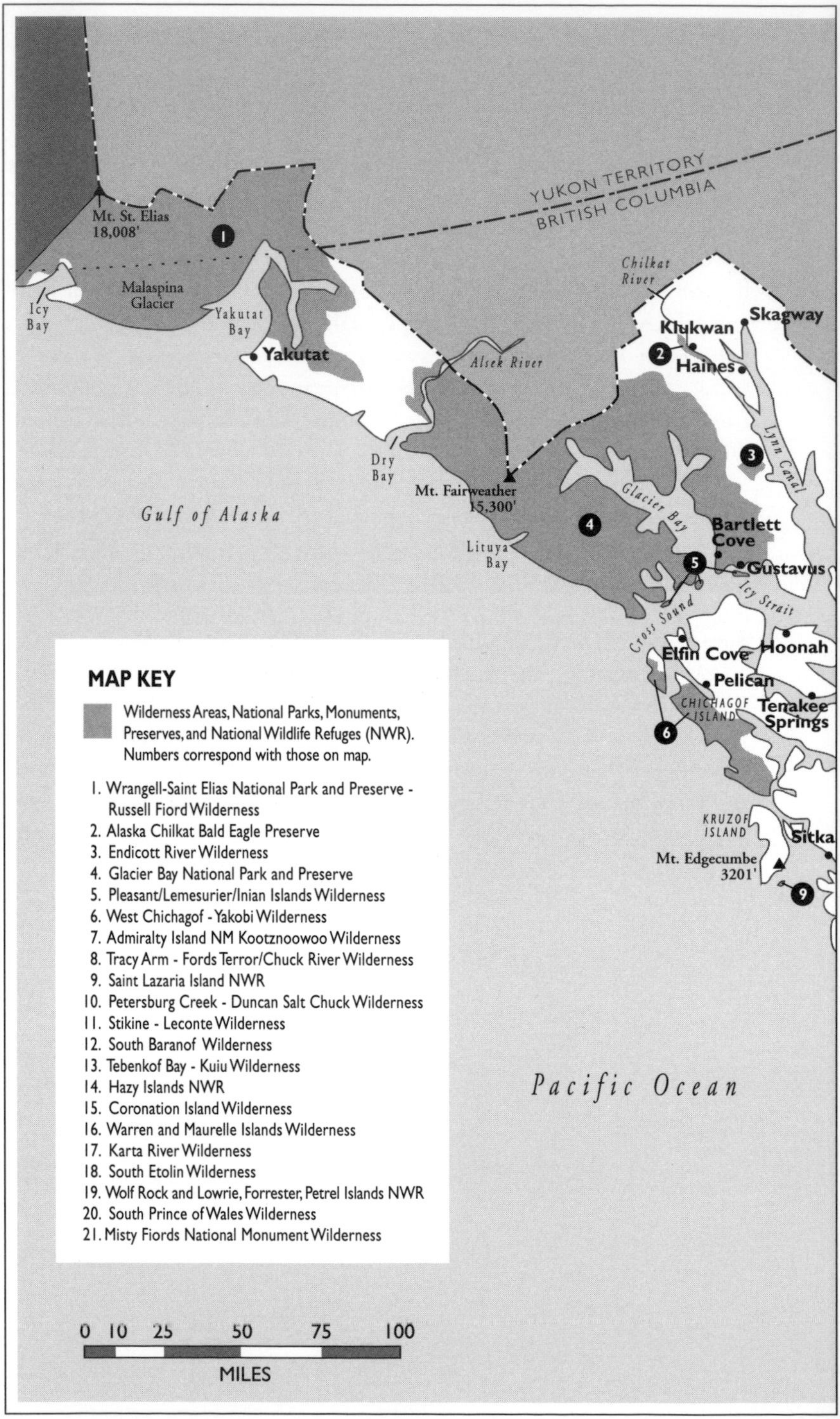

YUKON TERRITORY
BRITISH COLUMBIA

Mt. St. Elias
18,008'

Malaspina
Glacier

Icy
Bay

Yakutat
Bay

Yakutat

Chilkat
River

Klukwan

Skagway

Haines

Alsek River

Dry
Bay

Mt. Fairweather
15,300'

Gulf of Alaska

Lituya
Bay

Glacier Bay

Bartlett
Cove

Gustavus

Icy Strait

Cross Sound

Lynn Canal

Elfin Cove

Hoonah

Pelican

CHICHAGOF
ISLAND

Tenakee
Springs

KRUZOF
ISLAND

Mt. Edgecumbe
3201'

Sitka

Pacific Ocean

MAP KEY

Wilderness Areas, National Parks, Monuments,
Preserves, and National Wildlife Refuges (NWR).
Numbers correspond with those on map.

1. Wrangell-Saint Elias National Park and Preserve -
Russell Fiord Wilderness
2. Alaska Chilkat Bald Eagle Preserve
3. Endicott River Wilderness
4. Glacier Bay National Park and Preserve
5. Pleasant/Lemesurier/Inian Islands Wilderness
6. West Chichagof - Yakobi Wilderness
7. Admiralty Island NM Kootznoowoo Wilderness
8. Tracy Arm - Fords Terror/Chuck River Wilderness
9. Saint Lazaria Island NWR
10. Petersburg Creek - Duncan Salt Chuck Wilderness
11. Stikine - Leconte Wilderness
12. South Baranof Wilderness
13. Tebenkof Bay - Kuiu Wilderness
14. Hazy Islands NWR
15. Coronation Island Wilderness
16. Warren and Maurelle Islands Wilderness
17. Karta River Wilderness
18. South Etolin Wilderness
19. Wolf Rock and Lowrie, Forrester, Petrel Islands NWR
20. South Prince of Wales Wilderness
21. Misty Fiords National Monument Wilderness

0 10 25   50   75   100

MILES

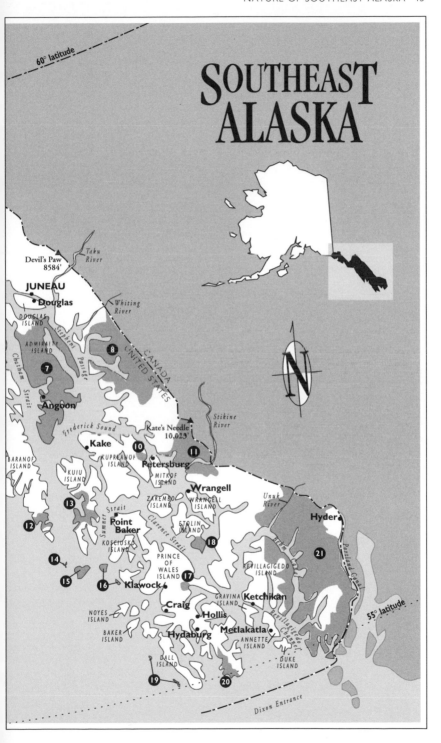

SOUTHEAST
ALASKA

60° latitude

Devil's Paw
8584'

Taku River

JUNEAU
• Douglas

Whiting River

DOUGLAS ISLAND

ADMIRALTY ISLAND

Chatham Strait

Stephens Passage

⑦

⑧

CANADA
UNITED STATES

• Angoon

Frederick Sound

Kate's Needle
10,023'

Stikine River

Kake

KUPREANOF ISLAND

⑩

Petersburg

⑪

BARANOF ISLAND

KUIU ISLAND

MITKOF ISLAND

Wrangell

Unuk River

ZAREMBO ISLAND

WRANGELL ISLAND

⑬

Sumner Strait

Point Baker

Clarence Strait

ETOLIN ISLAND

⑫

KOSCIUSKO ISLAND

⑱

Hyder •

Iskut

⑭

PRINCE OF WALES ISLAND

⑰

REVILLAGIGEDO ISLAND

㉑

Portland Canal

⑮

⑯ → Klawock •

• Craig

GRAVINA ISLAND

Ketchikan

Revillagigedo Channel

• Hollis

Metlakatla •

55° latitude

NOYES ISLAND

Hydaburg

ANNETTE ISLAND

BAKER ISLAND

DALL ISLAND

DUKE ISLAND

⑲

⑳

Dixon Entrance

N

HABITATS

. . .

CHAPTER 1

The overriding and underlying theme of Southeast Alaska is water, and inescapable moisture is the unifying feature of nearly all its habitats. From whales' permanent immersion to the banana slug's damp haunts, all our plants and animals must contend with it. Only when droughts shrivel the rest of North America do Southeast residents count their soggy blessings.

The amount and distribution of water is the most logical way to differentiate Southeast's many natural habitats. These range from ocean, lakes, ponds, and rivers, to frequently submerged salt marshes and stream flood zones, to perennially saturated bogs and other freshwater wetlands, to the usually drenched rainforest and alpine tundra. After a rare two-week drought, it's sometimes possible to sit in the forest understory without soaking our pants. But then the rains resume.

Then there are the habitats defined by solidified water—glaciers and high-country snowfields. The term "terrestrial" as applied to certain Southeast Alaskan habitats is somewhat generous; it actually means "occasionally free of water."

WHERE IS HERE? THE PACIFIC RAINFOREST—Southeast Alaska is a geographic unit defined by the open Pacific Ocean on the west and the boundary with Canada on the north, east, and south. In some cases the lines on maps are ecologically as well as politically significant. For example, if you climb east over the crest of the Coast Range into British Columbia (an expeditionary venture!), you enter more than just a different nation. Precipitation declines suddenly in the mountains' rainshadow. Flora and fauna are dramatically different. You've crossed a border in every sense of the word.

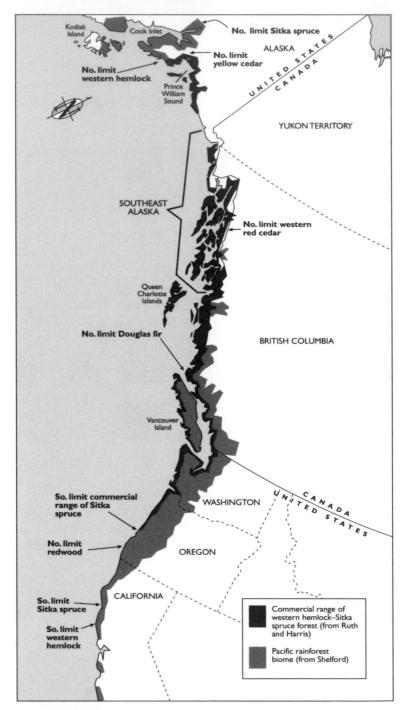

The Pacific Rainforest Biome

In other cases our political boundaries are ecologically arbitrary. Traveling south across Dixon Entrance into northernmost coastal British Columbia, one can detect no sudden differences in natural communities. In fact, many biogeographers would describe the immense North Pacific rainy coastline from Kodiak Island to Monterey, California, as a single ecologic unit or "biome," a geographic area with a distinctive plant community and climate. This unit extends as far inland as the influence of oceanic rain and humidity, from less than a mile in parts of coastal California to several hundred miles in Oregon and Washington.

Cool in summer and warm in winter, the Pacific rainforest biome is dominated by dense, wet, coniferous forest, with some of the greatest biomass (weight of living material per unit area) of any natural community in the world. Forest dominance grades from redwoods in California to Douglas fir, western red cedar, and western hemlock in Oregon, Washington, and southern British Columbia, to western hemlock and Sitka spruce in northern British Columbia and Southeast Alaska. The western hemlock–Sitka spruce forest also forms the seaward edge of the Pacific rainforest biome as far south as Coos Bay, Oregon, where coastal fog supplements summer rainfall, preventing drought. While western hemlock extends inland to the Rockies, Sitka spruce is intolerant of drought, and hugs the humid coast. Southward and inland from the coastal hemlock-spruce forest, the rest of the Pacific rainforest biome dries out enough in summer to be influenced by periodic fires. These fires need occur no more often than every 5 centuries or so to maintain the dominance of Douglas fir and, to the south, the coastal redwoods.

Relatively few new species of plants or animals are encountered as you travel northward from California to Alaska through the Pacific rainforest biome. Many species drop out, however, as they encounter climatic restraints or geographic barriers to colonization, or lose their favorite foods. The spotted owl and the Douglas fir extend northward roughly to the latitude of Vancouver Island. The mountain lion and the bigleaf maple reach the latitude of the Queen Charlotte Islands. Gapper's red-backed vole and western red cedar fade out in lower Southeast Alaska. A few species, such as the red-breasted sapsucker and shore pine, reach their northern limits in upper Southeast Alaska and are missing in Prince William Sound. Finally, these range limits are not static. In Misty Fiords some of the northernmost Pacific silver firs grow to 4 feet in diameter. These trees are certainly not at the limit of environmental tolerance, but are actively extending their range.

Glacial History of the Mendenhall Valley, near Juneau

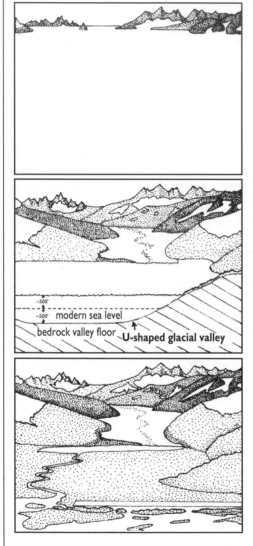

Top: **20,000 years ago, only summits higher than 5000 feet showed above the ice sheet. There were few plants or animals in Southeast Alaska.**

Center: **10,000 years ago glaciers had uncovered the valley, but the land remained depressed by the former ice load. The invading sea stood up to 500 feet higher than levels of today. There was little sediment on the sea floor, so "Mendenhall Bay" was nearly 1000 feet deep.**

Bottom: **Two events combined to put an end to Mendenhall Bay: the glacier dumped about 500 feet of sand, silt, and gravel into the bay; the land gradually rose, free of its burden of ice, lifting the bay bottom above sea level. This represents the valley today.**

GLACIAL HISTORY

Glaciers and their watery aftermath completely revised the topographic layout of Southeast Alaska, and glacial landforms now dictate the kinds and distributions of our upland, wetland, and aquatic habitats. About 20,000 years ago, at the height of the Wisconsin glaciation, almost all of Southeast Alaska was covered by ice. Above its highest extent, jagged, angular nunataks remain, peaks which once stood like islands in the sea of snow and ice. Below them, hills now gently rounded were completely overridden. Examination of this boundary between angular and rounded topography shows that the ice was 4000 to 5000 feet thick over the mainland, declining to about 2000 feet over the outermost islands.

GLACIAL LANDFORMS—Most of our large valleys were carved by glaciers into U shapes, with steep walls and fairly level floors. In contrast are the V-shaped valleys dug out since the end of the Wisconsin glaciation by streams, rivers, and associated minor landslides. These water-eroded drainages tend to occur on a smaller scale.

From Yakutat Bay at 60½ degrees north latitude to Portland Inlet at 55 degrees, all of the straits and inlets of the Inside Passage are glacial fiords. A fiord is simply a submarine U-shaped valley. The enormous thickness and weight of the geologically recent Pleistocene glaciers enabled them to gouge into the bedrock far below sea level. After the glaciers receded, salt water flooded these valleys.

Minor tributary glaciers couldn't gouge as deeply as the main trunk glaciers. They created so-called hanging valleys, with floors high above sea level. Streams emerging from them cascade steeply to the ocean. The 12,000 or so years since the ice left have not been long enough for stream erosion to rework the glacial contours.

SURFACE DEPOSITS—In addition to these tracks of glaciers on the bedrock of Southeast Alaska, the Wisconsin ice and its meltwaters were almost entirely responsible for the present distribution of loose, overlying materials. To make sense of our present mosaic of forests and bogs, lakes and wetlands, it helps to subdivide these surface deposits into glacial till, outwash, and lake-bed materials.

Glacial till ranges from huge boulders to cobbles, gravel, sand, silt, and clay. Some till is let down from stagnating ice (ablation till), whereas most till left by the Wisconsin episode was plastered down by the moving ice foot (lodgment till). A moraine is a ridge of till pushed up by an advancing glacier, or built by till melting out of the ice as a glacier pauses in its recession. The mix of coarse and fine materials in till gives it a moderate drainage that often supports forest communities.

Outwash, unlike till, is composed of particles roughly the same size. Formed by high-velocity waters gushing from the ice face, an outwash fan may be composed mostly of cobbles or even boulders. A cobble or gravel flat is "sorted"; the fine materials are washed away. As water velocity decreases downvalley, progressively smaller particles are found in the resulting outwash deposits. Coarse sorted outwash may also be buried under finer materials as the glacial source of meltwater

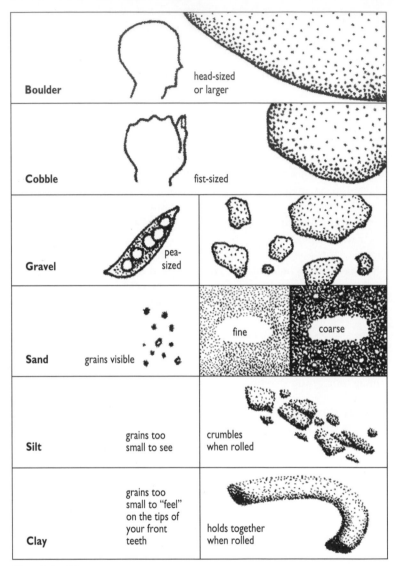

Boulder		head-sized or larger
Cobble		fist-sized
Gravel		pea-sized
Sand	grains visible	fine coarse
Silt	grains too small to see	crumbles when rolled
Clay	grains too small to "feel" on the tips of your front teeth	holds together when rolled

Particle Size

recedes up the valley and water velocity slows. Yet glacial rivers are always on the move, migrating back and forth across their floodplains. Therefore a wide variety of dominant particle sizes can be found on the suddenly abandoned outwash surfaces of any glacial valley. Rainwater percolates faster through coarse outwash materials than through unsorted glacial till, and these surfaces may even become excessively drained. Coarsely textured outwash flats are among the few sites in Southeast Alaska where roots of plants must occasionally contend with summer drought. Plants such as Nootka lupine with deep taproots are common on outwash (p. 186).

A constant settling of fine suspended sediments occurs in the large lakes at the snouts of glaciers. When these lakes eventually fill in, or when water levels drop, exposing bare mud to colonization by terrestrial plants, a very different succession begins. Former pond and lake beds, unlike till and outwash, are usually poorly drained. Sorted silts and especially clays may keep water continually at the ground surface. Trees often fail to grow here, and a freshwater wetland develops, which after many centuries can culminate in a bog or fen.

MARINE TERRACES AND GLACIAL REBOUND—During major ice ages, so much of the earth's water was locked up in the form of ice that sea levels dropped as much as 300 feet worldwide. But directly opposing forces operated near the centers of glaciation.

Throughout Southeast Alaska, the prodigious weight of glacial ice depressed the land twice as far as the global decline in sea level. For several thousand years after the Wisconsin ice sheet retired from the Alexander Archipelago, until the land rose again, ocean waves lapped against shorelines which today stand hundreds of feet above present sea level. Today's marine terraces are up to 500 feet above sea level and sometimes more than a mile inland from the coast. In addition to glacial rebound, mountain-building (tectonic) forces have raised some parts of Southeast as much as 8 vertical miles over millions of years. Separating postglacial from tectonic uplift, both of which vary in time and space, is a complex problem, currently under study by the U.S. Geological Survey.

SUCCESSION AND THE HABITATS OF SOUTHEAST ALASKA

The term "succession," fundamental to the study of natural history, means the change in plant and animal communities over time. The rate of change is usually greatest after a major disturbance. In addition to the dramatic glaciation of Southeast Alaska, other disturbances that punctuate the slow process of successional change are windstorms, floods, earthquakes, landslides, logging, insect infestation, and disease epidemics.

To study nature is to study change. Today's salt marsh may be forest in a century; today's forest may be bog in a millennium. To understand the present or to predict the future, we look into the past.

Succession is important to gardeners, forest managers, road maintenance crews, and beaver trappers. To unravel the mysteries of succession, ecologists try to start at the very beginning, searching out examples of disturbances so catastrophic that community recovery or "primary succession" must proceed almost from scratch. Virtually no living things or even organic soils are available on these sites; seeds and spores and colonizing animals must move in from elsewhere. The world's best examples are in such places as the suddenly emerged island of Surtsey off Iceland, and in Southeast Alaska, where retreating glaciers are still uncovering lifeless landscapes of till and outwash materials.

Each habitat has its own unique disturbance regime. For example, an avalanche may snap the trunks of spruce and hemlock but pass harmlessly over more flexible alders. Where avalanches happen every few decades, alder thickets may be maintained indefinitely. In old-growth forests throughout Southeast Alaska, the major disturbance is wind. Every few years a storm may topple some of the dominant trees, but subcanopy hemlocks grow up to fill the gap. Disturbance has some beneficial effects: uprooted trees expose fresh mineral soil; more light reaches down through the gap in the canopy; and understory plants are given a new lease on life.

FORESTS—For thousands of years after the great ice sheet receded, the initially cooler and drier climate resulted in alternating colonization by tundra plants, or alder and shore pine. Not until as recently as 7000 years ago did hemlock–spruce forests become well established on moderately drained surfaces. Today we find it hard to imagine Southeast Alaska without coniferous rainforests. Most of our *unforested* natural communities are either too wet (bogs) or too high (alpine/subalpine). Others are simply too young; that is, if given enough time without disturbance, a forest would develop there.

HIGH COUNTRY—Moving upslope from sea level, precipitation increases. More rain falls in summer, and more snow accumulates in winter. Combined with cooler temperatures and slower melt rate, this means that at the upper limit of tree growth, usually at about 2500 feet, the winter snowpack often remains until midsummer. Trees fail to establish here, resulting in a zone of lush subalpine meadows. The high bowls on Admiralty Island, for example, are filled with this meadow vegetation.

Proceeding upward from subalpine elevations, precipitation begins to taper off. Less snow falls in winter, and that which does, being drier and lighter, is often blown away by ferocious alpine winds. At these levels, we encounter true alpine tundra, a remarkably stable community that sustains itself in the face of unforgiving extremes of temperature and moisture. Tundra survives even on the nunataks at the head of Glacier Bay.

STREAMS, RIVERS, LAKES, AND PONDS—Because of their critical importance to sport and commercial fisheries, Southeast Alaskan streams and rivers are perhaps our most intensively studied natural habitats. Although they occupy only a small fraction of our total land mass, they could be viewed as a kind of circulatory system binding together the productivity of land and sea, mostly in the form of salmon and other fish which live in both fresh and salt water. Lakes and ponds further increase the productivity of any watershed.

FRESHWATER MARSHES AND WET MEADOWS—On terrain with good to moderate soil drainage, upland succession leads eventually to old-growth coniferous forest. But on poorly drained substrates, usually with fine sorted particles, a parallel successional process first leads to young freshwater wetlands and then culminates after many centuries in peatland. Dried-out or filled-in pond and lake beds, uplifted salt marshes, and annually flooded margins of streams and rivers are typical birthplaces of freshwater wetlands.

BOG—A youthful freshwater wetland has only a shallow depth of organic material overlying mineral substrate. If undisturbed, the undecomposed remains of mosses and sedges gradually build deep peat deposits. A true peat bog has at least several feet of this peat, which often represents many thousands of years of wetland succession. Bogs are also thought to eventually replace some old-growth forests, converting them to wetland over the course of millennia.

SALT MARSH—At the mouths of streams, and near the heads of protected bays and indentations in the coastline, fine sediments collect in the intertidal. Salt-tolerant species such as Lyngbye sedge and goose-tongue grow here. Salt marshes are coastal wetlands, of mid to upper intertidal elevations.

ROCKY INTERTIDAL—Most Southeast Alaska shoreline is quite steep. Thickly forested slopes plunge quickly into the ocean depths, and the horizontal extent of the intertidal zone is fairly limited. On these wave-pounded beaches the substrate is either bedrock or boulders. Here the vascular plants of the salt marsh cannot find a foothold, and the dominant organisms are seaweeds (marine algae) and invertebrates such as mussels and barnacles.

SALT WATER—This book emphasizes terrestrial and intertidal communities and species, but this is not to understate the importance of the

TRAFFIC

A great blue heron stands frozen in a tidal slough at the mouth of a river, eyeing a marine sculpin which, swallowed, it will carry to its roost in an old-growth spruce. The cutbanks reveal gray glacial silts, carried down from the grumbling ice face and trapped in the salt marsh by the leaves of sedges. Where the main channel slices through the mudflats, a hook-jawed salmon muscles its way into the cloudy currents, bound for a clear headwater spawning stream overhung with willow and alder. In the estuary traffic it passes mallards and dragon-flies that were born on the margins of a kettle pond in the upper valley.

As the bonds between species create communities, so the bonds between communities create watersheds and biomes, all of them shifting allegiances and fraying away at the edges, to the frustration and delight of those looking on.

ocean environment to the terrestrial and freshwater aquatic communities of Southeast. Rains blown in from the sea bathe our rainforests. Salmon battling up rivers feed bears, and their rotting carcasses nourish streamside vegetation. Nearly every terrestrial mammal, even the mountain goat, at some point comes down to the beach to eat. No one would consider the American robin or the yellow-rumped warbler to be seabirds, but even these species depend at times upon the ocean, scrounging for the goodies of the sea in spring when their terrestrial pickings are buried in the lingering winter snow.

PRIMARY SUCCESSION ON GLACIAL TILL

Glacial landforms left by the waning Wisconsin ice sheet dictate the arrangement of natural and human communities from Seattle to Manhattan. These areas have not seen large glaciers for 10,000 years. But in some wet coastal regions, cooling temperatures about 2000 years ago brought on another advance—the Neoglacial, or Little Ice Age. This episode was strongest in northern Southeast Alaska, where advancing glaciers reached their maximum downvalley positions as recently as the mid-1700s. Since that time most glaciers have receded, and in places such as Glacier Bay we can see in action the forces that once excavated Lake Superior, deposited the moraines of New England, and then slowly healed the devastated land.

Onto the raw surface creeps a procession of living things. From the first mosquito larvae, wriggling in puddles left by melting ice, to the woodpecker's nest in nearby old-growth forest, a story is written, perhaps the easiest reading in the world. By traveling from bare rubble at the ice face down-valley into mature forest and muskeg, we witness many of the same changes as those we would see if we were able to sit patiently on the rubble site for centuries. Ecologists have been coming to Southeast Alaska for just this purpose since the summer of 1914, when Professor William S. Cooper first visited Glacier Bay. Cooper's studies were continued and expanded by Professor Donald B. Lawrence, whose work, and ongoing support of further research, has established northern Southeast as a mecca for students of succession.

**Plumed seed of
dwarf fireweed**

THE PIONEERS—A chaotic jumble of rock and sand and ice lies at the glacier's snout. Even before embedded ice blocks finish melting, the first plant colonists arrive, wafted on breezes bearing tiny spores of mosses

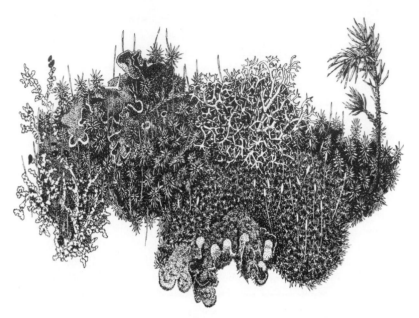

Pioneering plants on outwash or recently ice-covered sites. *Left to right:* **Easter and dog lichens, reindeer "moss" (actually a lichen), frayed-cap and haircap mosses, and seedling of Sitka spruce.**

and the plumed seeds of dwarf fireweed and willows. These extremely mobile seeds can travel miles from the parent plant, an advantage in upper Glacier Bay, where ice retreated so rapidly that vast wastelands distant from any seed source were uncloaked.

For a decade or more, only occasional sprouts and tufts of moss dot the gray till wreckage. Gradually green patches expand and merge over the bare mineral substrate. The frayed-cap moss is common in these pioneering stages, binding loose rubble and providing a moist seedbed for later colonizers. Northern horsetails and Drummond mountain avens move in, along with dog and Easter lichens. Also germinating are shrub and tree seedlings, not yet obvious, which in a short time will completely alter the face of the land.

Succession involves animals as well as plants. The first adventurers into deglaciated places include wolf spiders, hover flies, Dolly Varden, threespine sticklebacks, American pipits, black-legged kittiwakes, dusky shrews, and wolverines.

THE HOMESTEADERS—Pioneering plants are adapted to stressful environments and are usually small, quick to reproduce, and short-lived. They're soon replaced by more durable "homesteaders," such as willow and black cottonwood. These arrive in the first wave of colonization, but on the sterile soils they grow slowly, yellow-leaved and prostrate.

The first homesteader to thrive is Sitka alder. Alder is a nitrogen-fixer like beans and clovers. This thicket-forming species has a winged seed, which flies shorter distances than plumed seeds and may reach the site a bit later. Leaf litter from the alder adds even more nitrogen per acre to the soil than a farmer's alfalfa, and the willow and cottonwood respond with rapid upright growth. Within about 40 years from time of deglaciation, many cottonwoods stand well above the 15- to 20-foot alders.

Those few hardy souls thrashing through the alder thickets find lots of prickly saplings of Sitka spruce which, like alder, has a winged seed and usually arrives at about the same time. Spruces are intolerant of thick shade and may remain suppressed for decades in the thickets. But like cottonwood, they benefit from soil enrichment by alder-leaf litter, and when they eventually emerge into direct sunlight they grow rapidly.

Few low-growing plants survive the dense shade of

"Homesteaders." One-sided wintergreen in Sitka alder–leaf litter. Ground-cone at right.

alder thickets or the annual autumn burial under leaves. The bizarre ground-cone has solved both of these problems. Most commonly parasitic on alder roots, it produces no chlorophyll and has no need for light. Its stiff, upright stem is ideal for deflecting falling leaves. Other common species of the alder understory are the wintergreens, a genus of semisaprophytic plants. Saprophytes are the plant counterparts of scavengers, subsisting on dead plant and animal matter. While semisaprophytes are capable of photosynthesis, they can endure deep shade. Wintergreens need rich humus and are aided by fungi in their breakdown of organic materials. Their tiny seeds are easily carried by breezes. They appear with the alder and persist into the spruce forest stages, when the decline in soil nutrients starves them.

Mosses and lichens do poorly in the alder litter. Instead they take to the branches. There, as epiphytes (plants which grow on other plants), they escape smothering and find more light. They luxuriate as the alders mature and lean over, until the last dying trunks are enveloped in greenery.

The alder–willow thickets and mixed spruce–cottonwood forests, which mellow the harsh postglacial land, also support more animals. Black flies, fungus gnats, boreal toads, orange-crowned warblers, hermit thrushes, deer mice, snowshoe hares, and beaver all probably peak in population density during these successional stages.

THE BOURGEOISIE—The barren terminal moraines abandoned two centuries ago by Little Ice Age glaciers are now covered with even-aged spruce forests, a kind of ecological middle class. Cottonwoods are on their last legs, with a meager show of foliage high in the crowns, hemmed in and overtopped by conifers. An occasional remnant of the earlier alder jungles leans rotting at the edge of an opening. Most settled into the humus a century ago.

These stands are well on their way to old-growth conditions, but lack that aura of rich decadence found in fully mature old-growth stands. The spruces' growth may have slowed, but few are dying. Western hemlocks are only just beginning to share the upper canopy; most are less than half the diameter and age of the spruce. Hemlocks are far more shade-tolerant than spruce, and they reach into canopy gaps wherever these appear. Few small live spruce remain. Within another century, the dominance of these stands will begin to shift from spruce to hemlock.

Winged seed and cone of Sitka spruce (not on same scale)

Two centuries is just a moment in terms of soil development. If we dig through the duff on the forest floor we very quickly come to glacial till. The few down logs to be found are mostly in the early phases of decay. Rotting wood, standing and down, is the signature of old growth.

Mosses, now free of the smothering alder litter, can again cover the ground, but different species are involved. Step moss and little shaggy moss now blanket almost 100 per cent of the forest floor. There are only hints of the vascular floral richness that will grace the old-growth understory. The overhead foliage is interlocking and admits little light. Plants like bunchberry and blueberry are making their first tentative appearance.

Most lichens retain the epiphytic niche chosen during the alder-thicket successional stages, but new species now bedeck spruce trunks and branches. The fantasy world of the lichen community, studied by naturalists on their bellies in pioneering stages of postglacial succession, is still best viewed from 8 inches away. Conveniently, that's about the distance of a tree trunk from our noses, as we scramble into the high canopy.

Birds nesting in these young coniferous forests include Townsend's warblers, varied thrushes, Pacific-slope flycatchers, and winter wrens. Most of these species probably fare somewhat better in structurally more diverse old-growth forests, but we find no lack of them on the terminal moraines of Little Ice Age glaciers. Brown creepers, red-breasted nuthatches, and several woodpeckers, all dependent on snags for nesting and feeding, no doubt prefer old growth. But ecologists have yet to relate the habitat requirements of individual bird species to stand age in Southeast Alaska. As we cut down our old-growth forests, these questions beg for answers.

Population densities of porcupines and red squirrels probably peak in the even-aged forests and decline slightly with the transition to old growth. The reverse is expected for northern flying squirrels, which usually nest in snags. The most studied mammal in Southeast Alaska is the Sitka black-tailed deer. Partly because its critical winter foods are blueberry, bunchberry, and other low-growing evergreen plants uncommon in the young spruce forests, the deer is scarce in recently deglaciated regions. The northern red-backed vole is the most abundant small rodent in the forest and probably achieves greatest population density in old growth, where rotting down logs provide cover.

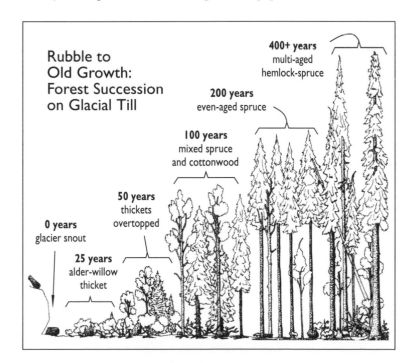

Rubble to
Old Growth:
Forest Succession
on Glacial Till

400+ years
multi-aged
hemlock-spruce

200 years
even-aged spruce

100 years
mixed spruce
and cottonwood

50 years
thickets
overtopped

0 years
glacier snout

25 years
alder-willow
thicket

SUCCESSION OF UPLIFTED MARINE TERRACES—Glacial recession since the end of the Little Ice Age has also driven successional development along our coastlines, miles away from those areas actually covered by ice. Just as the Wisconsin ice sheet pressed the land down, raising sea levels throughout Southeast, the Little Ice Age again depressed the land, but on a smaller and more localized scale.

In northern Southeast, studies of tidal gauges have revealed that the land is now rising relative to sea level. Near Glacier Bay, crustal uplift is occurring at about 1.5 inches per year. Along the seaward edge of the Gustavus Forelands (p. 85), scattered trees are colonizing the uplifted tideflats. Near Haines, the rebound rate is about 0.9 inch per year, and in Juneau about 0.5 inch per year. The land is now rising fastest where presumably it was most depressed. Geophysical evidence is accumulating, however, which suggests that glacial rebound is not the only cause of uplifting shorelines. Gravity studies indicate that in the Glacier Bay area tectonic forces may predominate over glacial rebound.

Whatever its cause, uplift leaves unmistakable evidence on beaches and in the immediate forest fringe. Rotting drift logs may be found, now overgrown by lush meadow. They were stranded there by high tides a few decades ago, when the land was several feet lower.

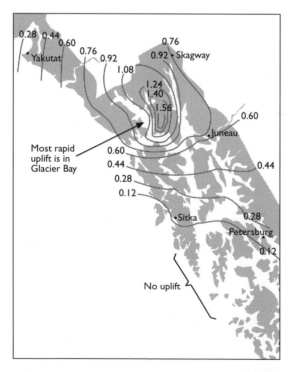

Rate of Crustal Uplift

Contours show inches of uplift per year (from Hicks and Shofnos)

Pushing back into the forest, we often find abrupt escarpments, now held in place by tree roots, but originally shaped by waves.

In most watersheds north of Petersburg and Sitka, the amount of recently uplifted shoreline far exceeds that of land uncovered by Little Ice Age glaciers. Post-uplift succession affects our coastal habitats, such as salt marshes and rocky intertidal beaches, which are even more valuable to people and wildlife than habitats developing in deglaciated valley headwaters. South of the area of active uplift, old-growth forests often come right down to the high-tide mark, and transitional meadows and thickets are less extensive.

Will uplift continue to provide new land along our coast? The greenhouse effect may introduce yet another factor. Predictions for worldwide sea level rise, as a result of warming climates and melting polar ice, range from 2 to 10 feet over the next 100 years. It isn't known whether northern Southeast Alaska's rising shoreline will continue to offset the rise in sea level.

OTHER KINDS OF SUCCESSION—Postglacial and post-uplift succession are only two varieties of community redevelopment on disturbed terrain. Although we can draw some conclusions based on the similarities and differences between these two examples, it's unwise to extrapolate too casually to other kinds of succession. While glacial rubble and raised beaches support primary succession, most other examples of succession are "secondary"; that is, the community dominants maybe killed, but abundant organic material, seeds, and surviving organisms remain to reoccupy the site. After logging, for example on Forest Service study sites at Maybeso Valley on Prince of Wales Island, conifers may spring up to close canopy in less than 20 years. This preempts the deciduous stages, minimizing growth of alder, cottonwood, and willow typical of primary postglacial succession, in turn providing less food for beaver, moose, and most warblers. And succession will be still different after avalanche, flooding, or storms that blow down trees.

OLD-GROWTH FORESTS

Much of what ecologists know about temperate old-growth forests has been learned since the late 1970s in the Douglas fir–western hemlock communities of Washington and Oregon. Meanwhile, Southeast Alaska has just begun to get the attention it deserves. Our western hemlock–Sitka spruce forests are in some ways comparable to the forests of the Oregon Cascades and coast ranges. In both areas, for example, it takes at least 250 years to produce true old growth. But the forests of Southeast are by no means carbon copies of their more southerly counterparts. Two significant differences are the lack of major forest fires here and the more critical role played by our old-growth forests as wintering habitat for black-tailed deer.

Old-growth forests are "multi-aged." Many age-classes of trees are present, from saplings to old-timers, assuring a sustainable cycle of decay and regeneration (p. 83). Trees weakened by insects and fungi are toppled during storms, opening gaps in the forest canopy that eventually are filled by the extension of tree branches and by young hemlocks and occasional spruces growing into the opening. Instead of fire, periodic gales, usually from the southeast, are the major disturbance to our coastal forests. The most damaging storms occur in fall and winter, usually in combination with heavy rain or snow.

UNDERSTORY PLANTS—The patchy old-growth canopy causes an equally patchy growth of herbs and shrubs on the ground below. In the resulting mosaic of ground cover, plants such as blueberry, bunchberry, five-leaf bramble, and fern-leaf goldthread may flourish. These plants are critical winter forage for Sitka deer. Many low-growing vascular understory plants are evergreen, an advantage in dimly lit places. Rather than relying too much on seed reproduction, they spread by extending rhizomes or runners, and can reach quickly into newly opened gaps when a tree falls.

Elaborate microcommunities of mosses and lichens live high above the ground on branches of conifers. These mosses and lichens are epiphytic—growing on, but not parasitizing the conifers. They subsist mainly on nutrient-containing dew, rainwater, and fog. Epiphytic lichens feed old-growth mammals like the northern flying squirrel, and when blown to the ground are eagerly consumed by Sitka deer. Many species are also nitrogen-fixers, and studies in the Cascades have shown that soil nitrogen benefits from litter-fall and the rain leaching off epiphytic lichens.

Southeast Alaska is a close runner-up to the Queen Charlotte Islands of British Columbia as the moss capital of the world. In old growth and in sphagnum bogs, moss serves as a sponge, moderating the effects of rainstorms, and preventing its vascular associates from being swept away to sea.

Coral-root orchids and the wintergreen relatives pinesap (p. 191) and Indian pipe live in old growth. All these plants are saprophytic; assisted by soil fungi they feed on organic materials in the soil and, unlike most green plants, don't use sunlight to make their own food. Some may be connected via fungi to the roots of green plants, parasitizing them. Because they don't need sunshine, these saprophytic plants thrive in dense shade.

OLD-GROWTH ANIMALS—Snags over 20 inches in diameter with

MARBLED MURRELETS

Although marbled murrelets are widespread in Southeast Alaska and number between 25,000 and 40,000, only one nest has ever been found here (p. 186). The nest was 51 feet above the ground in thick moss that covered a branch of a mountain hemlock tree, about three-quarters of a mile from salt water on the steep slopes of east Baranof Island. This nest and those found in other regions, as well as other evidence, has led scientists to conclude that marbled murrelets from Prince William Sound to California nest in and depend upon the old-growth coniferous forests.

Old-growth dependency may relate to the luxuriant thick moss on which females lay their single egg. According to one report, this moss does not appear on large branches of conifers of the Pacific Northwest until the forest is 150 or more years old. And old-growth trees have a more open crown structure, which would allow the birds access to and from their nests. Marbled murrelets, like all alcids, have short, narrow wings better designed for "flying" underwater in pursuit of fish than for aerial maneuvering and landing in tight places.

In British Columbia, where biologists estimate 20,000 to 30,000 murrelets live, the species is already listed as threatened. Meanwhile, the numbers of marbled murrelets in Washington, Oregon, and California (fewer than 9000 total) have only just recently been proposed to be listed as a threatened species under provisions of the Endangered Species Act. Like the spotted owl, murrelets are considered to be at risk from the logging of ancient coniferous forests. Unlike the spotted owl, however, the marbled murrelets face additional threats to their existence, from the continued discharge of large quantities of oil into their marine environment and from pervasive mortality in coastal gill-net fisheries throughout much of their range.

well-decomposed centers are valuable to excavating woodpeckers. Later, holes carved out by hairy woodpeckers and red-breasted sapsuckers may be renovated by so-called secondary cavity nesters—chestnut-backed chickadees, and small owls such as the northern saw-whet (p. 185), western screech, and northern pygmy. The availability of such cavities may limit population size for some birds.

Other characteristic breeders in the old growth are Townsend's warblers, Pacific-slope flycatchers, brown creepers, varied and hermit thrushes, winter wrens, red-breasted nuthatches, and marbled murrelets. Sharp-shinned hawks and northern goshawks find both breeding and hunting habitat in old growth. Bald eagle nests typically are found in the largest spruces of the coastal forest fringe.

Mammals of Southeast Alaska tend to use a wider range of habitats than do birds, and few spend all of their time in old-growth forests. On the other hand, there are very few mammals that never use old growth. Mammals with especially strong ties to ancient forests are the marten, Sitka black-tailed deer, and northern flying squirrel (p. 87). For others, the connection may be less clear but in some places just as critical. For example, some mountain goats descend into cliffy but forested habitats in winter, when their alpine range is buried in snow. River otters need old forests because roots of big trees provide the best den sites, and indirectly because of the value of old growth to salmon.

DEAD WOOD—A constant refrain among old-growth researchers is that nature never wastes dead wood. From death until they are completely rotted, trees give food and shelter to a complex succession of forest plants, animals, and fungi. A spruce log 30 inches in diameter may require 50 years or more to fully return to the soil. Spruce heartwood, high in lignin, rots slowly, but large hemlocks usually have heart rot even when living and decompose more rapidly. Wood-boring insects begin the breakdown, tunneling through sapwood, admitting oxygen, and transporting fungi and microbes. Bacteria in logs break down wood and fix nitrates usable by plants.

Fallen logs help prevent the erosion of forest soils, especially on steep slopes. A rotting log stays moist inside, even in times of drought. Down logs provide nurseries for hemlock seedlings. Logs without bark, in advanced stages of decay, provide the optimum rooting environment for trees that will dominate tomorrow's old growth.

Birds and mammals use rotting logs too. Bears tear them apart in search of insects, and small mammals use logs as protected runways through the forest. Some mammals and birds build their nests within the hollows of fallen logs.

Logs that fall across streams in the forest slow the current and create small pools, which dissipate the erosive energy of the stream, stabilize streambeds, and impound fine sediments, creating more diverse stream habitat. Stream logs also feed aquatic invertebrates. High populations of invertebrates, in turn, enhance the populations of many species of fish that feed upon them. The fisheries values of streams and rivers are therefore dependent on the quality of the forests surrounding them.

Small streams in the forest are protected by the canopy. This

Red-breasted sapsucker on western hemlock. The bird drills holes through bark and returns later to lick the sweet, congealed sap.

OLD GROWTH AND LOGGING

The Tongass is the largest national forest in the United States and contains some of the world's last extensive patches of commercially attractive temperate old-growth forest. Logging in this forest is highly controversial. In spite of the recent passage of the Tongass Timber Reform Act, which permanently protected many key drainages, clearcutting of ancient forests continues at alarming speed.

What exactly is in jeopardy? Although the Tongass National Forest contains about 17 million acres, only 7.8 million acres of this is forested (the rest is alpine, muskeg, wetlands, freshwater systems, etc.), and although much of this 7.8 million acres is very old forest, only a small percentage is considered to be really prime old growth dominated by massive conifers. These stands, of more than 50,000 board feet per acre, now make up less than 2 percent of the Tongass. The mean volume harvested per acre as of 1981 was 37,000 board feet, which included half of those stands of more than 50,000 board feet per acre which had existed in 1950. These stands are critical deer winter habitat and are essential to the stability of our finest salmon streams.

cover provides some degree of insulation, which can help keep small streams from freezing solid in early winter before snowfall is adequate to bridge them. Small fish in streams need running water to stay alive. The surrounding old-growth forest is also the source of much of the nutrient input to small streams in the form of dropped branches and leaves.

With all of the public controversy over management of old-growth forests, it behooves naturalists and researchers to decipher the true ecological role of ancient forest communities. It can be tempting to paint old growth as a paradise, rich in everything from berries to songbirds. But to most wildlife, the richest summer forage communities are those where frequent disturbance prevents establishment of conifer forest. As measured by ecologists, productivity is higher in early successional communities like salt marshes and lush subalpine meadows than in stable, mature forests. And young, unstable communities with strong annual pulses of "boom and bust" offer up more of their productivity to animals from neighboring communities than do old-growth forests, which tend to hoard their production. The problem with these "generous" young communities is that in winter they shut completely down. Vegetation dies back, and everything is buried in snow. Old growth then becomes survival habitat, not so plenteous and appealing to most animals as wetlands or upland meadows, but at least available in hard times.

Even the "productive" salmon streams of our stable, high-volume, old-growth forests are not the real source of fish biomass. Salmon fatten mostly in the ocean, not in the streams. Old-growth streams are not producers but *protectors* of fish, during the critical spawning and early rearing phases of their life cycle.

If young communities are nature's grocery stores, old communities are the banks, where productivity is hoarded and nurtured and carefully rationed out. Old growth is not our breadbasket. The real "resource" of old growth is buried in the bonds between species, in the elderly way the pieces fit together, in longevity, and in the thousand lessons we've not yet learned.

HIGH COUNTRY

If biologists know little about Southeast Alaskan old growth, they know even less about the mountains at our back door. This can't be from lack of romantic appeal. Watching a shaggy goat scale a nearly vertical cliff and disappear into a cloud should be enough to motivate any researcher. The reason for our ignorance is that agencies funding research deal with resources, and our most recognized commodities are trees and salmon. Timber harvest is not possible above treelimit, nor do salmon run that high.

Unlike circumstances in the Rocky Mountain and Pacific Crest states, mountain recreation is limited in Southeast Alaska. Except for Juneau (p. 82), few communities offer extensive networks of trails into the high country, and a stroll along most of our alpine ridgetops first involves 3000 feet of off-trail bushwhacking through forests and thickets. We are unaware of any popular book or magazine article on any aspect of the natural history of our mountain habitats. And local scientific literature on alpine habitats is scanty. To assemble the following picture of Southeast's alpine natural history and elevational zonation, we've relied on our personal experiences in the mountains of Juneau, Admiralty Island, Glacier Bay, Haines, and Skagway.

Mountain goat

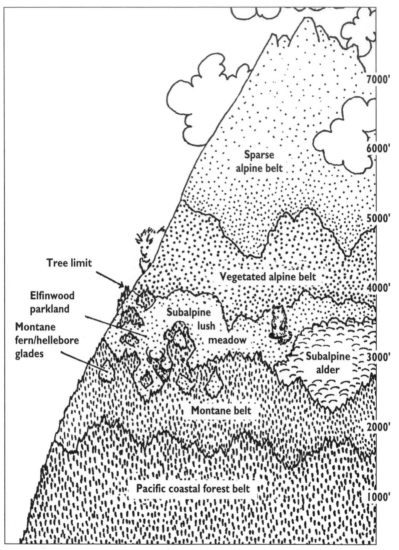

Mountain Communities

MONTANE FORESTS—At about 1500 feet above sea level, mountain hemlock begins to replace western hemlock as the dominant forest tree. Sitka spruce persists up to treelimit. Gradually trees become smaller and gnarlier, and the forest is more frequently broken by ferny glades, seeps, and brushy slide areas. Plants like false hellebore hint that we're nearing the upper limit of the forest. Invaders from higher communities, such as deer cabbage and Mertens' cassiope, appear in the understory. The scrubby high-elevation forests with their plentiful openings and "edges" have diverse and often luxuriant herbs and shrubs and are very important to Sitka deer. Mountain goats take refuge in cliffy forested areas during severe winter weather. Marten hunt the high montane forests for northern red-backed voles and other small rodent prey.

TREELIMIT—Extremely harsh winter conditions may be tolerated by trees, as long as the summer growing season offers enough warmth for reproduction. One of the most significant of all ecological transitions occurs where trees can no longer survive. Throughout the northern hemisphere, in those places where mean July temperatures run colder than 50 degrees F, trees cannot become established. This applies to both Arctic tundra, which is north of the 50-degree "mean summer isotherm," and alpine tundra, which lies above it.

The elevation of the 50-degree isotherm has not been determined for Southeast Alaska, but we suspect that on many slopes it lies much higher than the highest trees. Other factors such as slope steepness and direction, wind, soil water, and snow accumulation can depress treelimit well below the 50-degree isotherm potential. In humid coastal mountains, snow depth is especially important. Studies in the coast ranges of southern British Columbia found that depth of the late winter snowpack increased from sea level into the subalpine, where it peaked, and then declined at greater alpine elevations.

Maritime mountains also have much wetter snow than interior ranges. In spring, this saturated snow begins to creep slowly downhill. The woody-stemmed plants at treelimit, such as blueberry, Sitka alder, copper bush, and saplings of mountain hemlock, are either temporarily flattened or snapped off. Mountain hemlocks which endure decades of this "snowcreep" may eventually grow upright, but their bases bear evidence of the power of moving snow.

SUBALPINE MEADOWS—In some places one can step directly from montane forest to alpine tundra, but in Southeast Alaska this is quite unusual. More commonly we encounter a subalpine "ecotone," or interfingering of the elements of forest and alpine. On steep slopes just above treelimit with deep winter accumulations of snow, severe snowcreep and avalanches destroy all woody-stemmed plants. Instead, tall perennial meadow herbs spring up in June after snow melt and wilt back in the fall. These subalpine meadows are arrested by snowcreep in an early successional condition. Except for their

Snowcrook in mountain hemlock, caused in sapling stages by being flattened under the downward-creeping spring snowpack.

Spotted gentians, yellow mountain-heather, and starry cassiope.

steepness, they remind us of lowland coastal meadows and support many of the same species—cow parsnip, lady fern, and fireweed. Herbs more restricted to the subalpine meadows are deer cabbage, Sitka valerian, monkshood, and spotted gentian.

It would be hard to overestimate the value of subalpine meadows to the wildlife of Southeast Alaska. Deer spend the summer fattening here, and where the lush forage is close to cliffy escape habitat, mountain goats may venture. Bears sometimes just slide downhill on their bellies, raking herbs into their mouths as they go. Marmots grow so bulgy and wide that they could be run down by a fit human, and must remain close to their burrow entries. Female blue grouse (p. 185) flush underfoot, clucking warnings to their hunkered broods. Insects abound. Two ground-nesting songbirds common in our lowland beach meadows are also found in the subalpine—the savannah and Lincoln's sparrows. Where willow-lined creeks wind through subalpine bowls, the "Oh dear me" song of the golden-crowned sparrow may be heard.

The high country underwent dramatic changes in the Little Ice Age. Alpine cirque glaciers swelled, and even unglaciated slopes received more snow. Montane hemlock forests, especially in bowls, were erased by perennial snowfields. Treelimit in many places was lowered, and with the improving climate of recent decades, forests are painstakingly recovering lost ground. Succession takes much longer at high elevations, but has similarities to that of lowland glacial valleys. Dense alder thickets are common features of treelimit. As with Southeast's lush subalpine meadows, we believe subalpine alder thickets may in some locations represent successional stages in the return of montane forests to their pre–Little Ice Age elevations.

ALPINE TUNDRA—One commonly hears the misleading term "alpine" applied to all Southeast Alaskan habitats above treelimit. The moist fields of ferns and umbellifers just above the montane forest bear little resemblance to genuine alpine tundra, which is often hundreds of feet higher, with drier, thinner snow cover that is often blown away by violent winds. Alpine plants must be far more tolerant of desiccation than those of subalpine meadows, which are sheltered under deep snow throughout the winter.

The ability of wind to redistribute snow makes microtopography extremely important in the alpine zone, creating a vivid mosaic of tiny communities with very crisp boundaries. In a small hollow where snow-drifts persist throughout the winter, some plants, like the mountain marsh-marigold, may be fairly tender and succulent. Immediately next to this "late snowbed" community, on ridges or prominences, winter conditions can be so harsh that the ground is quite barren of plants except in the lee of boulders. This drier alpine habitat is referred to as a fellfield community, in which dwarfed creeping leathery plants, such as alpine azalea, and cushion plants, like moss campion, are the only vascular survivors. Lichens such as rock tripe, map lichen, and worm lichen cling to the rock and gravel.

But the classic alpine tundra of Southeast Alaska is the heath community of low woody-stemmed plants like Mertens' cassiope, starry cassiope, crowberry, arctic willow, dwarf blueberry, and bog blueberry. Tough plants like luetkea, Alaska saxifrage, sibbaldia, and mountain sagebrush are also found among the heathers.

Almost all of the large mammals of Southeast Alaska travel the high alpine ridges at times, but most are en route elsewhere. The lower subalpine meadows are more productive habitats for such creatures as Sitka deer and brown and black bears. The real mountaineers are mountain goats, so devoted to their craggy refuges that they rarely survive in captivity. Wolverines and wolves are also tundra travelers, tracing the alpine ridges.

Our most successful alpine nester is the American pipit which, like the less common rosy finch, often feeds on sluggish insects lying on summer snow patches. Male rock ptarmigan often sit atop prominences, entertaining us with display flights and strange nasal cackles. At times the alpine ridgetops become fair-weather hangouts for large collections of eagles and rowdy ravens ascending on thermals. We can't explain their presence in terms of food. Perhaps like us, they just enjoy the freedom of the hills.

STREAMS, RIVERS, AND LAKES

A subalpine snowpatch melts in the heat of June. Along its downslope margin, trickles merge and drop into a tiny ravine, carrying water at high speed toward the ocean 3000 feet below. This headwater stream, which hydrologists call "first order," is abrupt and businesslike, with none of the lazy meanders of its final lowland reaches. This mountain headwater stream contains many aquatic insects crawling about the pebbles and stones, but it lacks fish.

A very different first-order stream emerges from a spring on lower forested slopes. Fed by groundwater, this forest stream supports plentiful aquatic liverworts, a sign that water temperatures remain just above freezing in all but the harshest winters. This type of stream also has a relatively stable water flow, unlike those dependent on the variance of rainfall and snow melt. Adult coho salmon and Dolly Varden struggle almost to its spring-fed source, in order to spawn in the most stable environment our streams have to offer. Here their eggs and yolk-sac young can incubate and grow, protected from extremes of temperature and water level.

Where the mountain snow-melt stream and the forest spring-fed stream merge, a "second-order" stream is created. Where two second-order streams meet, a third-order stream begins, and so on. At each graduation in stream order, physical and biological properties change.

FOREST STREAMS—Small first- and second-order streams are heavily influenced by their forest surroundings. The uppermost headwater reaches usually don't have the brushy, deciduous margins of more powerful channels downstream. Shade of overarching conifer branches may prevent strong sunlight from reaching the stream, keeping the water cool. Mosses and liverworts are the only common plants within the channel.

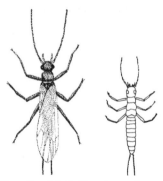

Stonefly adult (left) and nymph

The food base in these small streams derives largely from tree and shrub litter, rather than from plants that grow in the water. Invertebrates make their living by devouring wood, bark, and needles. Trees lie where they fall, since the stream is too small to move them. Down logs reach from bank to bank, forming small pools where organic and fine mineral sediments collect.

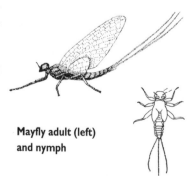

Mayfly adult (left) and nymph

POOLS AND RIFFLES—Between the pools are riffles, where faster currents scour beds of cobbles and gravel. The frequent pool/riffle alternation in first- and second-order streams results in a stepped downstream profile, which detains organic matter long enough to be efficiently used by invertebrate residents. For spawning and rearing fish, channel stability is just as important as high productivity. And in some situations, small old-growth streams offer fish the best of both worlds.

When first- and second- order streams pass over slopes of gentle gradient, beaver may find opportunities to dam short reaches. Here water surface area is vastly increased, sunlight warms the water, and a fringe of brush develops. By dragging streamside brush into the pools, beaver provide cover for fry and fingerlings. Beaver ponds scattered along an otherwise well-shaded old-growth stream can combine stability and productivity for rearing fish.

Coho fingerling

DEPOSITION—Downslope, as stream order increases, the creek exerts more influence on its surroundings. Instead of being confined to a narrow channel eroded into till or bedrock, it spreads out. During extreme high flows, sediments are deposited over neighboring floodplains, which widen to include more and more "terrestrial" habitats as streams become rivers. This alluvium, or water-sorted material, actually dictates the type of forest growing there. In Southeast Alaska our highest-volume forests, with the greatest percentage of Sitka spruce, are found on river-bottom floodplains and on steeper alluvial fans. Closer to the channel on regularly flooded sites, a deciduous fringe develops with red and Sitka alder, willows, black cottonwood, and berry bushes such as devil's club, salmonberry, and stink currant. Exposed to the sun, these streamside communities bustle with insects and songbirds and annually dump a nutritious load of leaves into the stream.

In third- and fourth-order streams, fallen logs may still span the channel, but here the greater volume of water is capable of dislodging them during storms, sweeping them down into debris jams. Pools become scarcer, and riffles dominate. These medium-sized channels are less stable than small first- and second-order streams, where logs may lie in place for many decades.

In late summer and fall, the riffle areas are hotbeds of biological turmoil. Pink (p. 187) and chum salmon, often in the thousands, compete with one another for a piece of stream substrate in which to excavate their nests and deposit their eggs. Male salmon fight viciously over spawning rights. Wave upon wave of new salmon enter the riffle areas, only to dig up previously buried eggs with their nest-building activities. Dolly Varden and sculpins dart about gorging themselves on these dug-up eggs. Gulls and bald eagles squawk and scream over the right to share in the bounty of the dead and dying salmon. Mergansers swim quietly through the turmoil, picking up eggs and young fish attracted to the eggs. On occasion the scene may be disrupted by a brown bear plunging after a salmon, or augmented by a mink, river otter, American dipper, belted kingfisher, or great blue heron.

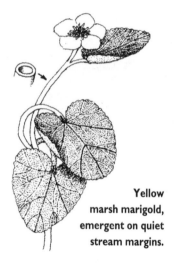

Yellow marsh marigold, emergent on quiet stream margins.

STREAM PLANTS—Algae now make greater photosynthetic contributions. The cobbles of fast mountain streams are the optimum sediment size for diatoms and green algae, which can quickly form a slippery coating over the rocks. As strands lengthen, they are constantly trimmed by the current and washed downstream. In gentler reaches downstream, finer sediments accumulate in eddies and quiet backwaters. Vascular plants such as speedwell, yellow marsh-marigold, forget-me-not, and yellow monkey-flower spread their leaves and flowers over shallow margins. On the bottom in the center channel, white water crowfoot and giant fountain moss provide excellent fish cover and support microcommunities of aquatic insects and epiphytic algae. Along the slowest and most sedate streams, plants characteristic of freshwater marshes and wet meadows may be found.

MEANDERS—Larger streams have more "room to move." A deflected current cuts into the bank, steepening it and even undermining roots of trees. Continuing downstream, the water is thrown onto the opposite bank, eroding there too, eventually creating a series of meanders in the channel. Sediments mined from steep outer bends are deposited on the inner bends where the current slows. Meanders offer a range of conditions for stream inhabitants: fast and slow currents, shady undercuts and sunny shallows, warm and cold waters, gravel and silt

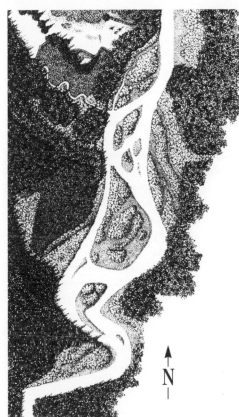

Raven's-eye view of Eagle River, near Juneau. The afternoon sun casts tree shadows across the water toward the northeast. The powerful glacier-fed current, moving north to south, has carved migrating meanders. Sitka alder thickets (pale) fringe the river on the active floodplain, framed in turn by the spruce–hemlock forest (dark). The small tributary stream, upper left, has been dammed by beavers, creating ponds and exceptional fish and wildlife habitat.

N

bottoms. On our larger meandering streams, the steepened outer bends are overhung by spruce and hemlock, while the bars on inner bends are colonized by younger deciduous shrub thickets.

On fifth-order and larger rivers, logs no longer span the channel and are piled on the banks during high flows. This is a further step in the "liberation" of the stream from the surrounding forest. Gradient typically decreases, and current slows except during high flows. The bed is now largely composed of sand and silt.

ESTUARIES—Where rivers meet the sea, their sediments create rich intertidal marshlands in the heads of bays, or delta formations protruding from more exposed shorelines. These estuarine "salt marshes" are focal points for many residents of the watershed.

GLACIAL WATERSHEDS—At first glance, turbid glacial lakes and rivers appear to be rather sterile environments. Since we can't see into the water, we assume that not much lives there. However, through the use of nets and traps designed to capture fish and insects, biologists find these murky waters may abound with life. Numerous Dolly Varden and some cutthroat trout were found in Mendenhall Lake near Juneau during a study by the Alaska Department of Fish and Game. Most fish were obtained near shore at water depths less than 15 feet. The fish began entering the lake in early August and left between March and May the following year.

We believe that most glacial lakes with access to the sea are used by Dolly Varden for overwintering. The high water turbidity and many months of ice cover make them sanctuaries offering a nearly predator-free environment. The low water temperature means the fish need little food to maintain themselves. We have generally noted that Dolly Varden obtained from Mendenhall Lake in March appear about as plump as when they entered the previous summer.

Glacial rivers are used by fish for spawning, rearing of young, overwintering, and as a highway to clearwater tributaries. Usually when salmon spawn in the main channels of glacial rivers, it is near sources of groundwater or springs. For instance, up to 500,000 chum salmon spawn in the spring-fed areas of the Chilkat River near Klukwan. In silty glacial rivers, as in clearwater rivers and streams, undercut banks, log jams, and backwaters abound with young coho salmon and Dolly Varden. Most king salmon young rear for one year among the log jams and side channels of the mainland river systems that are mostly fed by glacial waters.

Eulachon usually choose the lower portions of glacial rivers for spawning. Their eggs are adhesive and lie exposed, usually on a substrate of coarse sand and pea-sized gravel. Perhaps potential predators may have difficulty seeing the tiny eggs in the silty water.

LAKE-DOMINATED SYSTEMS—Lake-dominated systems are essential for certain species of fish. Sockeye salmon and cutthroat, rainbow, and steelhead trout are almost always associated with lakes. Most sockeye young live for 1 or 2 years in lakes fattening on the abundant zooplankton before heading out to sea. Resident cutthroat trout live year round in lakes, and the sea-run cutthroat overwinter in them. The outlets of lakes provide a more stable environment, as the lakes buffer periods of heavy rainfall, gradually releasing the accumulations. This seems to be important for steelhead, which usually choose lake outlets for spawning and rearing of young. Kokanee, a nonmigratory form of sockeye salmon, are found only in lakes. These small fish, in turn, provide excellent forage for the larger cutthroat trout.

Many of the lake-dominated systems in Southeast provide some of our finest and most diverse sport fishing. For instance, the Naha River watershed near Ketchikan contains high mountain lakes with Arctic grayling, landlocked lakes with large trophy-sized cutthroat trout, lakes and associated streams with sockeye, coho, chum, and pink salmon, both sea-run cutthroat trout and Dolly Varden, and a large river with an excellent run of steelhead. In the late 1970s the Alaska Department of Fish and Game's Division of Sport Fish submitted to the U.S. Forest Service a list of "quality" fishing waters that should be preserved from logging and other types of development. The majority of quality watersheds chosen were lake-dominated systems (p. 83).

MAJOR RIVERS—The largest rivers in Southeast Alaska originate in the interior plateaus of British Columbia and the Yukon Territory. The Stikine, Taku (p. 84), and Alsek rivers drain vast areas and form major biological pathways from Canada through the coastal mountains to Southeast Alaska. For example, the Stikine River drains an area of 20,000 square miles and snakes its way seaward for about 400 miles from its headwaters in northern British Columbia.

Various species use these great rivers as migratory highways. The most obvious mammal to enter Southeast from Canada by way of rivers is the moose. Moose populations are now established in the lower valleys of the Alsek, Chilkat, Taku, Stikine, and Unuk rivers.

Several species of birds regularly make their way to Southeast through these major river valleys, among them the pied-billed grebe, American bittern, warbling vireo, and western tanager. Also, many species of birds new (exotic) to Alaska no doubt arrive here in the same way. The green heron, Virginia rail, solitary vireo, northern oriole, rose-breasted grosbeak, swamp sparrow, and house sparrow probably came from Canada, where they commonly breed.

Records of some species of freshwater fish in Southeast come mostly from the major river systems: pygmy whitefish, round whitefish, longnose sucker, burbot, and slimy sculpin, for example. With only one or two exceptions, all king salmon that spawn in Southeast Alaska rivers utilize the mainland rivers. Our best-producing king salmon rivers are the Stikine, Taku, and Alsek.

Most amphibians found in Southeast occur within or near the major river valleys (spotted frog, wood frog, long-toed salamander). Even the widespread boreal toad may have entered Southeast via the Stikine River. Alaska's only reptile, the garter snake, has been sighted only along the banks of the Taku and Stikine rivers. However, our most common salamander, the rough-skinned newt, probably entered Southeast along the coast from the Pacific Northwest.

FRESHWATER MARSHES AND WET MEADOWS

A nondescript rodent swims through puddled marsh water and hauls out on a sedge hummock near the runway at the Haines Airport. The meadow vole is the most widespread vole in North America, but in

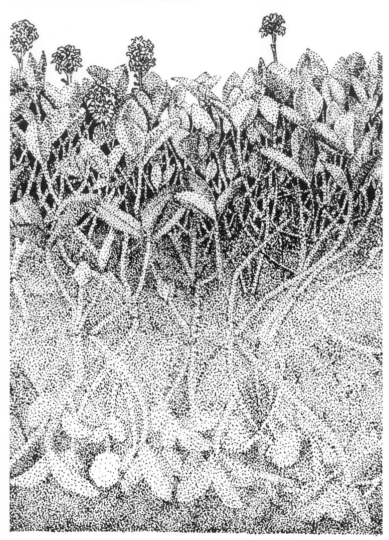

Buckbean, emergent on the margin of a stillwater pond.

Southeast Alaska, it is restricted mostly to large mainland river valleys. Its claim to fame is its staggering reproductive ability, and this soaked individual is one of a legion, at the peak of their 3- to 4-year cycle.

As it kicks the water from its gray pelage, the vole is pinned to the sedges by a short-eared owl. Migrating birds of prey are quick to notice dense populations of voles, and linger in the vicinity for days, "refueling." These freshwater wetlands bordering the Chilkat River host other "mousers" such as northern harriers, American kestrels, and northern shrikes. Larger hunters like northern goshawks may even snatch a muskrat from the banks of meandering creeks. In the marsh, a cow moose calmly raises a snout full of pondweed as the roar of a climbing plane overwhelms the songs of warblers.

Wetlands are "edge" communities, neither wholly aquatic nor upland. Aquatic habitats, according to the U.S. Fish and Wildlife Service, are covered by water more than 6 feet deep. Upland sites, at the other extreme, are characterized by well-drained soils. Wetlands are "in between," in areas of poor drainage.

Our local freshwater wetlands may be further subdivided into wet meadows, marshes, peatlands, and forested wetlands. Wet meadows and marshes are relatively young communities dominated by soft-stemmed herbaceous plants. Marshes have at least several inches of standing water, while wet meadows simply have waterlogged soils through much of the year. Sphagnum bogs and sedge fens (together called peatlands) are ancient freshwater wetlands with deep peat accumulating during thousands of years of wetland succession. Peatlands are very different from young wetlands.

MARSH PLANTS—Water depth determines plant growth form. This is best illustrated on the gently shoaling margins of muddy-bottomed lakes and ponds. With increasing depth, species grade from stiff, upright emergents, to limp but buoyant floating-leaved plants, to those entirely submerged.

Emergent plants are rooted in mud and partially covered by shallow water. Stems, leaves, and flowers project above the water. Some are tall and grasslike with narrow leaves, such as the tussock-forming water sedge and small-fruit bulrush. These emergents, and swamp horsetail, may form almost pure stands. Resembling the horsetails, but unrelated, is the common marestail (p. 187). Water hemlock is scattered through many young wetlands. Buckbean is an emergent in both young marshes and ancient peatlands.

Floating-leaved plants may either be rooted in the bottom or supported freely without anchorage. Yellow pond-lily is a frequent community dominant. Northern burreed may also blanket the surface of small shallow ponds. Pondweeds, a cross between floating and submerged plants, are excellent waterfowl foods.

Submerged plants have no need of the stiff supporting fibers found in upright terrestrial plants. Their stems and leaves are succulent and pliable, which increases their palatability to waterfowl. The plants are often hollow-stemmed,

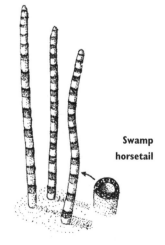

Swamp horsetail

which buoys them up in water and circulates oxygen. They lack the hard protective outer skin (cuticle, which in terrestrial plants prevents water loss), and they absorb dissolved gases through their entire surface. Leaves tend to be small and finely divided, which increases the surface area available for absorption. Spike watermilfoil is probably the most common submerged aquatic plant in Southeast Alaska. It grows in vast patches in the muddy shallows of lakes. Stoneworts are nonflowering algae, submerged in kettle ponds and brackish sloughs. They have a strange, crusty texture and are easily recognized by their meaty odor.

ORIGIN OF MARSHES AND WET MEADOWS—Wetlands develop on poorly drained surfaces. Retreating glaciers and the waters draining them create many such surfaces, usually of fine sands or silts, which precipitate in fairly still waters such as lakes, ponds, and quiet backwater areas adjoining outwash channels.

Kettle ponds form where ice blocks detach from the receding ice and slowly melt, leaving a water-filled depression. Larger lakes at the ice face become cloudy with "rock flour"—particles ground from rock by the glacier. Accumulation of fine sand and silt is rapid in these lakes. Usually they have shallow margins. When infilling or lowered water levels eventually remove shorelines from the reach of floods and grounding icebergs, a sedge hummock marsh or wet meadow may be the result.

UPLIFTED SALT MARSHES—When formerly marine surfaces are raised above the tides by glacial rebound, sediment size again determines the course of succession. On the coarse sands and gravels of storm beaches, drainage is good or even excessive, and a spruce forest develops. On the fine sands and silts typical of protected salt marshes, drainage may be poor. Intertidal sedge flats commonly have a compacted and nearly impermeable layer of glacial silt, bound by intertwined runners. Recently uplifted salt marshes of this kind in the lower Mendenhall Valley near Juneau now support freshwater sedge hummock marshes and wet meadows. *Sphagnum* moss is beginning to colonize, but deep peat has not yet accumulated. The most extensive freshwater wetlands in Southeast Alaska are found on the Yakutat Forelands, a vast marshy plain of willow and sweet gale on shallow peat over marine sands and silts, uplifted only within the past millennium.

LAKE AND POND MARGINS AND FLOOD ZONES OF RIVERS—The transitional nature of freshwater wetlands is most apparent on the quieter margins of lakes and ponds, where the wetland belts expand or shrink with the vagaries of their associated water bodies. Marginal wetlands are most extensive on the shorelines of gently shoaling lakes and ponds of lowland floodplains.

Wetlands are also found in the flood zones of some low-gradient rivers, or in quiet backwater areas protected from the current. Wetlands adjoining rivers, lakes, and ponds provide cover when they are accessible to immature fish. Even when inaccessible, wetland plants support a food chain that nourishes fish downstream.

WILDLIFE—Our salt marshes are famous for waterfowl, but the young freshwater wetlands of Southeast Alaska can be even more important to them at certain times of year. Mallards, green-winged teal, and other dabbling ducks which stay to breed in Southeast prefer to nest in freshwater wetlands where high tides can't reach their eggs. In the fall, when hunting pressure is heavy on tidal marshes, many ducks and geese retreat to freshwater wetlands in quiet valley headwaters.

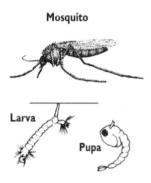

Mosquito

Larva

Pupa

Freshwater wetlands are feeding sites for large flocks of migrating birds. Because the visit may be brief and the site remote, many of these stopover marshes have not been documented. One well-known resting area for migrating sandhill cranes is the Dude Creek flats near Gustavus.

The birds with strongest ties to our freshwater marshes and wet meadows are great blue herons, belted kingfishers, common snipe, and several small breeding songbirds such as the common yellowthroat, northern waterthrush, and alder flycatcher. Formerly rare in Southeast Alaska, red-winged blackbirds are expanding their range, and their loud, clear "Konk-la-reee" now graces some of our freshwater wetlands.

In addition to these wetland specialists, many songbirds from neighboring forests and thickets venture into the wetlands to feed. Insect-eating swallows, warblers, thrushes, and flycatchers, which breed in upland habitats, all visit the wetlands, exporting the marsh's super-productivity back to nestlings hidden away in more sheltered locations.

Resident mammals of freshwater wetlands include beaver, muskrats, bog lemmings, and meadow, tundra, and long-tailed voles. Large mammals enter the marshes to graze and hunt. Like waterfowl, moose have developed a fondness for the succulence of floating and submerged vegetation.

Freshwater marshes are the breeding grounds of the widespread boreal toad, and of the less-common spotted and wood frogs. Marshes and wet meadows are prolific producers of aquatic insects, such as mosquitoes, dragonflies, water striders, and whirligig and diving beetles.

Our richest salmon streams are usually associated with extensive wetland systems. In a place where conservationists' concerns are so often focused on old-growth forests and coastal wetlands, it would be unwise to neglect our freshwater marshes and wet meadows.

PEATLANDS

The merlin comes barreling out of nowhere, its swift and lethal swoop across the bog punctuated by a soft *whump!* and an explosion of feathers. Later, those scattered brown and white feathers will be all that remains of a greater yellowlegs. The yellowlegs is one of the few birds heavily dependent on the peatlands of Southeast Alaska, where it nests in moss on the ground (p. 185).

Peatlands are ancient wetlands. They can be distinguished from younger wetlands by their greater depth of organic peat (at least a foot), which represents millennia of accumulation of dead mosses and sedges. The colloquial term "muskeg" refers to a complex mosaic of ponded peatlands, streams, and open, scrubby forest on poorly drained land. Peatlands are called bogs when dominated by sphagnum mosses, or fens when dominated by sedges. In both bogs and fens, trees are few and stunted, restricted to the drier hummocks. Peatlands have a diverse and very specialized flora (p. 82) and fauna.

Those who travel mainly by water in Southeast Alaska may be unaware of the many acres of peatlands hidden by the front ranks of tall evergreens, but even a short excursion by plane reveals how widespread they are—a far cry from the situation in the northeastern United States, for example, where botanists sometimes travel for hundreds of miles to visit a bog.

BOG HISTORY—Much of what we know about the last 14,000 years of vegetational history in Southeast Alaska derives from study of peatlands and associated lakes. The science of palynology involves the extraction of peat cores from bogs. Organic materials from these cores are radiocarbon dated, and unoxidized pollen grains and leaf fragments are identified to determine the species composition of the bog and its surrounding communities. Samples from varying depths in the peat document long-term successional changes.

But the question of bog origin and climax has always raised controversy. In Southeast Alaska, much of it centers around postglacial successional research conducted since the 1920s in Glacier Bay. There, some researchers suggested that peatlands appeared to eventually overcome old-growth forests, a process called paludification, and that the eventual climax community on many forested surfaces might be bog. Other workers have insisted the opposite—that many bogs are being invaded by forests. The dispute is far from resolution, and caused much debate at the 1988 Glacier Bay Science Symposium.

Peatlands originate in areas of poor drainage. As with hemlock-spruce forests, it took thousands of years after recession of the Wisconsin ice before bogs as we know them appeared in Southeast Alaska. In some cases bogs replaced open wetlands with shallow peat, similar to those described in the preceding section. This occurred roughly 7000 to 9000 years ago.

Peatlands also replaced forests. Rainwater percolating downward through the forest soil may carry minerals that precipitate out in deeper layers, forming hardpans impervious to drainage. In forests where frequent windstorms uproot trees, soils may be churned and rejuvenated, drainage improved, and paludification resisted. Otherwise, over the course of many centuries, waterlogged soils reduce the rooting environment for forest trees, which decline in vigor, and wetland plants like sphagnums invade the understory. Some researchers even suggest that *Sphagnum* is a causal agent of forest decline, rather than just a beneficiary of increased soil moisture.

In coniferous forests, a succession of sphagnums occurs. *Sphagnum girgensohnii* is the first species of its genus to colonize, usually becoming established on bare mineral soil of windthrow mounds, and from there spreading into wetter depressions. In standing water, *S. mendocinum* and *S. squarrosum* may grow. Much later, in open bog conditions, these early colonists are replaced by others such as *S. imbricatum* (one of several green species), *S. magellanicum* (reddish), and *S. fuscum* (brown). These peat mosses not only hold tremendous quantities of water in their tissues, thus maintaining a high water table, but also release phenolic compounds such as sphagnol and acids, which further discourage organic decomposition.

Since organic material is not being decomposed, the water of the developing peatland is low in nutrients. Phosphates and nitrates, especially, become critically short in supply. Meanwhile, at the periphery of the bog, trees may die when their roots become waterlogged, and the bog expands. But perhaps it's best to describe forest-bog dynamics as a ceaselessly shifting equilibrium, responding to both long-term climatic changes and to changes wrought by the plants themselves, rather than attempting to label either forest or bog as the ultimate "climax."

XEROMORPHY—Paradoxically, many of the plants in soaking wet bogs share features with plants adapted to dry conditions. Bog biologists refer to these plants as xeromorphs, but differ in their attempts to explain them. Possibly the acid waters of the bog are so inhospitable that many of the plants growing there are unable to use them, instead subsisting on whatever rainwater they can trap. Bog plants adapted to dry conditions would have a competitive edge over those requiring groundwater supplies. Alternatively, the hardened, evergreen leaves may not be responsive to drought stress, but rather to a cold substrate, a short growing season, winter dessication, or scarcity of soil nutrients.

Among the xeromorphs found in our bogs are many species of heather. Bog kalmia, bog rosemary, Labrador-tea, bog cranberry, and mountain cranberry are all bog-dwelling members of the heather family. Xeromorphic features found among these shrubs, and also in the closely related crowberry, include thick, waxy evergreen leaves with under-curled margins. Such leaves resist desiccation because their thickness and waxy cuticle decrease water loss from their upper surfaces, while their inrolled margins help prevent

Labrador-tea, in the heather family.

water loss from the delicate holes for gas exchange (stomata) on the lower surfaces. The stomata of Labrador-tea are further protected by a layer of rusty brown hairs on the leaf undersides. In addition, heather-family plants have special symbiotic fungi whose mycelia live on the plant roots. This association is called mycorrhiza; the mycelia pick up minute quantities of nutrients released into the waters of the bog from what little decomposition does occur and transfer these to the host shrub. The white and slender bog-orchids also have mycorrhizae.

Another xeromorphic bog plant is cloudberry. The fuzzy leaves of this member of the rose family have short hairs that cut down the wind speed across the leaf surface, decreasing desiccation. Such sedges as the water sedge, few-flowered sedge, many-flower sedge, spike rush, and the tall cottongrass all have exceptionally narrow grasslike leaves with reduced surface area, another xeromorphic feature.

Peat mosses *(Sphagnum* spp.) may have blue-green bacteria, such as species of *Nostoc,* associated with their tissues. These blue-green bacteria are able to manufacture nitrates from atmospheric nitrogen, and these nitrates nourish not only the peat mosses but probably other bog plants as well.

Lichens depend directly on rainwater for nutrients, so they luxuriate in the well-lit bogs. Some species such as the reindeer "mosses" form thick mats on the surface of the bog. Others form heavy encrustations on tree branches, while old man's beard and several species of *Bryoria* hang in long strands.

Peatland plants lacking the specializations discussed above may barely make a living. The bunchberry, for example, has deciduous leaves relatively poor in nutrients when growing in peatland, but in nearby forests the leaves are higher in nutrients and are evergreen. Similarly, the stiff clubmoss appears yellowish and sickly in bogs, but a rich, dark green when growing in the forest. Shore pine, western hemlock, and mountain hemlock grow very slowly, taking bonsai forms. These conifers often have yellowish needles and are susceptible to many fungal diseases. Shore pines, for example, are sometimes parasitized by the western gall rust, which attacks the branches, forming swellings that may girdle and kill the branch. In June the galls crack, releasing clouds of orange spores, which can settle and germinate on other nearby shore pines, thus spreading the infection directly without the alternate host needed by most other rust fungi. Pines might not survive in our bogs at all, were it not for suillus and other mushrooms which are mycorrhizal on their roots.

Pit ponds support buckbean and the yellow pondlily. Buckbean prefers shallow pools and the edges of deeper ponds, while the long stems of the yellow pondlily enable it to colonize deeper waters.

Among the aquatic insects found in bog ponds are the predaceous diving beetles. These beetles have paddle-shaped hind legs and must come to the surface to obtain air. Their larvae, called water tigers, are predators that often tackle prey much larger than themselves. Water striders (p. 188) skate over the surfaces of ponds, feeding on myriads of mosquito larvae and other insects. Above these ponds, the Sitka darner and other dragonflies form baskets with their hairy legs and strain small flying insects from the air (p. 187). The Sitka darner lays its eggs in wet peat moss, while its carnivorous larval stages develop in bog pools.

The peatlands of Southeast Alaska have few truly characteristic birds or mammals. Plant growth in the sterile bogs is so hard-won that most species can't afford to be eaten, and protect themselves with antiherbivore compounds like ledol, a narcotic in Labrador-tea. Relatively low herbivore use of bogs also means fewer predators. Bogs do produce delicious berries that compensate for their relative sparseness with incomparably distinctive flavor. Sedge fens, in comparison to sphagnum bogs, offer much faster-growing and less toxic forage for grazing mammals.

In addition to the greater yellowlegs, other birds using the peatlands include several species of woodpeckers, which search in the rotting wood of dead snags for insects, and such ground-feeding birds as

Steller's jays and dark-eyed juncos. Blue grouse, especially females with young, forage in bogs for berries and insects. At the forested bog edges, raptors like great horned owls, sharp-shinned hawks, merlins, and American kestrels may sit quietly, waiting for an unsuspecting vole to venture into the open. We've seen kestrels and olive-sided flycatchers capturing dragonflies in flight over the peatlands.

Among the mammals found in the peatlands of Southeast Alaska are the masked shrew, an insectivore, and the herbivorous northern bog lemming. These species neither migrate nor hibernate, but remain active all year. Wolves, black bear, brown bear, short-tailed weasels, wolverines, and Sitka black-tailed deer all may forage in peatlands. In the November deer-rutting season, we find freshly thrashed shore pines, about 3 feet high and a few inches in diameter, many of their needles knocked off by argumentative bucks. Perhaps they offer just the right amount of resistance to simulate a sturdy rival. These stunted shore pines may actually be nearly a century old. Their slow growth is mostly a result of wet, nutrient-poor soils, but certainly cannot be improved by generations of black-tailed deer using them for punching bags.

SALT MARSHES

Salt marshes are intertidal wetlands vegetated locally with sedges, goose-tongue, and other salt-tolerant plants. They usually develop on sand and mud deposits at river mouths and in bay-heads protected from wave action and longshore currents. Although salt marshes account for less than 1 percent of our total land mass, there are few Southeast Alaskan birds, mammals, or fish that do not benefit, directly or indirectly, from our astonishing salt-marsh productivity.

In the summer of 1987, we conducted a salt-marsh study on the Mendenhall Wetlands (p. 83) northwest of Juneau, to assess impacts of a planned airport expansion. From early-morning bird counts, to stream mapping, to soil pits, to seining of brackish ponds and sloughs, we were immersed in the fascinating life of the intertidal marsh. Perhaps the most lasting impression left by this work was a sense of interconnectedness. A salt marsh is a "giveaway" system; it continually sends the fruits of its seething productivity to the surrounding ocean and forests. Notice in the illustration that most "arrows" move outward from the salt marsh to other systems.

For example, consider the life history of the Pacific staghorn sculpin. This medium-sized marine bottomfish of our shallow coastal waters lays its eggs in February, often under a clamshell, at moderate subtidal depths. By late March, the Pacific staghorn sculpin fry begin to appear in the brackish sloughs and lagoons of Southeast Alaskan salt marshes.

Until ice drives them out in the fall, these 2- to 6-inch juveniles

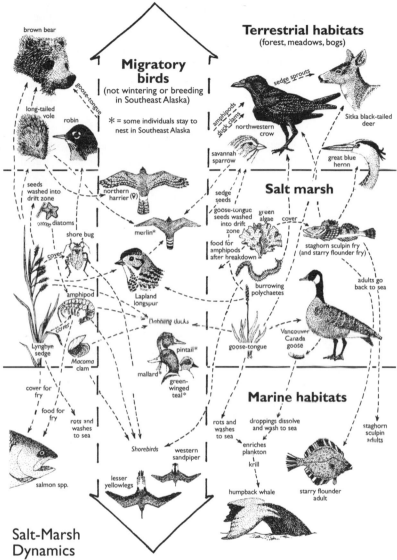

Salt-Marsh Dynamics

The salt marsh exports its production to neighboring terrestrial and marine habitats, and feeds migrants from distant lands.

fatten in the warm waters. When you see a great blue heron stalking in the marsh puddles, chances are good that staghorns are its quarry. Kingfishers and terns plummeting into the shallows carry other staghorns to their nestlings. Mergansers and mink cash in too. In some of our study area sloughs we captured dozens in a single seine haul. The staghorn fry is a "converter" of salt marsh productivity into forms attractive to terrestrial predators.

This productivity is then removed. The "work" of the sculpin fry doesn't end up in the salt-marsh soil. In fact, the salt marsh hardly even has a soil. The tides carry any decomposing organic material to the sea. And what about the fry that survive? They return to the subtidal zones at season's end, eventually to nourish marine animals such as seals and halibut. The salt marsh is a forbidding place in winter and has few year-round residents bigger than a clam.

VEGETATION—Intertidal plants are also an elite group. Only a dozen or so have learned to tolerate periodic submersion in salt water. But the relative lack of shading and root competition results in annual growth matched by few other natural communities or agricultural lands. Where the marsh is steadily blanketed by fine river-carried silts, Lyngbye sedge dominates. On coarser sands and gravels, lower-growing species like goose-tongue, Pacific alkaligrass, and sea milkwort (p. 192) are found.

The basis of salt-marsh production is plant photosynthesis. The salt marsh is like a forest in this respect, but with the difference that almost all of the annual green production of the marsh is either eaten by invading herbivores or dies back in the fall to rot and wash into the sea. This annual cycle draws hordes of visitors—Pacific flyway migrants from Mexico to the North Slope, and closer neighbors from our rainy woods and sea. Compared to the terrestrial plants of meadows and forests and bogs, salt-marsh plants are delightfully succulent. Most of them except the grasses and sedges can be eaten raw by humans, even with our relatively unsophisticated digestive apparatus. For grazers, like geese, deer, and bears, the salt marsh is a giant salad bowl devoid of thorns and woodiness.

ZONATION—As in the rocky intertidal, elevation determines duration of submergence and exposure. Few vascular plants can survive much lower than extreme high water neap (EHWN), or the upper limit of neap tides. In the Juneau area this elevation is about 13 feet above mean lower low water (MLLW, or "sea level" as given in the tide books). The vegetated marsh is therefore confined to the mid to upper intertidal, bounded by sand or mudflats below, and supratidal forest or meadows above. The salt marsh itself is sometimes divided into low and high marsh. Low marsh is dominated by sedges, goose-tongue, and Pacific alkaligrass, whereas high marsh is usually dominated by taller grasses such as tufted hairgrass, beach rye, and foxtail barley. For most birds, mammalian grazers, and fish, the low marsh provides far more valuable habitat. Throughout both the low and high marsh, two-way sloughs carry plankton as well as silt and detritus, bathing the flats in nutrients.

At the upper limits of the salt marsh, above the highest reaches of the tide but below the edge of the forest, a meadow community is often found. These supratidal beach meadows are particularly common in northern Southeast Alaska, where the coastlines are rising relative to sea level. Salt marsh is literally lifted out of the intertidal, and these lush coastal meadows are early successional stages that will eventually become spruce forests.

REARING FISH—Salt marshes are extremely important as nursery areas for salmon. Young coho salmon grow faster in the intertidal portions of streams, where the water is warmer and food more abundant than farther upstream. Fry of chum and chinook are also particularly abundant within the marshy areas of estuaries. The young salmon prey easily on swarms of invertebrates such as amphipods. The invertebrates in turn feed upon algae trapped in the sedges as the tide advances and recedes. Aside from sculpins and salmon fry, other fish drawn to our salt marshes include Pacific sand lance, capelin, Pacific herring, three-spine stickleback, and starry flounder.

Salt-marsh values sometimes surprise us. By the end of our Mendenhall Wetlands study, we came to regard what we called "Impact Pond"—a brackish, unsightly, rectangular dredge pit—as a nearly priceless wetland asset. Yet it had been created by human disturbance! The bottom of this shallow pond was covered with ditchgrass, a five-star aquatic forage plant for geese and dabbling ducks. The ditchgrass beds sheltered breeding sticklebacks and isopods which turned the pond into a nourishing soup.

Impact Pond was mostly filled for a taxiway extension. In straight-up-and-down country like Southeast Alaska, the flat expanses of salt marshes are often the only level sites for airports, farming, and other human activities. On coastal wetlands we can destroy wildlife habitat or we can improve it—even accidentally, as on Impact Pond. But we need to remember that coastal wetlands offer far more than building sites and a pleasant relief from rainforest claustrophobia.

The muck of the marsh is a gift.

ROCKY INTERTIDAL HABITATS

A kayaker, recently returned from a long journey through the Alexander Archipelago, said that he felt like an intertidal creature. He'd slept in the splash zone at extreme high water, gathered his dinner at low tide, and paddled hundreds of miles with his rear end below waterline and his head above it. He was not alone; most Southeast Alaskan terrestrial mammals and birds are happy to wet themselves in salt water in search of a meal. And their marine counterparts, the seals and cormorants and ocean fishes, also dine on intertidal bounty, whether they actually come up from the subtidal to forage, or simply wait for it to drift or swim out to sea.

Rocky intertidal habitats compose the vast majority of about 15,500 miles of marine shoreline (p. 82). In Southeast Alaska, beachcombing isn't a diversion; it's a way of life.

TIDES—The seashores of Southeast Alaska are subject to mixed semidiurnal tides; that is, there are two high tides and two low tides per day, and all four differ in amplitude. The tides are caused primarily by the gravitational pull of the moon and sun on the earth's seas. Tidal heights and times are modified by the shapes of shorelines and offshore basins, and by weather. Atmospheric highs can depress low tides below predicted levels, while onshore winds can drive waves above the predicted high. The lowest low tides and highest high tides of each month and the strongest shallow-water currents are associated with the full and new moons; such tides occur in the daytime in spring and

Heart cockle in the drift line

summer and at night during the fall and winter. The highest high tides range from about 12.6 feet at Sitka to 20 feet at Juneau.

Marine waters of Southeast Alaska range the full spectrum from the wave-exposed outer coast with waters of relatively high salinity (about 33 ppt, or parts per thousand) to sheltered inland bays with waters diluted by freshwater runoff. River runoff is highest in summer and fall due to snow melt and heavy rains, and salinity of inland waters is lowest in those seasons, dropping to 19 ppt or less. Only those intertidal and subtidal species tolerant of such lowered salinities are found in the inland waters. Invertebrates living only on the outer coast, such as the pinto abalone, ochre sea star, red sea urchin, and purple sea urchin, may be intolerant either of the lowered salinities of inland waters or of the more fluctuating temperatures there. In addition, rivers carrying glacial runoff spew plumes of silt for miles offshore, restricting penetration of sunlight into the water, fouling filter-feeding mechanisms, and inhibiting the growth of marine algae. Bull kelp beds (p. 86) are more common on the outer coast than in inside waters. Decreased plant growth in turn lowers the productivity of all other trophic levels.

We've found about 170 species of macroscopic (easily visible with the unaided eye) invertebrates in the intertidal zone of Southeast Alaska, and doubtless many more exist. Here we will mention just a few of the more abundant forms, according to their favored elevational zones.

UPPER INTERTIDAL ZONES—Here we find several species of barnacles, limpets, and periwinkles (tiny snails). Barnacles filter plankton from the water during high tides, while limpets and periwinkles scrape delicate algae off the rocks using a belt of chitinous rasping teeth called a radula. The high intertidal zone often appears more barren and desolate than either the mid-intertidal or supratidal zones which enclose it. Some naturalists consider it a "no-man's-land," too infrequently flooded for most marine creatures, yet too salty for most terrestrial invaders.

Lichens colonize high intertidal and supratidal rocks in the spray zone where mosses and vascular plants fail to grow. Inconspicuous yet ubiquitous black encrusting lichens may form continuous belts on rocks several feet below extreme high water. Above them are brighter splashes of white and orange lichens.

MID-INTERTIDAL ZONES—Extensive beds of rockweed occur in the mid-intertidal zone. Like the upper intertidal, this zone harbors barnacles, limpets, and periwinkles, but in addition has green burrowing anemones, several species of nemerteans or ribbon worms, chitons, snails, sea slugs, mussels, and various crustaceans. The anemones are predators, catching prey with their stinging tentacles. The nemerteans are also predators, throwing a long muscular proboscis around their prey. In some species, the proboscis is armed with piercing stylets and associated poison sacs.

Chitons are mollusks with 8 overlapping plates on their backs; they rasp primarily red and brown algae with their toothed radulas. Some of the mid-intertidal snails called whelks use their radulas to drill holes in the shells of mussels and barnacles. Sea slugs of the mid-intertidal zone include the small rough-mantled sea slug, a specialist predator feeding on barnacles. The blue bay mussel often blankets the mid-intertidal. It's a filter-feeder and frequently is contaminated with toxins from certain species of phytoplankton, which can result in paralytic shellfish poisoning if the mussel is eaten by vertebrates. Among the mid-intertidal crustaceans are several species of isopods (flattened top to bottom), amphipods (flattened sideways), and hermit crabs living inside abandoned snail shells. Many of these crustaceans are scavengers.

LOWER INTERTIDAL ZONES—These areas also support many of the species mentioned above, as well as invertebrates not common in the mid and upper levels—sponges, hydroids, other species of large anemones, chitons, limpets and snails, many bivalves, octopus, tiny colonies of encrusting animals called ectoprocts, many species of segmented worms (polychaetes), spoon worms, shrimps, crabs, sea stars, brittle stars, sea cucumbers, and fish.

From 1 or 2 feet above sea level (MLLW) down into the shallow subtidal zones, dense kelp jungles often completely obscure the rocky bottom. Ribbon kelp and sugar kelp are the dominants of distinctive communities, feeding the invertebrate grazers and offering cover for both residents and visitors from the deep. This reminds us that not until these lowest intertidal reaches do plants regain the visual and ecological importance that they held in most terrestrial environments; in the upper and mid-intertidal zones, the organisms blanketing the rocks are animals, such as mussels and barnacles. Highly branched species of red algae are common in both low intertidal and subtidal areas, and encrusting species of coralline algae (calcified reds) often paint the lower intertidal rocks, especially where exposed to waves. Beds of eelgrass, a flowering plant in the pondweed family, grow on the shallow sands of protected bays or river deltas.

The life of the beach rocks and tide pools mesmerizes children and sourdoughs. Each spring during SeaWeek, a statewide program of environmental field trips, grade-school classes throughout Southeast spill onto the beaches, noisy, wide-eyed, variably reverent, and invariably engaged. Maybe it's because intertidal animals can be almost extraterrestrially weird, or maybe because the tidy arrangement of elevational zones appeals to our sense of order, so often frustrated by nature's lively chaos. For many born-and-raised Southeasterners of the past few decades, it was a SeaWeek field trip that first immersed them in the grasped-yet-unfathomable wonders of the land's edge.

MAMMALS

· · ·

CHAPTER 2

Southeast Alaskans live among the last remaining healthy populations of "deep wilderness" mammals, such as the wolf, brown bear, mountain goat, and wolverine. Because these animals fare poorly near civilization, in the southern 48 states they are now restricted to protected national parks and wildernesses. In much of Southeast, they still range freely. And any reader of travel brochures soon comes to associate Southeast Alaska with visibly thriving populations of marine mammals. Breaching humpback whales are second only to calving glaciers as attention-getters in the advertising trade; seal-pup-with-mom-on-iceberg probably runs a close third.

MAMMALIAN PARADISE?—Our marine mammals and our deep-wilderness land mammals are matchless attractions. Considering only these "heavyweights," Southeast must be ranked as a mammalian paradise. In one sense this is true; Southeast Alaska retains its original complement of mammals, a claim made by few other regions of North America. While populations of some marine mammals are much lower now than in the 1700s, we needn't wonder about the contents of (as Thoreau

Sitka black-tailed bucks in subalpine deer cabbage meadow

once described Massachusetts) a book from which the best pages have been torn.

On the other hand, Southeast Alaska's actual list of mammals is short by comparison with those of other states or the Canadian provinces. Compare our 50 or so terrestrial mammals with the 85 mammals in Alberta or the 67 mammals in Texas's Big Bend National Park alone. And of our 50 terrestrial mammals, a dozen are very rare or found only in scattered enclaves, perhaps introduced by people, or just sneaking over the borders of Southeast Alaska from interior regions.

TERRESTRIAL MAMMALS

The features of Southeast Alaska which limit distribution of terrestrial mammals are heavy rains, deep winter snows, geographical barriers such as the ice-draped coast ranges, dissecting rivers, and wide marine channels. Another feature is time. Except possibly for the occupants of a few ice-free refugia, all mammals were evicted from Southeast during the great Wisconsin glaciation. The intervening 12,000 years have not yet allowed recolonization by all those mammals that could live here. Subterranean homebodies like moles and ground squirrels and pocket gophers are conspicuously missing; our only true burrower is the hoary marmot, and it is found only on the mainland.

The exact distribution and subspecies status of many of the small mammals remains unknown, and exotic new arrivals, such as the mountain lion, continue to surprise us; one was shot near Wrangell in 1989 and, more recently, sightings of them have been reported near Petersburg and Haines. But we now have a pretty good idea *where* each of the 50 species of Southeast Alaskan terrestrial mammals can be found. *How* and *when* they got there are the difficult questions. One way to approach the question of distribution in Southeast Alaska is to categorize our mammals geographically, in ways that provide clues to their points of origin and means of dispersal.

UBIQUITOUS SPECIES—A first category might be called ubiquitous mammals, or species found throughout the mainland on nearly all of the major islands of Southeast. This group includes only 11 species. One, the little brown bat, obviously has little trouble with water crossings. Others, such as the beaver, Sitka deer, brown bear, mink, and river otter are nearly as comfortable in the water as on land (although sightings of beaver in salt water are curiously rare). It was almost inevitable that these creatures would eventually overcome the 5-mile ocean crossings that isolate some of our islands.

Our most ubiquitous small mammals are the short-tailed weasel, the masked and dusky shrews, the long-tailed vole, and the deer

Native Mammals of Southeast Alaska

mouse. While all are good swimmers, their small bodies would not endure lengthy crossings. Several hypotheses could explain their wide dispersal. Pregnant females could have hitched rides in sea-going Native dugouts, as did a shrew we once uncovered while hauling crab pots from a modern fiberglass canoe. They could also have been swept into the water with landslide debris, floating to distant islands aboard the resulting log rafts. Such slides were probably quite common following the Wisconsin glaciation, when destabilized mountainsides hadn't yet "settled down."

MAINLAND SPECIES—The largest geographic category of Southeast's mammals are those found widely throughout the mainland, but missing on 1 or more of the largest islands. This includes 14 species: the water shrew, 3 small rodents (northern red-backed vole, jumping mouse, and northern bog lemming) and 5 larger ones (bushy tailed woodrat, red squirrel, northern flying squirrel, hoary marmot, and porcupine), 4 carnivores (wolf, black bear, marten, and wolverine), and the mountain goat. Most of them could probably survive quite well on the islands, given suitable amounts of their preferred habitat, as evidenced by the successful introduction of the marten and red squirrels to Baranof and Prince of Wales islands in 1934. Others simply haven't had the opportunity.

For some mammals, however, presence or absence on islands may depend less on colonizing ability (swimming or hitching rides) than on auspicious or inauspicious species combinations. Black and brown bears don't mix well on the islands. While the two often live together on the mainland, blackies are not found on the "ABCs" (Admiralty, Baranof, and Chichagof islands), and brownies are rare on Prince of Wales. In contrast, wolves may be unable to sustain themselves indefinitely on islands *without* large populations of their friends the deer, beaver, or marmot.

The assemblage of mammals on a particular island, a product of the interplay of time, chance, predation, wanderlust, and resistance to drowning, has fascinating consequences. Admiralty Island lacks wolves. Without efficient predators, Sitka deer periodically reach high densities there. Certain deer forage plants are highly palatable but, unlike blueberry and bunchberry, are unable to survive repeated cutbacks of their entire annual growth. Therefore, highbush cranberry, willow, black cottonwood, and beach strawberry are all quite rare on Admiralty. And the island's subalpine meadows, packed with deer all summer, lack the rich herb diversity of the mainland's wolf-patrolled high country with fewer deer. An island's fauna is not just icing on the ecological cake, but a strong influence on its vegetative character.

INTERIOR SPECIES—A third large geographical category is composed of the 13 mammals found only in northern Southeast Alaska, or at the mouths of our largest rivers. These might be described as "interior" species, best adapted either to drier climates or to deciduous forests and thickets, which are scarce or of small acreage in most of Southeast. The Alsek, Taku, Stikine, and Unuk rivers provide two features needed by mammals of this interior group: an abundance of deciduous forage and cover on broad alluvial floodplains, and a lowland corridor into British Columbia through the otherwise impenetrable coast ranges and ice fields.

The clearest example of a mammal unable to cope with Southeast's precipitation is the collared pika, found only on the "dry side" of

Chilkat and White passes. A hay maker, instead of hibernating like the marmot, the pika collects herbs and grasses in the fall to sun-dry outside its burrow, later caching them underground. Sun-drying green plants in the alpine in October in Southeast Alaska would be a futile undertaking!

The interior group also includes the snowshoe hare, muskrat, and meadow vole. The tundra vole lives in northern mainland Southeast, plus on Baranof and Chichagof islands. Carnivores in this group are the coyote, red fox, least weasel, lynx, fisher, and mountain lion. Hoofed mammals in the interior category are the moose and, possibly, the Dall sheep. The Alaska Department of Fish and Game has records of sheep entering the U.S. border north of Haines. Dall sheep, like other bighorns, depend in winter upon fairly dry slopes where strong winds blow snow off the vegetation. This habitat is lacking in most of Southeast.

SOUTHERN SPECIES—A botanist could assemble a long list of plants found in southern but not northern Southeast Alaska. These species probably recolonized Southeast by working up the Pacific coast at the end of the Wisconsin glaciation. By contrast, few mammals are re-stricted to the southern part of Southeast Alaska. While seeds and spores of plants easily blow (or fly inside birds) across miles of water, the countless fiords of coastal British Columbia must have been a for-midable barrier to terrestrial mammals. It's much easier to imagine them entering Southeast through the big river valleys than by moving north up the tortuous Pacific shoreline.

The Gapper's red-backed vole reaches north only as far as Thomas Bay. Five species of bats in addition to the ubiquitous little brown bat have been recorded in Southeast. Of these, three are known only in the southern portion. Technically, the Sitka black-tailed deer could be classified as "southern," since it hasn't quite colonized the northernmost parts of Lynn Canal. And our Alaskan subspecies *(Odocoileus hemionus sitchensis)* is more closely related to the Columbian black-tailed deer of coastal British Columbia, Washington, Oregon, and northern California than to the big mule deer of interior B.C. This sug-gests that our deer returned to Southeast via coastal B.C., developing their distinctive features in the last 10,000 years. Still, after seeing a Sitka blacktail on the Haines Highway in 1989, we decided it belongs in the "ubiquitous" category.

OUTER COAST SPECIES—Two rodents cling solely to outposts on the westernmost islands. The Coronation Island vole is closely related to the ubiquitous long-tailed vole. It is found on only a few small islands standing well out to sea beyond Prince of Wales Island. And similar isolation has produced the Sitka mouse, which some biologists consider to be a species distinct from the cosmopolitan deer mouse. Some outer coast islands were probably ice-free throughout the Wisconsin glaciation, contributing to the high diversity of mammal subspecies in today's archipelago.

INTRODUCED SPECIES—Many of the mammals discussed above, which are "native" to at least some parts of Southeast Alaska, have been introduced to islands by people within historical times. And it seems probable that Native Southeast Alaskans conducted their own transplants, intentional and otherwise. But in addition to this shuffling-around of local species, several mammals entirely unknown in Southeast prior to the arrival of white explorers have been experimentally and accidentally released here. In the early 1900s, arctic (blue) foxes were placed on many small islands by trappers. Unlike the case in the Aleutians, where foxes persist to this day, no known wild populations remain in Southeast. This is extremely fortunate; in the Aleutians foxes have had tragic impacts on nesting seabirds and waterfowl. Even in our area, they caused local extinctions of birds and small mammals.

Raccoons were introduced near Sitka and on northern Prince of Wales Island in the 1940s and '50s. Like the arctic fox, raccoons are potentially devastating to nesting birds, but thankfully they seem not to have survived in the wild.

The house mouse and the Norway rat are the "weeds" of the mammal world. Like their vegetative counterparts common plantain and sheep sorrel, they've followed European colonists into nearly every pocket of "civilization" on the globe. Unlike plantain and sorrel, they're not usually considered edible!

Encouraged by successful transplants on Afognak Island, the Alaska Department of Fish and Game introduced 50 Roosevelt elk to Etolin Island near Wrangell in 1987. The elk have spread to nearby Zarembo and Wrangell islands, and even to the mainland. Biologists fear they are not containable, and may displace native Sitka deer.

MARINE MAMMALS—Salt water is habitat rather than a "barrier" for our marine mammals, which are discussed more thoroughly on page 101. The most common range throughout the inland waters of Southeast: humpback and minke whales, orcas or killer whales, harbor and Dall porpoises, harbor seals and Steller's sea lions. Most humpback whales migrate to Hawaii in winter, but a few remain in Southeast throughout the year. Also occasionally seen along the outer coast are gray, fin, and Pacific pilot whales as well as the northern fur seal.

The sea otter, a seagoing member of the weasel family, is restricted mostly to the outer coast. However, they have recently penetrated as far inland as Glacier Bay. Protected since 1911, several hundred sea otters were relocated to Southeast Alaska in the late 1960s, in connection with underground nuclear testing on Amchitka Island in the Aleutians. By 1988 about 4500 of these playful animals graced our area.

BROWN AND BLACK BEARS

Most Southeast Alaskans are authorities on bears. Bears infest our imagination and quicken our love of the land. Comic, ominous, endearing, disgusting, incredibly beautiful, bears are our own wilder selves. When conversation lags, we revive it with bears. There's no need for Sasquatch in Southeast Alaska; we have Brown Bear.

ORIGINS—Bears diverged from doglike ancestors about 20 million years ago. Originally carnivorous, they turned to eating plants. Today bears are neither honed killers, like the cats and weasels, nor sophisticated herbivores, like the cud-chewing deer. They have the canine teeth of wolves but the molars of pigs and people. Their carnivore's gut tolerates only the highest-quality vegetation, like fresh sprouts, berries, and the more tender roots. Predators-turned-herbivores, bears met *Homo sapiens*—herbivores-turned-predators—coming the other way. Each of us straddles a dietary divide, and the position is often uncomfortable. As we do, bears survive by their wits and their penchant for experiment.

Also as we did, bears underwent physical and psychological revisions during the ice ages of the last 2 million years. Black and brown bears, our 2 Southeast Alaskan species, took different bites from the postglacial pie. The black bear is truer to standard bearlike behavior, an agile climber and furtive seeker of dense cover. The brown bear or grizzly has given up climbing except in cubhood, and often uses open tundra and preforest communities. The classic brown bear is actually the interior grizzly, which once ranged over almost all of North America. Our coastal brownies are the same species, but somewhat atypical—larger because of salmon diet and a longer foraging season. Big males can exceed 1000 pounds.

When brown bears moved into open country, females couldn't send their cubs up trees for protection. They then grew larger, and more aggressive toward potential predators, including wolves, people, and especially male brownies, who eat cubs whenever possible. A mother black bear, in contrast, will often hide from danger once her cubs have treed.

Most of the field marks that distinguish brown from black bears

Brown and Black Bears

Both tracks were 5½ inches across. Unlike the human foot, the big toe is on the outside.

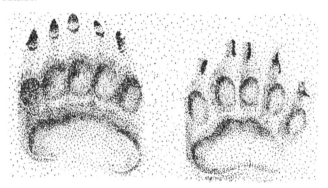

Small brownie, right front. Toes close together, almost in line. Long claws.

Large blackie, left front. Toes spread, aligned in strong arch. Claws less than 1½ inches from toe tips.

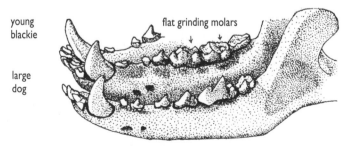

Lower jaws compared. Bears have carnivore jaws, but flattened molars for grinding plants. Dogs, cats, and weasels have sharp molars for shearing and breaking.

BEARS AND PEOPLE

Visitors to Southeast usually ask 1 of 2 questions about bears: "How can I see them?" or "How can I *not* see them?" The best way to see bears is from a boat or observation platform in an unhunted place like Pack Creek on Admiralty Island (contact the Forest Service first) or Glacier Bay, or with a knowledgeable guide. The best way not to see bears is to stay home (although in Southeast sometimes even that doesn't work) or to read *Bear Attacks, Their Causes and Avoidance,* by Stephen Herrero, who is an authority on bear encounters. We feel that this book says it all about safety in bear country, but 2 recent technological aids are worth mention.

Counter Assault™ is a new aerosol spray that has accumulated both positive and negative testimony over the past few years. Bear spray is especially appreciated by outdoorspeople who don't feel comfortable with firearms. And even if you do carry a gun for more serious encounters, the spray is more humane. But it may not stop a truly enraged bear!

Another newly available item is a bearproof food cannister, now required for kayak campers in Glacier Bay National Park and Preserve, where bears of both species have been unhunted for so long that food-related bear encounters are escalating.

Elsewhere in Southeast Alaska, bears are hunted during the spring and fall, and normally take to cover when they see people. Brown bears are killed mostly as trophies, usually on Admiralty, Baranof, or Chichagof islands, where about 60 animals are taken annually. A special tag is required, and females with cubs are not legal. Black bears are hunted for food by some residents.

With increased logging and mining in Southeast, wildlife managers are concerned about the future of brown bears, whose populations declined drastically during similar developments in the "lower 48." One of the many problems in field camps and small communities is garbage dumps. Habituated bears become menacing nuisances and often are destroyed.

People and bears have been like magnets to each other throughout our evolution, drawing and repelling in mutual fascination. When the bear is gone from our mountains, the heart is cut away. It's a privilege to live where we can still be frightened by a bear.

(p. 88) also date back to the brownie's shift from forest into more open country. The brown bear's tree-climbing ancestors, like today's black bears, had more widely spaced, grasping toes, and shorter, more tightly curved claws. Brownies traded these clinging claws for longer, straighter digging claws, and their toes became almost bound together, probably to reduce damage to them when the bear plows up boulder fields. The brown bear's hump is actually an enormous set of shoulder-blade muscles, also a digging feature. Both black and brown bears will dig, but brownies seem to enjoy it. Shallow scrapes for angelica sprouts in a coastal meadow, the mosses delicately overturned, are usually black bear sign. Brownies collecting alpine sweet vetch roots leave sign more suggestive of rototillers.

Color is fairly useless in distinguishing black from brown bears. Both can range from black to blond. Admiralty's brownies can be especially dark, and "cinnamon" black bears are common. The famous rare glacier bear, found mostly in the Yakutat area, is a blackie with a bluish-gray coat.

Black and brown bears may differ, but bears are opportunists and love to break rules. We've seen blackie tracks 20 miles from cover in the barrens of upper Glacier Bay, where only brownies are "supposed" to go. And we've watched a 200-pound brownie hitch her way easily up a 30-inch-diameter hemlock. The sudden appearance of a bear flusters us, and we forget to look for humps and dish faces and claw length—it's just a BEAR! Only later do we remember to wonder if it was black or brown.

LOCAL RESEARCH—The Alaska Department of Fish and Game has been following radio-collared brownies on Admiralty and Chichagof islands since 1981, and much has been learned about black bears recently from tagging and radio-collaring of "problem bears" in the Juneau area. Much of the following comes from Alaska Department of Fish and Game studies.

Researchers estimate there are from 6000 to 8000 brown bears between Yakutat and the Ketchikan area, with the highest density population, about 1 bear per square mile, occurring on Admiralty Island. Over 17,000 black bears are estimated to live in Southeast. The home ranges of coastal brown bears are about 40 square miles for males and 10 for females. On Admiralty Island, home ranges overlap wherever food is concentrated, with the resultant high population density.

In the spring both brown and black bears forage on south-facing avalanche slopes where snow disappears first, eating the nutritious roots and young shoots of skunk-cabbages and angelicas. They also venture onto salt marshes for newly emergent sedges. Before the arrival of Europeans in Southeast Alaska, the intertidal and its fringing meadows were like cafeteria serving-lines for bears. Hunters scanning the beaches from boats have evicted bears from much of this critical habitat, and only in protected places like Glacier Bay National Park can we get a true impression of bears' fondness for the coastline.

In summer, bears' diet expands to include devil's-club berries, salmonberries, blueberries, and currants. By midsummer, most brownies move to salmon streams, although some females with alpine territories eat no salmon at all. When salmon are abundant, particularly late in the summer, we have observed that bears foraging on spawned-out salmon carcasses tend to eat only the fat-rich brains, leaving the rest of the fish for other scavengers, such as bald eagles. Other foods include winter-killed deer, fawns, and long-tailed voles. Black bears have similar diets, although they may refrain from fishing if brownies are on the streams. When food runs out late in the fall, bears enter dens.

Brownies may dig dens in old-growth forests at 1000 to 2000 feet elevation under a large spruce or in the base of a snag. Many dens, however, are dug above tree line. The average elevation of 86 dens located by the Alaska Department of Fish and Game on Admiralty Island was 2339 feet. Individual bears probably don't reuse dens in successive years. Once it has denned, a bear's metabolism slows, but its temperature stays fairly high. During this winter sleep it neither urinates nor defecates. Bears den from about the end of October until the beginning of May, with time of emergence depending on spring snow melt. The first brown bears to den are females with cubs, followed by females without cubs, and finally by males. The following spring this order is reversed, with males emerging first; cubs weighing less than 10 pounds would be very vulnerable if they emerged earlier.

In Southeast, most female brown bears breed for the first time between the ages of 4 1/2 and 6 1/2 years. Black bears probably reach sexual maturity at 3 to 4 years for females and a year later for males. Mating occurs between May and July, and 1 to 4 cubs weighing about a pound each are born in midwinter to sleeping mothers. Emerged females with cubs try to avoid the cannibalistic males, but not always successfully. On Admiralty Island brown bear cubs suffer 60 percent mortality in their first year.

After reaching sexual maturity, brownie sows generally produce cubs only once every 4 years. Coupled with the high mortality of cubs, this gives brownies a low reproductive potential and a high sensitivity to overexploitation.

Some brown bears live 20 years or more. The age is determined by pulling a small premolar tooth from an immobilized or hunter-killed bear and sectioning this tooth to count the annual growth rings.

Short-tailed weasel with deer mouse in Sitka alder thicket

THE WEASEL FAMILY

From largest to smallest, the Southeast Alaskan members of the weasel family (Mustelidae) are sea otter (discussed with marine mammals), wolverine, river otter, marten, mink, short-tailed weasel or ermine, and least weasel. All have long bodies and stubby legs, with 5 toes on each foot. Their fur is dense, fine, and valuable. Their anal scent glands emit a characteristic skunky odor (the skunk doesn't occur here but is also a mustelid), which serves as a territorial marker and, in some, a defense against larger predators. Skinning a mustelid that has discharged these glands requires a tolerant nose.

No member of the dog or cat family is so widespread throughout Southeast as the short-tailed weasel, mink, marten, or river otter. And although our largest terrestrial weasel, the wolverine, hasn't fully colonized the islands, its range approximates that of the wolf—the non-mustelid runner-up for carnivorous ubiquity. The wolf and the wolverine need greater prey diversity and more room to wander than most of the islands can provide.

Because so many species of weasels live together here, all of them eating meat, they've specialized to avoid competition. One kind of specialization lies in the size sequence outlined above, with each species selecting prey appropriate to its strength and dimensions. A wolverine can drag down a mountain goat, and an ermine can squeeze into a mouse hole. Males of each weasel species are larger than females and often concentrate on different prey, reducing competition between the sexes when females are supporting families.

Wolverine skull

HABITATS—Habitat specialization is also important. Wolverines are tireless wanderers, fondest of our ridgetops and the barrens near glaciers, seeking marmots, ptarmigan, and carrion. Sea otters are so aquatic that they rarely come ashore, feasting on bottom-dwelling (benthic) invertebrates and fish. The river otter's diet overlaps somewhat with the sea otter's, but they are more tied to the land, working our coastlines, salmon streams, and lakeshores. And they apparently compete with mink; trappers notice that high river otter populations usually mean low mink numbers. Mink (p. 88) use the same marine and fresh waters as otters, but spend less time swimming. Their scats contain more mouse and vole hairs. The one habitat that every mustelid in Southeast eventually visits is the beach, so rich a food source that competition and encounters with larger predators are tolerated.

Martens (p. 88) are the old-growth forest specialists. They probably evolved as tree-climbers and windfall-denners under pressure from dangerous competitors like fox and lynx. This pressure is mostly lacking in Southeast, and here martens often risk forays along the beach and into shrublands and subalpine habitats. But most of the year, martens remain in the forest, feeding on northern red-backed voles, deer mice, and berries in season.

The short-tailed weasel probably uses more habitats than any other Southeast predator including the wolf, since it penetrates into microsites which the wolf can only sniff. Its paired line of dime-sized tracks meanders from rockweed to mountain heathers, through the densest cover and widest openings.

ANCESTRY—The weasel family is one of the ancient lineages of the order Carnivora. Two of the North American subfamilies of weasels— the Lutrinae, including river and sea otters, and the Mustelinae, including weasels, mink, marten and wolverine—went their separate ways 30 million years ago. This was before seals or sea lions had colonized the oceans, before early bears had diverged from the canid line, and before the Hominidae (the family that eventually produced humans) had split from the apes.

If you place the skulls of the members of the Southeast Alaskan weasel family side by side, the similarities overwhelm the differences. The ermine skull looks just like a scaled-down wolverine. Faces are snakelike in profile, with eyes far forward. The lower jaws are almost locked into the skull, moving up and down like hinges, unable to grind sideways. The most unique skull is the sea otter's, which has flattened molars for pulverizing shell, a divergence parallel to that of bear molars from the standard carnivore type.

For their size, mustelids are startlingly powerful. One of the few safe ways to experience this strength is to tie a piece of meat firmly to a string and go "fishing" for a short-tailed weasel. It takes a bit of teasing, but once frenzied, this 5-ounce terror will brace itself against a chair leg and try to rip the string from your fingers. In its winter white, with never a disheveled hair, the ermine blends daintiness with applied fury. Wolverine fishing isn't recommended.

Left foot of mink, with 5 toes typical of weasel family.

Mink tracks in fine sand on riverbank. Left hind foot above, left front below.

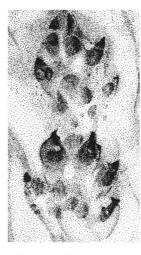

|◄——— 1¼" ———►|

|◄——— 1½" ———►|

THE RULE OF THUMB AND OTHER HANDY REFERENCES

Because most mammals shun humans, tracks and other sign are essential to students of mammal behavior. Some people even feel that bears leave droppings intentionally on our trails, to help prevent surprise encounters and let us know what and where they've been eating. We've long since overcome our inhibitions at disassembling mink or porcupine scats, even in the presence of students.

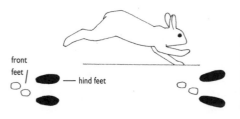

front feet / — hind feet

Snowshoe hare's hopping gait. Hares place one front foot slightly ahead of the other.

Tracks are equally engaging, and when you've graduated from basic identification to story-telling through tracks, the land begins to speak. Naturalist Greg Streveler of Gustavus has invented a rule of thumb for identifying tracks of local members of the weasel family. Footprints the size of your thumbnail are probably the short-tailed weasel's. If the diameter matches the distance from your thumbtip to your first joint, the track probably belongs to the weasel's bigger cousin the mink. Marten are only slightly heavier than mink, but have larger feet for flotation on snow, measuring from your thumbtip to your second joint. Tracks larger than these are probably river otter or wolverine.

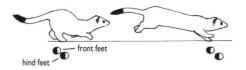

— front feet

hind feet —

Weasel's bounding gait. Front feet leave the prints, which the hind feet also land in.

Of course there are other nonmustelid possibilities in all of these size classes. Other clues, such as the gait, or arrangement of tracks, must be studied. To teach yourself to track mammals, first learn what species could occur in your area, and then read Murie or Halfpenny, excellent introductions to tracking.

Continued on page 89

The Hubbard Glacier at the mouth of Russell Fiord, near Yakutat, August 1989. The fiord was dammed by ice here in 1986, briefly creating an enormous lake. (D. Job)

▲ Peatland near Mole Harbor on Admiralty Island, with shore pines and yellow pondlilies.

▲ Rocky intertidal at Graves Harbor on the outer coast of Glacier Bay National Park and Preserve. (D. Job)

▲ The alpine tundra of Mount Jumbo keeps watch over Juneau, Alaska's capital city, nestled under Mount Juneau.

▶ The Mendenhall Wetlands near Juneau include some areas that are dominated by fresh water.

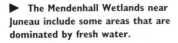

▼ Old-growth forest, with 7-foot-diameter western hemlock at Eagle River near Juneau.

▲ Many lakes dissect the old-growth coniferous forests on Admiralty Island. (J. Hyde)

▲ The Mendenhall Wetlands salt marsh near Juneau is a sea of sedges that supports large numbers of water birds and fish.

▲ Mendenhall Valley from Mount Meek, on Douglas Island. Subalpine meadows in foreground. (C. Pohl)

▲ The Taku River is one of the few major rivers that penetrate through the Coast Range of British Columbia to the sea. (D. Job)

▲ Lake Dorothy, at 2,423 feet, is an alpine sapphire near Juneau.

▶ Juneau Icefield. Devil's Paw in background on Canadian border.

▲   Young spruce spring up on recently uplifted tidelands at Gustavus Flats.

▶   Steep mountains thrust above a pristine cove in Misty Fiords National Monument. (A. Kimball)

▼   Dundas Bay, in Glacier Bay National Park and Preserve, shows the intimate relationships among mountains, glaciers, forests, and sea so typical of Southeast Alaska. (J. Hyde)

Fast-growing bull kelp on the outer coast of Baranof Island. (D. Job)

▲ **Large ears and eyes distinguish deer mice from the related voles.**

▲ **Killer whale breaching.** (J. Hyde)

◀ **Northern flying squirrel.** (R. Wood)

▲ **Northern red-backed vole, a forest dweller.**

▲ **Benjamin Island in Lynn Canal is an important sea lion haulout.** (D. Job)

▼ **Humpback whales are often seen breaching in Southeast Alaska.** (J. Hyde)

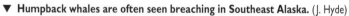

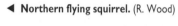

▲ Black bear near Anan Creek, a major salmon stream. (J. Hyde)

▲ Porcupine feeding on spruce needles.

▲ Marten, the most "catlike" member of the weasel family.

▲ A mink eating a sea urchin. (D. Job)

▼ Brown bears interacting at Pack Creek on Admiralty Island. (J. Hyde)

Especially around humans, mustelids prefer to hunt under cover of darkness. But in midsummer, night shrinks to a few hours, and every member of the family forages by daylight. And beach-cruising mustelids may be more keyed to stage of tide than time of day. The most observable of our mustelids are the mink and the river otter, runners of beaches and salmon streams, happy to borrow a fish from your stringer or to scent-mark the deck of your boat.

REPRODUCTION AND ABUNDANCE—Our mustelids give birth between late winter and early summer, so that the rapidly growing carnivore pack places greatest demands on mom only at the peak of prey availability. The wolverine, slower to mature, gets a head start, as early as January. Most species mate in summer. As a result, gestation takes more time than the rapidly growing embryos actually need. Mustelids solve this problem by delayed implantation; the fertilized ova remain dormant, floating freely in the uterus until the last month or so of pregnancy. Only the mink has a relatively short gestation, mating in early spring and birthing in early summer. But delayed implantation occurs even in this species.

Most mustelids are capable of breeding in their second summer. Only the river and sea otters take longer. Life expectancy varies roughly with size. Few short-tailed weasels live more than a year or two, but wolverines may survive a decade. Litter size averages 3 or 4 in most species.

Mink, river otter, and ermine can sustain a fairly high population density as predators go, and removal of some by trappers may locally depress numbers but doesn't appear to affect regional density. Wolverines hunt beyond the range of most trap lines, and are so thinly distributed that few are taken in Southeast. Marten glean most of their food from old growth, a less productive habitat than beach or streamside. But while marten are less abundant than mink, they're easily trapped. In the contiguous 48 states, marten have repeatedly been overtrapped, and their current range is much reduced. They've also been eliminated from some areas by logging of old-growth forests. The Alaska Department of Fish and Game recently started a radiotelemetry study of marten on heavily logged northern Chichagof Island, to see if marten have been impacted there.

SITKA BLACK-TAILED DEER

For many of us, the Sitka black-tailed deer has come to symbolize the old-growth forests and subalpine meadows of Southeast Alaska. The deer distills our vast acres of coastal hemlocks and high-country parklands into one small package of flesh and blood. Deer have received more attention—scientific, romantic, and culinary—than any other local mammal.

MULE AND BLACK-TAILED DEER—Sitka blacktails are one of 7 subspecies of *Odocoileus hemionus*, a species that includes both black-tailed and mule deer. Black-tailed deer, in contrast to mule deer, have smaller bodies and antlers and less strikingly patterned coats, use denser cover, and are less gregarious. Sitka blacktails have the thickest-diameter guard hairs of the species. The branches of their small antlers are thick relative to their length, and brow tines (points near the base of antlers) are larger and more common than in the closely related Columbian blacktails, which occupy the coast ranges from northern Vancouver Island south to California. Sitkas tend to be stockier and shorter-faced than Columbians, but the two blacktail subspecies intergrade on mainland coastal British Columbia.

DEER HABITATS—Ecologist Victor Shelford, in his book on the geographical life zones, or biomes, of North America, described Southeast Alaska and coastal British Columbia as the "hemlock–Sitka deer–Sitka spruce association." In so doing, he recognized not only the wide range in habitat use by Sitka blacktails, but the major influence our deer have on their environment. Blacktails can be seen from 4000-

Sitka black-
tailed deer in
old-growth
forest

foot summits down to the intertidal. Their grazing and browsing leave unmistakable evidence in forests, thickets, meadows, and beaches.

Most months, it seems that the bulk of our deer are at snow line, following its climatic whims up and down the mountainsides. In spring, deer are selective feeders, preferring the first unfolding leaves and sprouts spread in the wake of the receding snowpack. Summer is devoted to replenishing fat stores, nursing young, and growing antlers, and the best place for this is the fertile subalpine meadows, where high-protein herbs flourish in almost continual daylight.

With the first high-country frosts, subalpine meadow herbs begin to wilt (p. 84). Deer move down into the mountain hemlock stands, beginning the shift from herbs and shrub leaves to evergreen plants and the stems of blueberry bushes. Especially where they are heavily hunted, deer wait at high montane elevations until deepening snow forces them down.

DEER AND OLD GROWTH—A controversy involving Sitka deer came to a full boil in the late 1980s, spilling out of the hands of local land managers right onto the floor of Congress. The resulting Tongass Timber Reform Act and subsequent skirmishes will greatly influence the future of the Tongass National Forest. The debate included, among other problems, the winter habitat needs of Southeast Alaskan deer and the consequences of logging their high-volume old-growth winter refuges. In fact, the Sitka deer/logging debate has caused deer researchers nationwide to rethink some of the most basic and unquestioned principles of wildlife biology.

It was long assumed that deer responded favorably to the stimulation of forage plants in recent clearcuts, and that "what's good for loggers is good for deer." This idea was and is especially prevalent in Washington and Oregon, and in other places where winter snow accumulations rarely prevent deer from moving into clearcuts to feed. As recently as the 1970s, wildlife biologists considered "mature old-growth forests" almost useless as deer habitat.

Southeast Alaskan old-growth researchers finally pointed out the fallacy in this assumption. The supposed "old growth" so barren of deer and other wildlife was, in fact, even-aged forest less than 2 centuries old, mature only from a timber harvester's viewpoint. The lowland high-volume forests of the northwestern states have been so extensively logged and burned that there are few genuine old-growth stands remaining to study!

Exhaustive fieldwork by the Alaska Department of Fish and Game has shown that clearcuts here are little used by deer compared to adjacent old-growth forests, where low-growing evergreen plants such as bunchberry and shrubs such as blueberry sustain them. The multi-layered tree canopy of old-growth forests intercepts winter snows, yet admits enough light in summer for growth of understory forage species. The key is snow-free forage; early growth after clearcutting provides forage but is buried in snow, while dense second growth intercepts snow but has poor forage.

Throughout North America, deer of all kinds need "edge," the proximity of open foraging habitat and dense cover. In most states, where old growth was erased centuries ago, edge means the contact between a thick young forest and a meadow or farmer's field. Edge takes on subtler meaning in Southeast Alaskan old-growth forests. The patchwork understory of an ancient forest offers countless *internal* edges. A doe might rise from her December bed under a bushy subcanopy hemlock, take several steps, and find a healthy evergreen clone of five-leaf bramble only lightly dusted by snow, while in nearby muskegs and clearcut openings, the snow is up to her belly!

Even summer habitat may be inferior in young clearcuts with superficially abundant forage. Research by the Forestry Sciences Laboratory in Juneau showed that leaves of blueberry, bunchberry, five-leaf bramble, and skunk-cabbage from open clearcuts all tested higher in tannins and were less palatable to deer than leaves of the same species in nearby shaded forests.

Now that old growth has become a catchword and rallying cry of environmentalists, we are perhaps in danger of accepting another unquestioned dogma, the reverse of the old one, expecting high-volume old-growth forests to be year-round game paradises. This isn't true, least of all for deer.

In the mild winters of 1983 through 1988, with only shallow snow accumulations even in openings, we noticed deer tracks mostly in scrubby, low-volume, old-growth forests of little interest to loggers. These stands, with widely spaced smaller hemlocks, admit more light to the shrub and herb layers than most high-volume stands, and usually offer more winter food for deer. Stepping from these low-volume stands into high-volume forests on alluvial fans, the light is dimmer, and shrubs and herbs fewer. Tracks show that deer are avoiding the big timber.

But look closer—those scattered low blueberry shrubs have been browsed down below knee height by deer. Periodically, even in mild winters, large numbers of deer are forced by snowstorms to retreat together into these high-volume stands. And during severe winters they may have to spend months on end there.

Wintering deer do best in a mosaic of high- and low-volume old-growth stands, each with a different balance of forage and protection from snow. As snow depth fluctuates, deer move. High-volume stands, however, are relatively scarce. These giant trees repeatedly become the key to survival for Sitka black-tailed deer. And they're the trees we are logging right now. It may be 300 years before there are again similar trees to shelter large numbers of deer.

BEAVER, PORCUPINE, AND HOARY MARMOT

In order of size, the 3 largest rodents of Southeast Alaska are the beaver, the porcupine, and the hoary marmot. While their habitats could hardly be more different, they use those habitats in similar ways. Their physiques, "personalities," and reproductive strategies are also alike.

RODENTHOOD—A rodent could be defined, with apologies to kangaroo rats and other racy exceptions, as a plump and visually unimpressive body designed to transport a truly impressive set of curved, chisel-tipped, ever-growing, self-sharpening incisors. The incisor has been for rodents what gunpowder was for the European invaders of the New World. Rodents have followed these revolutionary front teeth into holes, up trees, and under water, thereby diversifying into about 1700 species, more than that of any other mammalian order.

REPRODUCTION—The incisor patent has spawned a staggering fecundity on the part of some of the smaller rodents. But beavers, porcupines, and marmots are not prolific. In fact the porcupine has one of the slowest reproductive rates of North American mammals. This may be hard for some dog owners to believe. A walk in the woods with a good porky hound quickly demonstrates the prevalence of this rodent; there must be some advantage to the porcupine's conservative reproductive effort! What are the pros and cons of speedy versus slow reproduction?

Speedy reproduction includes species that are short-lived, promiscuous, have many offspring, often with multiple litters per year, and care only briefly for the young. The most often cited rodent example is the meadow vole, which lives a year at most, and within a month of birth begins turning out litters of about 6 babies, up to 3 times per summer. This high turnover rate is appreciated and assisted by weasels! Speedy reproducers can immediately respond to unpredictable bonuses like bumper seed crops or beached whales.

Slow reproduction is found in individuals that live for many years, are often monogamous, give birth to few offspring, and have prolonged child-rearing. Classic examples are elephants and humans, but among rodents the extreme cases are the beaver, porcupine, and hoary marmot. These may all live for well over a decade, don't mate for at least 2 years, have 4 or fewer young per litter (only 1 for porkies!), and have only 1 litter per year. While speedy reproducers simply die off when their environment degenerates, slow reproducers prepare for and weather the slump by educating their young.

FEEDING BEHAVIOR—Beavers, marmots, and porcupines have realized the full potential of the ever-growing incisor. Only a perpetually renewed and self-sharpening tooth could meet the demands of bark removal and severing of gritty roots, let alone the actual felling of trees by gnawing into undecayed heartwood. Wood chips at the base of a 12-inch beaver-dropped cottonwood are as big as the flakes from a razor-sharp axe. And though the work of beaver and porky teeth is seen everywhere in the woods and streamsides of Southeast Alaska, the accomp-

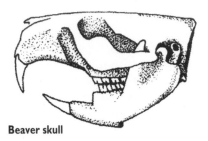

Beaver skull

lishment of marmot incisors is hardly less impressive—they are employed in devouring tough willow rootstock and carrying rocks from burrows. As with all rodent incisors, those of beavers, marmots, and porcupines depend on constant heavy wear to prevent them from growing too long to use.

Although beavers and porcupines have reputations as tree eaters, the consumption of inner bark and twigs is only a part of their annual foraging routine. Like their cousin the marmot, and like almost all herbivores, beavers and porkies shift in summer to a diet of juicy, fastgrowing, nutritious sprouts. Beavers take sedge tips, pondweeds, and other aquatic vegetation, while porkies move out from forests into

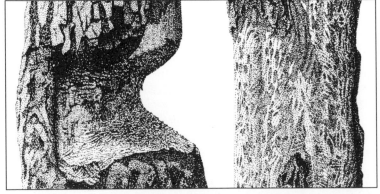

Beaver-gnawed cottonwood on left was partially cut many years ago but survived, and bark is beginning to grow back over the corner of the wound. Porcupinegirdled spruce, right, was killed, the cambium mostly removed.

coastal wetlands to graze on beach greens or yarrow, or into subalpine meadows to share the marmot's fare of coltsfoot, paintbrush, and buckwheat. The use of woody foods by beavers and porcupines is an answer to the same problem which the marmot solves by hibernating; there's nothing else to eat in winter. The porcupine is fortunate in that its treetop escape habitat is also its winter larder (p. 88). The frozen beaver pond has no such access to food, so the beaver puts down a cache of submerged willow and cottonwood branches in autumn to sustain it through the winter. Beavers and porcupines go into low-energy mode when the snow flies. Meantime, marmots are in almost zero-energy mode. Along with bats and jumping mice, they're the only true hibernators in Southeast Alaska (bears' body temperature stays high).

LARGE BELLIES, SOCIAL LIFE, AND THE COST OF SEDENTARY HABITS—Portly rodents are not swift. Only marmots can reach the feeble velocity of 10 miles per hour. Partly as a result of this insecurity from predation, the beaver and marmot are sedentary, not wandering far from water or burrows. The porcupine, defended by quills, is freer to roam. But alarmed porcupines take to a well-known tree if possible, aware of their vulnerability to people, and to wolves which, when hunting cooperatively, can kill porkies by biting repeatedly at their unquilled faces. And because its winter diet of cambium is unlimited, a porcupine, like a beaver or marmot, can live on a very few acres. Even in summer we see the same individuals week after week, grazing the same narrow strip of beach.

The porcupine is normally solitary, except for mother-and-young pairs and brief but spectacular mating encounters. By contrast, the marmot and beaver are extremely social. Marmots, also known as whistle pigs, live in noisy colonies for security against predators. The same holds for tail-slapping beavers, with the added benefit of close teamwork in dam building and maintenance. Young marmots and beavers spend their first winter with their mothers. This is unusual among rodents, and allows for more learning and less dependence on "hard-wired" instinctual behavior. While most young marmots and beavers must leave the parent homestead, a lucky few will inherit valuable property, with several generations of investment in tunnel digging or dam construction.

Like human civilizations, though, marmot towns and beaver workings come

Hoary marmot

and go with the rhythms of natural succession. Beaver gradually exhaust the supply of streamside brush near their lodge, and must leave the site fallow for a time. And while gnawers and grazers rearrange the vegetation, predators rearrange the herbivores. In areas lacking deer, most valley-bottom wolf scats we've examined contain bones and hair of beaver, while wolf scats on high ridges are often composed of the frosty-tipped guard hairs of the hoary marmot. A family of wolves can extinguish a marmot colony in a summer, and brown bears excavating marmot burrows can make some highland pastures uninhabitable, restricting marmots to bedrock outcroppings or fields of boulders too large to move.

Sedentary habits, combined with formidable appetites, means that our 3 large rodents leave unmistakable imprints on their environment. Marmots "farm" the subalpine meadows, as if tethered like horses to their burrow entries, clipping, plowing, trampling, and fertilizing. Porcupines are often the dominant herbivores in Southeast Alaskan forests, grazing and browsing herbs and shrubs in summer, and switching to inner bark of conifers in winter, occasionally killing trees by girdling. And the beaver is a creator and modifier of wetlands, a factor as significant in the course of succession as landslides or wave erosion.

RED SQUIRREL

The red squirrel is the most easily observed mammal in Southeast Alaska. It's even easier to hear one of its seven recognizable calls, which it rehearses at every opportunity. Red squirrels are diurnal in habit and don't hibernate in winter. They're usually most active in the morning and evening, but in winter they go about during the warmth of midday. In summer they have energy to spare, running up and down tree trunks headfirst and leaping 10 feet between branches. They can also run along the underside of branches. They rarely fall, but when they do, they usually escape injury.

Red squirrels forage mostly in conifers. In early spring they consume tender buds, and in August they cut unopened green cones from the upper branches of Sitka spruce. To extract and eat the seeds, they hold each cone in the

Red squirrel

forepaws and rotate it rapidly while chewing; cone scales fly in all directions. In late summer and fall, most cones are not eaten but are deliberately cached by each squirrel in its own midden, a large pile of cones on the forest floor, or in chambers connected to underground tunnels. The midden is usually located near the base of a large, productive spruce tree. These cones sustain the squirrel during the lean winter months. In some years the spruce cone crop is meager, while the western hemlocks produce a heavy crop. Squirrels may then consume more hemlock cones, but because they are so much smaller than spruce cones, the squirrels often harvest them by cutting an entire twigful at a time. Because of their preference for spruce and ability to thrive on little else but its seed, red squirrels fare better in the early, impoverished understory stages of forest succession than most other local mammals.

Studies have shown that in the interior of Alaska, red squirrels consume about 144 white spruce cones per day, and that a single midden may contain up to 16,000 cones. As much as 70 percent of the white spruce cone crop may be harvested. Peculiarly, some squirrels have been observed caching empty cones, while other squirrels remove a few scales from each cone, apparently checking to make sure it contains seeds. Juvenile squirrels cache fewer cones, which helps explain their higher mortality rate.

The red squirrel is fond of sap and will drive the red-breasted sapsucker away from its carefully drilled holes in trees. Squirrels also cut mushrooms and lodge them in branch crotches, possibly to keep them from neighbors. They consume even the poisonous fly agaric with no apparent ill effects. They may also eat small mammals such as shrews, and small nestling birds. In turn, the squirrels are eaten by large birds of prey and by marten. But an adult red squirrel is a formidable creature, and predation seems to be less of a factor in population dynamics than territorialism and food supply.

The red squirrel's home-range size is also controlled by food supply, and varies from ½ to 6 acres. It defends its territory against both sexes, striking a brief truce only at mating time. Each red squirrel typically constructs several nests. It builds arboreal nests of twigs and leaves, or grasses when available, on a limb not far from the trunk of the tree. The squirrel also may nest in hollows inside tree trunks, which it carefully lines with plant material, or it may construct a den underground. The squirrel sleeps in its nest at night and may spend several days there to wait out a severe storm.

Red squirrels reach sexual maturity at about 1 year of age, but not all females breed each year. Of 17 squirrels we once live-trapped in June, only 2 were nursing females. Breeding occurs in March or April and is preceded by mating chases; the female scampers away, with the male in hot pursuit. After a gestation period of 36 to 40 days, a litter of

3 or 4 young is born in May or early June. The young squirrels are naked, blind, and deaf at birth and are totally dependent on their mother. They develop rapidly and are weaned at about 5 weeks of age, but they will usually remain with their mother until they are about 18 weeks old, when they are almost adult size. The life span of red squirrels in nature is unknown, but individuals have lived in captivity for 10 years.

SHREWS, MICE, AND VOLES

Shrews, mice, and voles are the nickels and dimes of nature's currency, eaten by such diverse predators as great blue herons, northern shrikes, house cats, and even red squirrels. Shrews belong to the order Insectivora and are only distantly related to mice and voles, which are members of the order Rodentia. We discuss them together here because they share a position at the base of the mammalian food pyramid.

SHREWS—Shrews are among the smallest mammals in the world; an adult of the smallest species weighs less than half a pat of butter. Because they are so tiny, shrews lose heat rapidly, and to fuel a warm-blooded metabolism they must eat relatively enormous amounts of food. Shrews typically consume more than their own weight in meat every day. We have watched a 2-inch shrew consume an entire earthworm in a sitting, devouring each segment as it was pulled out of the ground. Shrews' diet consists mainly of insects, but includes other small invertebrates such as snails and spiders, and occasionally plants and fungi. If shrews are prevented from eating by being caught in a trap, they quickly die. This

Masked shrew on western hemlock cone. These cones are about the size of a penny.

makes them difficult to study, and the biology of most species is poorly known. The pulse rate of a frightened shrew may elevate to 1200 beats per minute, and they may be literally scared to death if you pick them up and handle them.

Shrews twitter constantly at frequencies inaudible to us as they forage in leaf litter and under logs with their long, pointed, flexible snout. Like bats, they find their prey by echolocation, monitoring the echoes of emitted squeaks in order to discern moving objects. Shrews attack and eat animals larger than themselves, such as mice and even small birds. In turn, shrews are eaten by such predators as hawks, owls, and the forest-dwelling members of the weasel family, although a musk gland on each flank makes the shrew rather unpalatable.

The masked shrew is a species found throughout Southeast Alaska, except on Prince of Wales and neighboring islands. An adult masked shrew is about 4 inches in length, half of which is tail, and weighs about a fifth of an ounce. Like those of other shrews, its eyes and ears are so tiny they are barely discernible.

The female masked shrew bears 2 or 3 litters per season. After a gestation period of only 17 or 18 days, an average of 5 or 6 young are born in a nest built of grass and concealed beneath a fallen log or rotting stump. The life span of the masked shrew is probably less than 14 to 16 months.

Also common in Southeast Alaska is the dusky shrew, found everywhere except on Baranof and Chichagof islands. The water shrew is less well known in Southeast, but has been found on mainland lakes and streams. This is a giant among shrews, reaching the size of a mouse.

DEER MICE—Deer mice are larger than shrews and have blunter snouts. Their large round ears are bare and they have big eyes (p. 87). Deer mice are primarily nocturnal. Although the deer mouse looks like a house mouse, an introduced Old World species, it's more closely related to voles and muskrats.

Deer mice are found throughout Southeast Alaskan conifer forests, thickets, and even bare glacial rubble. Most backwoods cabins resound at night with the scamperings and territorial scratchings of this lovely species. The adult's coat color resembles a deer's, reddish brown above, with white underparts and feet. Deer mouse scats are somewhat less lovely, however, especially in frying pans and coffee cups.

Deer mice are little dynamos. Their diet is catholic, consisting of seeds of grasses, herbs and conifers, fruits, berries, tender grass stems, insects, and other invertebrates. They transport seeds to a cache near the nest, for consumption mostly in winter when other foods are scarce.

Each mouse forages within a home range of about 2 acres, but home ranges of several mice may overlap in bounteous environments like cabins. In winter deer mice remain active, dashing over snow or tunneling beneath it, so they're often caught by owls. Other important predators include weasels, mink, and marten.

Deer mice use fine plant material to construct cup-shaped nests in tree cavities, beneath upturned roots, or nestled into your ceiling insulation. A female reaches sexual maturity when barely more than a month old and produces several litters per year. The gestation period is 3 to 4 weeks, and the average litter size is 4. Young deer mice depend on the care provided by both parents, and the mother will usually defend the territory around the nest. Juvenile deer mice are driven off before the next litter arrives. The deer mouse population bottoms out in spring after the rigors of winter, but after the summer's fecundity, their numbers are much higher. Few individuals survive an entire year, however.

Shrew and Mouse Skulls

Masked shrew (top): Pointed snout, large hooked leading incisor.

Deer mouse (bottom): No canine teeth. Long gap between flat molars and curved, chisel-like, deeply rooted incisors.

VOLES—Voles and mice are both rodents of the family Muridae, but voles have fatter bodies and their legs appear shorter. Their noses are more rounded, and their eyes and ears are smaller, almost concealed beneath the fur. Most voles have relatively short tails. They seem less jumpy and hyperactive than deer mice.

The northern red-backed vole (p. 87) is about the size of a deer mouse. Its coat bears a broad reddish stripe down the center of the back, accounting for its common name. Like deer mice, red-backed voles are mainly nocturnal, but in summer the hours of darkness are so few that they're forced to forage in daylight. Red-backed voles are abundant in the forests and thickets of Southeast Alaska, consuming the foliage, twigs, and fruit of shrubs as well as wintergreen and bunchberry plants. The vole's nest may be constructed on the surface of the ground or in a short underground burrow. They produce 2 or 3 litters during the summer, with an average size of 6. The young are naked, blind, and deaf at birth, and heavily dependent on parental care, but they develop rapidly, and in only 18 days are weaned and leave the

Recently unfolded sprout of Nootka lupine, nipped by a long-tailed vole while still closed.

nest. The Gapper's or Southern red-backed vole is a closely related species which replaces the northern red-backed vole on the mainland and some islands south of the Stikine River.

Several other species of voles occur in Southeast. The most ubiquitous is the long-tailed vole, which lives primarily in beach fringe and subalpine meadows. As its name implies, the tail is longer than that of other voles, nearly as long as that of the deer mouse. Every few years, long-tailed voles reach very high population densities. As the winter snows melt back, their clippings, shrub girdlings, root diggings, runways, and scat piles are highly visible among the flattened mulch of coastal meadows. Ordinarily, though, it takes keener senses than ours to detect the presence of these voles. Harriers and hikers' dogs listen for their high-pitched squeaks and rustlings, while minks and weasels sniff them out. At low population levels, their runways are inconspicuous.

Other small rodents are the tundra vole of early successional habitats on the northern mainland, the meadow vole and jumping mouse, and the northern bog lemming, which lives in our mainland fens and wet sedge meadows.

MARINE MAMMALS

Sitka was established by the Russians in 1799 as a center for the collection of sea otter pelts. Marine mammals have been commercially important to Southeast Alaska ever since, mostly in ways we'd rather forget. As sea otters neared extinction, whaling stations appeared, such as the one at Port Armstrong on south Baranof Island, which operated between 1912 and 1922. And now, with most whales endangered, they're deemed more valuable alive and spouting for tour vessels than rendered into oil and burning in our lamps.

The marine mammals of Southeast belong to two separate orders. The order Cetacea includes whales, dolphins, and porpoises, and the order Carnivora includes sea otters, seals, and sea lions. Some biologists place the seals and sea lions in a third order, Pinnipedia or "finfeet." Others believe that seals descended from early members of the weasel family and that sea lions are separately derived from early bearlike creatures that became aquatic. If this interpretation is correct, the order Pinnipedia is an artificial category.

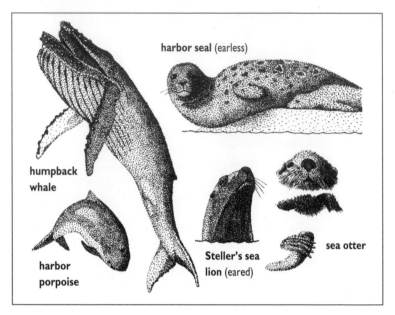

Representatives of Major Marine Mammal Groups
Baleen whales, dolphins, eared and earless seals, and the weasel family.

CETACEANS—The Cetacea appear suddenly in the fossil record about 50 million years ago. Their closest contemporary relatives are in fact even-toed ungulates like pigs ("porpoise" comes from Latin words meaning "pig-fish"). Cetaceans are now totally aquatic, even bearing young in the water, while other marine mammals haul out onto beaches or icebergs to give birth. Cetaceans have no hind limbs, while other marine mammals retain 4 appendages, although they are highly modified in the seals and sea lions.

Cetaceans include toothed whales—sperm whales, killer whales, and porpoises; and baleen whales, which have fringed baleen plates made of keratin suspended from the upper jaws, to trap small prey as water is expelled through the plates. Since baleen whales have teeth before birth, it's believed they evolved from toothed species.

Humpback whales belong to the rorqual family of baleen whales, which have pleats along the throat and belly that allow the body wall to expand as they take in huge quantities of water during feeding. Humpbacks "lunge feed," swimming open-mouthed through dense concentrations of krill (shrimplike crustaceans) or schooling fish. Another method, first described by Dr. Charles Jurasz of Juneau, is "bubble-net feeding," in which the whale spirals upward, blowing a curtain of bubbles which concentrates the prey. The whale then bursts through the surface at the center of the "net," trailing foam and fish.

A CLOSE ENCOUNTER IN CHATHAM STRAIT

Cynthia D'Vincent, director of Intersea Research, a national research group based in Friday Harbor, Washington, has frequent contacts with whales in the course of her work. She emphasizes that her studies "are conducted unobtrusively out of respect for the whales...and because our research is concerned with the observation of nonmanipulated behaviors." Feeding whales offer such quiet opportunities, but occasionally high drama takes over. D'Vincent reports:

"On one such occasion I was sitting in our 13-foot Boston Whaler observing a group of 9 whales.... My boat was dead in the water with a hydrophone over the side.... While the whales were singing, I scanned the placid water for any sign of where they might surface. Sometimes they blew a bubble net simultaneously with the song [but] more often there was no sign at all, except in that fraction of a second before they emerged, when thousands of herring flew into the air in a last attempt to escape. The whales would then burst through the surface in a powerful lunge with mouths wide open.... Over and over again the performance was repeated as they tirelessly worked the productive reef.

"The day had been long. I was parched and burnt...and decided to head back to the ship. The whales had been down a long time, and then I began to hear the song without the aid of the hydrophone. At once all of the nearby herring stopped their surface swimming. An ominous silence fell upon the stillness of the day.... Nervously I glanced over the side...just in time to see the white flash of pectoral fins racing to the surface.... I grabbed my camera as the whales broke through and snapped a picture—as I thought, my last. Tremendous jaws encased my boat, baleen surrounded me and herring shot through the air, landing at my feet. Within a split second, the whales saw me and they veered, collided, then sank back into the deep.... Nothing else in my life has ever produced such a combination of thrills, alarms, and excitement...." (From *Voyaging with the Whales*, by Cynthia D'Vincent)

Noting that whales are sensitive to sounds, D'Vincent advises motor sailors to avoid danger by letting their engines idle. Kayakers and those under sail should bang their hulls from time to time, to let whales know of their presence.

Sometimes several humpbacks blow bubble nets in a tightly coordinated group. It's a good idea not to be inside a bubble net in a small boat!

Between about April and November, humpback whales feed in the rich fiords of Southeast Alaska, fattening for migration to winter calving grounds in Hawaii (a few humpbacks do overwinter in Southeast). Mating occurs on the wintering grounds, and since pregnancy lasts about 11 months, the calves are born there the following year. Since the calf is also nursed for up to 11 months, babies are produced only every other year. Over their life span females may bear up to 15 calves. A 1991 estimate of the North Pacific humpback population was only 1398 to 2040, or about 8 to 13 percent of the population prior to commercial whaling; for Southeast Alaska it was 300 to 350.

Humpbacks are often seen breaching—leaping out of the water— or slapping the surface with their long flippers (p. 87). They have a small "humped" dorsal fin well back on the body, and many lumps, or "stovebolts," on their head and jaws. Much of their skin is covered with barnacles, a different species from those on intertidal rocks. These barnacles filter plankton and don't parasitize the whale, but they do create drag, so whales sometimes come into shallow waters to rub them off on the rocks.

Minke whales look much like small humpbacks and are the second most often seen baleen whale in Southeast's inside waters. Gray whales aren't residents of Southeast, but large numbers move past our outer coast twice yearly between summer arctic feeding grounds and winter calving grounds in the lagoons of Baja California. In addition to straining plankton with their short baleen plates, gray whales also scoop mud off the bottom and sift out marine worms and shellfish, a unique behavior among whales.

PORPOISES AND DOLPHINS—The cosmopolitan killer whale, or orca, is actually the world's largest dolphin (p. 87). Probably several hundred live here year round, although no accurate estimates have been made. Orcas reach 31 feet and have about 2 dozen blunt teeth resembling huge Brazil nuts. Their prey includes all of our marine mammals plus fish, such as cod and flatfish. Seen from a kayak, the dorsal fin of the orca is memorable—it stands 2 or 3 feet high on females, and 6 feet on big males.

Dall and harbor porpoises abound here. Even without a close look, their different swimming styles immediately distinguish them. Harbor porpoises are usually seen close to shore, backs and dorsal fins rising and falling sedately. Dall porpoises are the ones seen sprinting, kicking up spray in mid-channel, or riding the bow wave of larger boats. With their black-and-white markings, Dalls look like miniature orcas.

SEALS AND SEA LIONS—These are the finfoot counterparts of the harbor and Dall porpoise, similarly distinguishable by their behavior. When a round head comes up quietly, turns 90 degrees or so to take in the view, then slips gently under, it's a harbor seal. When you hear a vigorous "whoosh," and see a bearlike head plowing purposefully through the waves, it's a Steller's sea lion. Harbor seals play at the surface only on special occasions, but sea lions do it almost constantly, rolling, slapping, sometimes leaping completely out of the water.

Harbor seals eat squid, shrimp, and fish, especially pollock and capelin. Steller's sea lions consume all these and more cod and herring. Seals fish more often in estuaries and take more sand lance and eulachon than do sea lions. Seals stay down longer, a behavior that allows them to hunt solitary or hidden prey such as octopus, while sea lions target mostly near-bottom schooling fish.

Both seals and sea lions may give birth on rocks, but harbor seals especially favor the iceberg-strewn waters near tidewater glaciers. Pups on icebergs are free from predation by terrestrial predators such as bears, and even orcas avoid the cloudy bay-head waters. Newborns need only be defended from gulls and eagles, who eye them while scavenging afterbirths. Tracy Arm and upper Glacier Bay have famous seal-pupping grounds. Important haulout sites for sea lions occur at Forrester Island, at the extreme southwestern corner of Southeast Alaska, and Benjamin Island (p. 87), near Juneau.

Like the gray whale, the northern fur seal isn't resident in Southeast but may pass by our outer coast en route between pupping grounds in the Pribilofs and wintering waters as far south as California.

SEA OTTERS—These marine weasels grow to be 5 feet long and 80 pounds, and live in the nearshore habitats of our outer coast, especially submerged reefs off rocky beaches. Sea otters often live in kelp beds. They can give birth at any time of year. Pups stay with the parents, who introduce them to a diet of chitons, mussels, snails, rock oysters, clams, octopus, crabs, sea urchins, sea stars, and fish.

Sea otters are a keystone species in our waters because of their predation on green sea urchins, abalones, and other important herbivores. In the absence of otters, these grazers flourish and decimate kelp beds, which are important habitats for many fish and crustaceans. Removal of urchins by otters favors the kelp beds and their inhabitants. In feeding, otters may carry a rock on their chest, to use as an anvil to smash urchins or other hard-shelled prey. During storms, otters ride out the surf by wrapping a strip of kelp around their middles for stability.

UPS AND DOWNS—The chance to watch marine mammals in their natural habitat is a large part of the lure of Southeast Alaska. Although currently guarded by the Marine Mammal Protection Act of 1972, many species of marine mammal are recovering from population sizes once reduced almost to vanishing. As a result, they have probably lost much of their genetic diversity and may remain vulnerable to environmental changes long after their populations return, if ever, to original levels. And the Protection Act doesn't prevent people from loving marine mammals to death. The growing popularity of sea kayaking threatens newborn seals on icebergs, who easily get separated from their mothers. Sightseers too close to sea lion rookeries can trigger avalanches of flesh, as the animals flee into the water, an even more thrilling form of harassment.

Each of our marine mammals has in some way run afoul of human recreation or enterprise. Some conflicts have been reduced, but when commerce is involved, protective regulations may lose their teeth. Humpback whales ignited a lively argument over tour vessel use in Glacier Bay National Park after the humpbacks' puzzling mass exodus from traditional feeding grounds in 1978. One interpretation held that vessel traffic had reached intolerable levels; another that whales left when their prey naturally decreased. Both responses—to harassment and to prey availability—have since been demonstrated.

Declines in prey species, over longer terms, are not always "natural." American fisheries follow the Japanese example by targeting fish that are progressively lower on the food pyramid. Escalating Pacific herring and walleye pollock harvests compete with even the baleen whales for food. Pollock accounted for over half of sea lion diet in a recent Gulf of Alaska study. In 1990 the Steller's sea lion was listed as threatened under the Endangered Species Act, the world population having dropped to one-quarter of its size in the 1950s. A sudden increase in the rate of that decline coincides disturbingly with the explosive onset of the Alaskan trawl fishery.

Marine mammal populations also cycle independently of human causes, although it's increasingly hard to separate natural from human influences. As tidewater glaciers back up onto dry land in upper Glacier Bay, fewer icebergs enter the water, and seals must pup on shore, or possibly find other tidewater glaciers. Icy Bay, at the extreme northwestern tip of Southeast Alaska, might partially replace this lost habitat, but doesn't offer the legal protection of Glacier Bay National Park.

Our marine mammals are at the top of the marine food chains, which means that any pollutants picked up by smaller organisms can ultimately be transferred to them. These toxins include naturally occurring substances, such as the poisons produced by some species of phytoplankton that cause paralytic shellfish poisoning (PSP) in mammals. In 1989, 14 humpback whales washed up dead on Cape Cod, Massachusetts, from eating herring that had fed on small crustaceans, which in turn had eaten toxic phytoplankton.

Recent research in Kodiak, Alaska, indicates that sea otters may be capable of distinguishing and avoiding clams containing PSP toxins. One researcher has speculated that the historical absence of sea otters from the inside waters of Southeast Alaska may be correlated with the common occurrence of toxin-tainted butter clams here.

BIRDS

• • •
CHAPTER 3

More than 300 species of birds have been documented in Southeast Alaska. This represents about 75 percent of the 425 or so species recorded for the entire state. Of these, 160 species have nested in the region.

Nowhere else can you see black oystercatchers, harlequin ducks, varied thrushes, blue grouse, and rock ptarmigan in just a few hours of birding. It's possible to cross several habitat zones by starting at a rocky seashore and moving inland through saltwater wetlands, muskegs, deciduous woodlands, old-growth coniferous forests, and finally alpine areas, all in a relatively short distance.

The close proximity of habitats allows birds to nest in one and forage for a variety of foods in others. At least two-thirds of our species regularly visit more than one habitat. Bald eagles, for example, nest in old-growth forests yet easily survey the saltwater beaches for dead fish or cruise the alpine slopes for adolescent marmots.

Southeast Alaska's outer coastal islands are important nesting grounds for substantial numbers of sea birds, such as ancient murrelets, Cassin's and rhinoceros auklets, fork-tailed storm-petrels, and Leach's storm-petrels. Forrester, Hazy, and Saint Lazaria islands have been set aside under the National Wildlife Refuge system especially for these nesting sea birds. From tour boats you can usually see tufted puffins (p. 186), Kittlitz's murrelets, and occasionally horned puffins in Glacier Bay, where they nest. Saint Lazaria Island, near Sitka, is another fairly reliable place to see tufted puffins by boat.

Other extremely small rocky islands provide nesting places for the unusual-looking black oystercatcher (p. 185). In Glacier Bay, oystercatchers are less restricted to islands, and commonly nest at the high tide mark on rock or gravel beaches. From evidence of numerous pairs of marbled murrelets along coastal inlets and bays, the adjacent timber or mountains must provide ideal nesting sites for this elusive sea bird.

Some nesting birds quite common or fairly common in Southeast Alaska are accidental in other regions of the state. You will see blue grouse, red-breasted sapsucker, and Pacific-slope flycatcher, for example, only in this region on a regular basis.

Many common nesting birds in the region migrate south for the winter, among them the spotted sandpiper, rufous hummingbird, tree swallow, hermit thrust, ruby-crowned kinglet, Townsend's warbler, and Lincoln's sparrow.

Sandhill cranes migrate through Southeastern Alaska.

Many other birds use Southeast Alaska as their permanent home. The Vancouver Canada goose, harlequin duck, bald eagle, rock ptarmigan, great horned owl, Steller's jay, common raven, northwestern crow, chestnut-backed chickadee, American dipper, and several others can be seen here any month of the year.

Many birds normally do not enter western or northern Alaska because of natural barriers such as mountains or arctic climatic conditions, but often move into Southeast Alaska by way of the valleys carved by the major rivers originating in Canada. Usually such birds are more common in the valleys and mouths of such rivers as the Unuk, Stikine, or Taku than elsewhere in the region. These birds include the pied-billed grebe, American bittern, warbling vireo, common yellowthroat, and western tanager. Others, such as the western grebe, make their way up to Southeast Alaska by way of the seacoast from lower British Columbia and the Pacific Northwest.

Waterfowl and shorebirds often stop to rest and refuel in our numerous undeveloped estuaries, salt and freshwater wetlands, and lakes during their long migrations to and from their more westerly and northern breeding grounds. These include the tundra swan, northern pintail, American golden-plover, red-necked phalarope, long-billed dowitcher, pectoral sandpiper, and dunlin. Some, like the red-necked phalarope, occur in enormous numbers; over 15,000 have been observed on the waters of Glacier Bay in late summer.

Numerous land birds also use Southeast Alaska for a refueling and resting area on their way to and from nesting grounds. These birds include the northern harrier, American kestrel, short-eared owl, horned lark, northern shrike, Lapland longspur, and white-crowned sparrow.

Many sea ducks find Southeast Alaska, with its relatively mild winters, protected inlets and bays, and abundant marine invertebrates, a suitable place to spend the winter. These include several species that usually nest farther north: common goldeneye, Barrow's goldeneye, bufflehead, oldsquaw, and surf scoter. You can often see enormous flocks of these birds along the inside waters during winter.

Some land birds that nest farther north also find our climate and habitat suitable for overwintering: Bohemian waxwing, northern shrike, and dark-eyed junco (slate-colored subspecies). Some shorebirds that nest farther north spend the winter in Southeast—sometimes in flocks of several hundred birds—the dunlin and the rock sandpiper, for example.

BIRD HABITATS

Birds are far from randomly distributed among the marshes, shrub thickets, pole timber, tundra, muskeg, and old-growth habitats of Southeast Alaska. Each bird has its own foraging and cover requirements. In time, the naturalist learns to identify these habitat needs. At that point, a cottonwood grove, for example, takes on a new dimension. It's more than a certain collection of canopy and understory plants on a predictable soil type with a given successional history. It's a home—for Wilson's and yellow-rumped warblers, ruby-crowned kinglets, and hermit thrushes. It might even shelter one of the rarer songbirds of Southeast—a warbling vireo or a western tanager. The songs of these birds are as much the "signature" of the grove as the smell of young leaves of the cottonwood, or its plumed seeds drifting in the summer breeze.

BIRDS OF THE BEACHES—"When the tide is out the table is set!" This saying applies not only to human clam-diggers and seaweed-gatherers, but to birds of many varieties. Sandpipers and plovers, geese and ducks, crows and ravens, eagles and gulls, all noisily collect the ocean's bounty. Some graze the low salt-marsh vegetation, some forage for intertidal invertebrates, some go fishing, and others scavenge tidal debris. The beach offers the riches of both land and sea, often massed into convenient piles at the high-water line. In fall, the debris zone may look as though someone had dumped bags of bird seed, so concentrated are the seeds of sedge and goose-tongue. They draw flocks of American pipits and snow buntings, which, unlike most of their songbird relatives, dare to feed in open coastal spaces lacking vegetative cover.

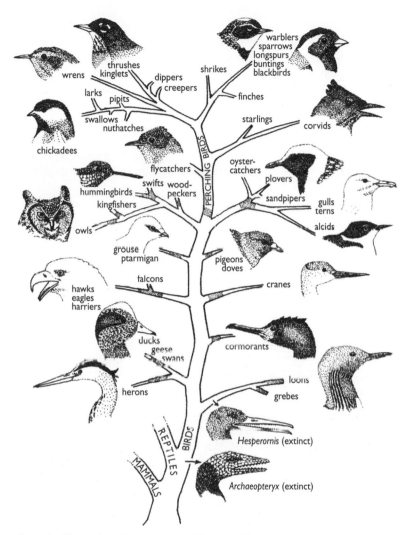

Family Tree for Southeast Alaska Birds
(adapted from Welty and Baptista)

CONIFEROUS FOREST—This habitat offers forage for some birds and cover for many more. Although it is not really a prolific producer of bird food (except for the seed-eating pine siskins and crossbills), the great value of our hemlock–spruce forest to birds lies in its structural complexity. The multilayered canopy and abundance of standing and fallen dead wood provide cover for nesters and winter residents.

Woodpeckers are more important in our forests than their numbers would suggest. Digging nest cavities in rotten snags, they provide future homes for "secondary" cavity dwellers—chickadees, swallows, the smaller owls, and even some diving ducks. Tiny insectivores like brown creepers and winter wrens use other elements of forest cover, such as upturned root wads or sheets of bark sloughing from dead logs.

Townsend's warblers, Pacific-slope flycatchers, and golden-crowned kinglets sing from high in the canopies of old-growth forests. The male blue grouse, or "hooter," is likewise best located by sound in the spring and early summer. Although he hoots near the treetops and may forage on fibrous needles in winter, his mate nests on the ground, and her young feed on nutritious insects in lush meadow and shrub vegetation, as do the nestlings and fledglings of most other terrestrial birds.

MEADOWS AND THICKETS—The importance of insects to baby birds (and many adults) brings us to meadows and shrublands. These early stages in vegetational succession green up suddenly each spring and die back as quickly each fall. Closely timed to the boom-and-bust of deciduous leaves is a corresponding flush of creeping, flying, and burrowing insects. Protein-rich insects of these young deciduous communities in turn feed most of our arriving songbirds, including

Coastal meadows on an uplifted spit. Ground-nesters in this community include Lincoln's and savannah sparrows.

almost all of our common warblers, flycatchers, and swallows, most nesting sparrows, and many thrushes.

Although we tend to group birds by where they nest or where they are most frequently seen—forest, beach, meadow—we also need to keep in mind the dependence that most have upon more than one habitat. Many people, for example, consider the varied thrush, or "rainbird," a symbol of Southeast's old-growth forests. One May we examined the gizzard of a dead varied thrush. It was packed with the wing covers of adult leaf beetles, which browsed the willow and cottonwood saplings where the thrush had been foraging. The varied thrush, like many others, may nest in conifers, but it often feeds in younger, deciduous habitats.

VARIATIONS IN BIRD SOUNDS

From May to early July, our resident and summer nesting birds can easily be located by their songs. Territories have been staked out, and the "owners" loudly and enthusiastically proclaim their rights. The woods and meadows resound with hoots, twitters, squawks, and trills. These sounds are often most intense between 4:00 A.M. and 6:00 A.M.; afterward the birds quiet down. Ornithologists now think the early calling is to remind rivals of territory boundaries which may have been forgotten overnight. The ensuing silence results because the hungry birds are feeding voraciously.

While most spring bird vocalizations you hear in Southeast are from males establishing the boundaries of their territories and attempting to attract a mate, there are exceptions, as with most aspects of biology. For example, the female red-necked phalarope, which breeds in Glacier Bay and the Yakutat Forelands, engages in courtship displays and calls to attract a mate. After laying her eggs, she repeats her displays and calling and leads her mate to the nest, where he then incubates the eggs and cares for the young.

Some birds make sounds in unusual and nonvocal ways. Probably the most bizarre of these in Southeast Alaska is the courtship display of the common snipe. This bird displays by circling upward, then diving down toward earth. With the bird's tail well spread, the air rushes over the extreme outer pair of tail feathers, causing them to vibrate. The airstream over these tail feathers is broken about 11 times per second by quick wingbeats, thus producing a loud winnowing or throbbing sound.

Woodpeckers also use nonvocal sounds. These birds establish territories by loud drumming, usually on resonant, hollow, drumming trees. In contrast, a feeding woodpecker may rather quietly chip away pieces of bark while looking for insects. We once nailed a wooden model of a black-backed woodpecker on a tree and played a recording of one drumming. The male in whose territory we did this responded by viciously pecking the model on the head until he knocked it to the ground. He then appeared satisfied at having "killed" the intruder and flew off to feed quietly nearby.

Song sparrow male, singing

Duetting is an interesting form of bird vocalization. It occurs when one bird inserts notes with beautiful precision into the songs or calls of its partner. Duetting is most common among birds of the tropical forests, where they employ it to keep in contact with each other as they forage in the thick foliage. In Southeast, duetting occurs in paired Vancouver Canada geese. The "A Honk Hink" call you often hear is actually produced by two birds. The male gives the "A Honk" and the female follows immediately with a higher "Hink." The whole performance sounds as if it were given by one bird. In species such as Canada geese that may remain paired for life, mutual identification and maintaining contact between mates is very important; duetting is one way they accomplish it.

Besides calling to stake out territories and attract a mate, many birds call to provide an outlet for excess energy. One could speculate that it serves as a regulator of stress—it certainly is much safer to sing or make noise at an intruder than to do physical battle. Some ornithologists even think that birds may also sing for pure pleasure.

SOUND RECOGNITION BY BIRDS

Each species of bird has a unique song, call, or sound. Birds can detect minute pitch differences, enabling them to recognize different individuals of their own kind. Studies of certain colonial nesting seabirds, for example, have shown that while still in the egg, the chicks learn to distinguish the voices of their parents from others in the same colony. While photographing Arctic terns at a nesting colony, we noticed that newly hatched chicks would emerge from beneath one parent to prepare to accept fish (p. 185) from the other parent before it landed! Apparently the chick could recognize its own parent's voice among those of the many terns constantly circling and calling from above the colony.

WINTER ADAPTATIONS

Many of the 425 or so species of birds documented in Alaska leave for the winter. Slightly more than 100 species commonly remain year round in Southeast Alaska, compared to just 4 species along the North Slope. In both areas, most overwintering species must contend with food shortage. Winter feeding is further complicated by less daylight in which to forage, less available habitat because of ice and snow cover, and the need to keep warm.

In general, birds are more resistant to cold than are mammals of comparable size. The coat of feathers on a bird's body serves as excellent insulation, and birds lack mammals' projecting fleshy ears and tails, which lose heat. Birds living in cooler latitudes typically have more feathers and more fat for insulation, and have higher standard metabolism per unit body weight.

Some birds, such as ptarmigan, ruffed grouse, and snow buntings, insulate themselves from winter cold by plunging into and under the snow, where the temperature may be many degrees warmer than at the surface. Some may even stay under snow both night and day in order to survive our occasional winter storm.

Many of our smaller birds conserve heat by roosting closely together in sheltered places. Chestnut-backed chickadees, for example, may pack together in holes in trees. Some birds, like the ptarmigan, possess a crop, a food-storage organ, that can be filled during a short winter day and the contents digested at night, allowing the bird to keep its metabolism and body temperature high during a cold winter night. Another example is the redpoll's enlarged esophagus, which acts like a crop. Redpolls quickly eat a large amount of food just before roosting for the night.

Other species, such as Steller's jays and chickadees, store food during times of plenty, retrieving it during lean periods. At feeders, jays seem to fill their throat pouches with as much as they can cram in before flying off, and chickadees seem to be constantly taking our offering of sunflower seeds to some secret hiding place.

Small birds must feed every day in order to survive the winter cold spells, and they must be able to find a sheltered area in which to spend the night. Feeding birds is one way to help them through the winter. However, once our resident birds become dependent on the food, it's a good idea to be a consistent provider throughout the winter. We find that a variety of food is needed: unsalted sunflower seeds attract chickadees; smaller commercial blends are good for juncos and redpolls, and suet for woodpeckers.

One of the joys of feeding birds in winter is the chance of attracting a rare bird, and many bird records for Alaska have been established at feeders. In Southeast a few of the rare birds that you might attract include the northern pygmy-owl (looking for small birds to prey upon), Clark's nutcracker, mountain chickadee, white-throated sparrow, Harris's sparrow, and purple finch.

Although most birds that commonly winter in Southeast do not, at first glance, appear to be as specialized for cold as the ptarmigan, they do have physical, physiological, and behavioral adaptations that work well. We can't ignore the fact that more species winter in Southeast Alaska than in any other region of Alaska, owing to the moderating marine influence on temperature and the greater food availability in the coastal habitats. Still, winter conditions in Southeast can at times be very severe. It is truly remarkable that chickadees, nuthatches, and

Chestnut-backed chickadees in Sitka spruce

kinglets survive, and one can only wonder how an Anna's hummingbird in Juneau was able to tolerate several winter snowstorms.

VANCOUVER CANADA GOOSE

The Vancouver Canada goose lives and nests along coastal Southeast Alaska from northern Southeast southward to northern Vancouver Island, British Columbia. It is an essentially nonmigratory subspecies, and most live year round within this area. Authorities believe that the numbers of Vancouver Canada geese have remained about the same over the years, probably because their nesting and wintering habitat remains mostly in pristine condition. Also, they are lightly hunted compared to other Canada goose subspecies which migrate over major human population centers. In spring we briefly see some of these other migratory geese on our wetlands; most are smaller and paler than the Vancouver subspecies.

One study of the nesting habits of Vancouver Canada geese, conducted in Seymour Canal on Admiralty Island, revealed fascinating and unique habits. Surprisingly, most of the nests in this study were found in the forest among dense shrubs, although nests of other subspecies of Canada geese are usually associated with established water bodies, such as lakes, ponds, or bays. Most of the nests were on the ground, but one nest was at the top of a spruce snag, and an earlier study found a nest 48 feet above the ground on a moss-covered bough of a Sitka spruce. Vancouver Canada geese have also been found nesting in muskegs, along stream banks, and adjacent to lakes and estuaries throughout Southeast Alaska.

Around their nests, the geese were commonly seen perched in the upper portion of the nearby trees. When the pair returned to the nest site, they usually landed in the trees and remained perched for 10 to 45 minutes before flying to their nest. While the female incubated her eggs, the male usually remained perched in a nearby tree.

During nesting, the item most commonly eaten by the geese was leaves of the yellow skunk-cabbage. Geese are rather inefficient at digesting their food; hence they must eat a lot of food in a short period of time. The huge green leaves of skunk-cabbage are thought to provide the necessary bulk food for Vancouver Canada geese.

Although Vancouver Canada geese can be found throughout Southeast Alaska, the Mendenhall Wetlands near Juneau is probably the easiest place to observe them. In late winter and spring, the geese usually feed on the Wetlands right up to the Egan Expressway, where they forage for seeds, roots, and young shoots of sedges. In spring, a walk along a dike separating some freshwater ponds and marshes (p. 82) from the salt marsh (p. 83) will often yield amazingly close-up looks at these magnificent geese. About 500 to 600 Vancouver Canada geese spend the winter on the Mendenhall Wetlands. Although these intelligent birds vacate the Wetlands during hunting season, by mid October they often come in to feed at night when the hunters are elsewhere.

Soon after hunting ends in mid-December, the geese return to the Wetlands, where they stay day and night. By early April, the paired adults move to their nesting sites at such areas as Seymour Canal on Admiralty Island. The adolescents remain on the Wetlands until late June, and in July these nonbreeders fly to secluded inlets in Glacier Bay or to other remote areas, where they molt, shedding their worn flight feathers and growing a new set. During this 3- to 4-week molting period, the geese cannot fly and avoid people and other predators. They seek open flats with abundant forage near expanses of water, to which they can escape if disturbed. If approached by boaters, molting geese take to the brush. In August the new families and these adolescents gather again on the Mendenhall Wetlands, where they spend the rest of the year, except when they are chased out by an extreme freeze-up or by hunters.

THE FAMILY LIFE OF CANADA GEESE

Once mated, Canada goose pairs usually stay together for life. Geese with families have higher status in the flock. Studies indicate that families of geese are dominant over mated pairs without families, and mated pairs are dominant over single adults and yearlings.

Geese stay together as a family unit after breeding. Migratory subspecies even travel south as a family, wintering together and returning together to their northern breeding grounds. Only when they reach their breeding grounds do the young of the previous season separate from their parents. These young join other subadults to form flocks, often at considerable distance from their nesting parents. Adolescents will not nest until they are 2, 3, or even 4 years old.

There are many advantages of staying together in family groups and flocks. Parents teach their young about feeding areas, migration routes, and life-threatening dangers, thus enhancing their chances of survival.

Places like the Mendenhall Wetlands provide food necessary for our Canada geese to survive the winter and to build up energy reserves for nesting. Remote areas such as tidelands and adjacent forested parts of Seymour Canal are critical to nesting success. And finally, areas such as Adams Inlet in Glacier Bay, far from human disturbance and lacking many of the predators found elsewhere in Southeast, are necessary for their survival during molting. The protection of these interconnected habitats will help insure the perpetuation of this subspecies of Canada goose.

SEA DUCKS

About 1 million ducks winter in Southeast Alaska, according to the U.S. Fish and Wildlife Service. About 75 percent are species of sea ducks, and the rest are mallards (dabbling ducks), scaups (pochards), mergansers, and a few eiders.

Sea ducks are stocky, short-necked diving birds that generally winter and feed together along our saltwater bays, channels, and inlets. All 8 species found in North America can be seen in Southeast: black, white-winged, and surf scoters, harlequin ducks, oldsquaws, Barrow's goldeneyes, common goldeneyes, and buffleheads. Scoters and goldeneyes are the most numerous of the sea ducks here, but significant numbers of other species also occur.

Sea ducks obtain most of their food on or near the sea bottom and hence must dive to a variety of water depths. Oldsquaws are the

Harlequin pair in rocky intertidal (male on left)

champion divers and have been reported to reach depths of 240 feet. In general, oldsquaws feed farther offshore than the other species and so have little competition for food. Scoters often dive for food at water depths greater than 20 feet, but the goldeneyes, buffleheads, and harlequin ducks seem to prefer water depths of about 10 feet or less.

Sea ducks eat a variety of food, with some species having obvious preferences. For example, scoters may gorge themselves almost exclusively on blue bay mussels. A scoter commonly swallows several dozen mussels whole, shell and all, during one short feeding period. In fact, one surf scoter was reported to contain 1100 small mussels in its gizzard!

Harlequin ducks are specialists in prying limpets, mussels, and chitons off rocks and swallowing them whole; amazingly, they can do this while swimming underwater. Their gizzards can crush shells that we must open with a blow by rock or hammer. In streams we have observed harlequin ducks pushing up rocks with their upper bill, then grabbing the dislodged aquatic insects while swimming underwater against the swift current. Sea ducks also eat small crabs, clams, shrimp, amphipods, barnacles, sea urchins, sea stars, marine worms, small fish, and algae.

Birds and people can tolerate only up to a 1 percent concentration of salt in their blood and other body fluids. This is less than a third of the salt concentration in open ocean water. If we were to drink sea water, our kidneys would excrete the excess salt by drawing additional fluids from our body, and dehydration would result. A bird's kidneys are even less efficient than ours at getting rid of excess salt. However, birds living on salt water have special glands in a depression just above each eye. Excess salt is picked up by the ducks' blood and transferred to these salt glands. The concentrated salt solution then flows via ducts to their nostrils, where it is excreted.

Sea ducks begin courtship antics while still on the wintering ground. Male goldeneyes court females by dipping bills in the water, raising their heads straight up, and then bending them clear over on their backs while uttering a peculiar whistle. Male buffleheads conduct a head-bobbing, chin-up display with their head feathers erected. Male oldsquaws become quite excited and spring into flight, dash madly about, and then abruptly splash back down into the water.

Despite all the courtship antics by sea ducks in Southeast, only the harlequin duck commonly nests in the region. This sea duck has the unusual habit of nesting beside fast-flowing streams. Other species nest mostly in the more northerly parts of Alaska near the stiller waters of lakes, ponds, marshes and inlets, and bays of the seacoast.

Sea ducks do not nest until they are 2 years old, and the subadults, especially scoters, remain in Southeast and are joined in early summer by males returning from the northern nesting areas soon after their mates have finished laying eggs.

Most communities in Southeast have shoreline roads from which you can watch sea ducks. From January to May, look for their courtship antics. Also watch the feeding flocks of surf scoters. Often, for no apparent reason, they will form a long line, almost single file. First the leader will dive; then each one, like dominoes falling, will follow suit. With binoculars you can see them bringing mussels to the surface, which they will gulp down whole.

Listen for the unusual vocalizations of the oldsquaw. Also look carefully for the beautiful male harlequin duck perched on the larger beach rocks, preening or sleeping. Despite their gaudy appearance, they blend in well with their surroundings.

Scoters from all along the Pacific coast migrate slowly to Southeast in April before heading inland for nesting. One can sometimes see flocks of 20,000 to 30,000 feeding in unison or flying. This is one of the grandest bird sights in our region.

Southeast Alaska, with its numerous protected and relatively ice-free bays, channels, and inlets, its pristine unpolluted waters and abundant food supply, provides ideal habitat in which sea ducks can spend the winter.

BALD EAGLE

The U.S. Fish and Wildlife Service estimates that there are 10,000 adult bald eagles (with white heads) in Southeast (p. 186). Immature ones (with dark heads) blend in so well with their surroundings that they are difficult to count; however, at least several thousand immatures also live here. These numbers are thought to be similar to the number of eagles that existed here prior to European settlement.

While most raptors have pair-bonding displays, with the female and male touching talons briefly in flight, only eagles hang on, cartwheeling down. This heart-stopping maneuver sometimes ends only a few feet above the ground.

BALD EAGLE BOUNTIES AND LEGISLATION

A predator control program from 1917 to 1952 resulted in the killing of 101,000 bald eagles in Southeast Alaska. The bounty, established in 1917 by the Alaskan territorial government, was 50 cents per bird until 1923, when it was increased to $1. After 1941, the Legislature failed to appropriate bounty money, and the system was discarded in 1946. A new bounty act was passed in 1949, paying $2 per bird and remaining in effect until nullified by federal protection of the eagles in 1952. Eagles were killed in order to reduce their alleged predation on salmon; however, later research revealed that eagles usually scavenge only salmon that have already spawned.

Bald eagles are now protected under specific federal legislation, commonly termed the Bald Eagle Protection Act, which makes it illegal to kill or possess any part of an eagle. Penalties under this act can range up to a $10,000 fine and 2 years in jail for repeat offenders. One interesting provision of this act allows up to one-half of the fine to be paid to the person or persons giving information leading to conviction. The act also makes it illegal to disturb eagle nesting sites.

On national forest lands in Southeast Alaska, bald eagle nests are further protected by a cooperative agreement between the U.S. Fish and Wildlife Service and the U.S. Forest Service. Under this agreement, a 330-foot buffer zone of uncut trees is to be left around each nest tree, and a suitable perching tree or group of trees is to be left for every 100 yards of beach front.

Additional protection was afforded to eagles in Southeast in 1982 by state legislation which created the 48,000-acre Alaska Chilkat Bald Eagle Preserve and the adjoining Haines State Forest Resource Management Area.

Impressive numbers of bald eagles occur in Southeast wherever fish concentrate in shallow water to spawn. The largest number of eagles feeding on spawning fish occurs on the Chilkat River near Haines. Here over 3000 eagles may gather during October and November to feed on the carcasses of spawned-out chum salmon. During April, from 500 to 1500 eagles have been counted feeding on spawning eulachon in the

Stikine River near Wrangell. Spring concentrations of spawning herring may also attract hundreds of eagles to several other places in the region.

Radio tracking of eagles indicates that most adults remain year round in Southeast Alaska, and in fall and winter wander widely throughout the region in search of food. During the 6-month breeding season, however, nesting eagles remain close to their nesting sites. Some radio-tracked nonbreeders, on the other hand, leave the state in winter, and one was recovered as far south as the Washington–Oregon border.

Nesting eagles in Southeast Alaska typically choose a large old-growth spruce (most frequently) or hemlock within 220 yards of salt water. In one study, the chosen trees averaged 3.6 feet in diameter and were approximately 400 years old.

On the average, about 1 eagle nest can be found per 1¼ mile of shoreline in Southeast. The highest density of nests (1.05 nest per mile of shoreline) was found on Admiralty Island. In Juneau, 130 eagle nests have been found between Berners Bay and Point Bishop (including Douglas Island).

According to the U.S. Fish and Wildlife Service, the picture is not entirely rosy for the bald eagle in Southeast Alaska. Starvation (particularly in young birds), poisoning, and accidents cause the death of many eagles. Several eagles are shot each year in Southeast; the total number is unknown, as is also the case for eagles killed or injured when caught in traps set for furbearers. Some destruction and alteration of bald eagle habitat continues to occur on public and private lands through logging, road construction, community expansion, and other developments.

The Fish and Wildlife Service continues to monitor the number of eagles in selected index areas within Southeast Alaska. In addition, it is analyzing blood samples from Southeast eagles to detect any accumulation of such heavy metals as lead, mercury, zinc, or copper.

NORTHERN HARRIER, SHORT-EARED OWL

The most easily observed birds of prey that migrate through Southeast Alaska in spring and fall are the northern harrier (formerly the "marsh hawk") and the short-eared owl. Only the short-eared owl is known to nest in Southeast, and then rarely, but both are prominent visitors to our coastal salt marshes and inland freshwater wetlands.

Hawks and owls are only distantly related, but we've chosen to describe these birds together because of their remarkably similar appearance and behavior. The harrier has facial disks like an owl's, and both birds hunt for voles by day over our thick beach meadow vegetation. Flight patterns are subtly different. The harrier flies with several shallow wing strokes, punctuated by a glide, with wings held at an angle above the horizontal. The short-eared owl flies with deeper and faster strokes; observers liken it to a huge moth or butterfly, the resemblance

The northern harrier glides with wings held in a shallow V. The short-eared owl glides with downturned wingtips.

heightened by its stubby, cigar-shaped body. The short-eared owl is such a lightweight bird that the wings' upstroke seems to drive the body down slightly, causing a "wavier" trajectory than that of the harrier, whose longer tail provides more stability.

To observe predation in the field is a rare experience. But northern harriers and short-eared owls often provide exceptions to this rule. With binoculars one can identify them almost a mile away, flapping languidly just above the tall coastal grasses. And to watch hawks and owls hunting nearby is an instant cure for spring fever.

Such closer views are fairly easy to come by. On occasion we have set out an old fish head in the marsh and then crawled into a blind and watched. Harriers often found the food within minutes. The larger female harriers always displaced the smaller males. Usually the male stood by until the food was nearly gone and the female had left. Perhaps this obvious dominance of the feeding females is why we see fewer males hunting in our salt marshes. Possibly the males migrate through Southeast Alaska at higher elevations along the mountain ridges, especially when southbound in fall.

Female harriers sometimes fought among themselves for the fish head (p. 186). On one occasion, a larger red-tailed hawk came in and immediately displaced 2 female harriers. On another, a short-eared owl investigated the situation and gave its barking call, which seemed only a passing annoyance to the feeding harrier.

Throughout our observations, physical contact between rival birds of prey was rare. Usually the larger easily displaced the smaller bird. If both harriers were the same size, one would wait a few feet away while the other fed. Then a threatening spread-winged hop toward the feeding hawk would drive it away.

We once observed a harrier kill a green-winged teal. The harrier

Short-eared owl, with ear flaps erected.

Regurgitated pellet of short-eared owl, with pelvis, leg, and rib bones of long-tailed vole at surface. Usually there are intact skulls within.

was gliding along close to the ground, and swooped in and landed on the teal. As it began tearing into the teal, a bald eagle dived from its perch in a nearby spruce and stole the harrier's prey. The eagle flew off with the teal in its talons, and the harrier resumed hunting.

Aside from being easy to observe directly, northern harriers and short-eared owls are some of the easiest of all predators on which to perform feeding studies. This stems from their habit of regurgitating "pellets," which consist of the undigested fur, feathers, bones, bills, and teeth of prey species. Often numerous pellets can be found near roosting areas. We have carefully examined about 40 pellets from short-eared owls, and a few from harriers, all found in the beach meadows around Juneau. In these marshes the owls seem to feed almost exclusively on the long-tailed vole, as evidenced from the molar patterns of skulls found in their pellets. The harrier seems only slightly less specialized.

Harriers and short-eared owls must be able to hear their prey. Voles scurrying about beneath thick grass cover cannot be spotted from a perch, or by soaring. Instead, these raptors hunt by cruising slowly and silently, almost brushing the vegetation, listening for ultra-high-pitched squeaks and inopportune rustlings. An owl's facial disks can be repositioned by erectile flaps in front of its ear openings. Perhaps these manueverable disks serve not so much to pick up prey sounds as to muffle the unwanted sound of wind. For harriers and owls, silent flight may be more important in allowing the bird to listen than in sneaking up on prey.

PTARMIGAN

Our most memorable encounter with ptarmigan was on a crosscountry ski trip. We had skied up the icebound Herbert River near Juneau, almost to the Herbert Glacier, when our leader motioned us to stop. There, with the glacier as a backdrop, stood two white-tailed ptarmigan in about as beautiful a setting as can be imagined. The only disturbance

Male rock ptarmigan feeding on tips of young alpine sedges

of the freshly fallen snow was two sets of dainty ptarmigan tracks leading from some willows to the center of a small clearing. One ptarmigan had buried itself so that only its head and upper shoulders appeared above the snow. The other remained motionless, in full view, by its side. The skiers filed by about 30 feet away without causing the ptarmigan to flush.

This encounter was especially enjoyable because these were the first white-tailed ptarmigan we had seen in Southeast Alaska. Of the three ptarmigan species in the region, white-tails are the least abundant and the smallest, and tend to live at higher elevations than the other two. Rock ptarmigan are the most numerous, with the willow ptarmigan in second place. All three species are year-round residents and, aside from elevational movements, probably do not migrate long distances.

Ptarmigan are well designed for living in the white, cold environment of an Alaskan winter. Their white winter plumage not only is excellent camouflage but also insulates better than colored feathers. This is because white feathers are completely hollow, unoccupied by pigment, and this provides additional dead air space. Ptarmigan also are well designed for walking about in winter. In late fall they grow a dense mat of stiff feathers on their toes, which serves as "snowshoes" for walking on top of the lightest of snow. Long, sharp claws serve as "crampons" for traction over icy slopes.

In winter ptarmigan eat mainly willow twigs and buds. In summer they feed on a variety of green plant shoots, buds, flowers, berries, and insects. To help them digest woody material of rather low caloric value, their crops contain special bacteria.

As soon as the snow melts, female ptarmigan molt into a dark summer plumage and begin nesting. They nest on the ground and usually lay 6 to 10 eggs. Around late June to early July, after an incubation period of about 3 weeks, the chicks hatch.

The males retain their white winter plumage longer for display purposes and as a decoy for predators. Males, especially willow ptarmigan, are very territorial. They stand guard while the females incubate their eggs, and fearlessly attack any intruders. We once saw a male willow ptarmigan pounce on the back of a northern harrier and successfully drive it away.

Male willow ptarmigan also help care for their chicks, a habit unique among North American grouse and ptarmigan. If the female is killed, the male will take over all family responsibilities. This habit, along with its beauty and widespread distribution, makes the willow ptarmigan a good choice as our official state bird.

SHOREBIRDS

Plovers, sandpipers, and oystercatchers are the shorebird families found in Southeast Alaska. Within these families 38 species visit our region, and 10 species nest here. The abundant islands, lakes, marshes, rivers, and tidal flats of Southeast Alaska provide extensive shorelines and ideal habitat for shorebirds. Our region is important to these birds during 3 phases of their life cycle. First, Southeast Alaska provides necessary resting and feeding areas for shorebirds during their long migrations to and from their more northerly breeding grounds in Alaska. Second, many species use the region for nesting—the most abundant nesters are semipalmated plover, black oystercatcher, greater yellowlegs, spotted sandpiper (p. 186), least sandpiper, and common snipe. Third, a few species overwinter here. The most abundant is the rock sandpiper; others are dunlin, black turnstone, common snipe, surfbird, sanderling, black oystercatcher, and killdeer.

The distances traveled by shorebirds during migration are generally much greater than those of most other birds. Many species that nest in Alaska spend their winters in the southern coastal United States and throughout Central and South America.

Careful watching of shorebirds in Southeast Alaska can reveal some interesting, bizarre, and sometimes humorous behavior patterns. Perhaps the most obvious and peculiar is the courtship display of the common snipe. Their loud winnowing or throbbing sound can be heard most often over marshes early in the morning or late into the evening. When approached by humans, some nesting shorebirds behave rather unusually. The distraction displays of the semipalmated plover and killdeer are particularly interesting to watch. In this display the parent bird flutters on the ground as though crippled and utters pitiful cries in hopes of luring you away from its young or nest. If you happen upon a muskeg in which a pair of greater yellowlegs is nesting, you will be greeted by a shrill, incessant cry, which is repeated over and over until you leave the area. These cries are usually given from the top of a shore pine while the bird clumsily balances itself with feet not at all adapted for gripping tree limbs.

If you approach a small rocky nesting island of the black oyster-catcher by boat, you may be greeted by this bizarre black shorebird with its long, bright red bill and pink legs and feet (p. 185). Often it circles around your boat, sometimes quite close, until its curiosity is satisfied.

We always enjoy watching shorebirds feed. The smaller least and western sandpipers dart this way and that, grabbing flies that have been momentarily trapped in the surface tension of the advancing tidewater. Greater yellowlegs prowl our shallow tidal sloughs, grabbing young staghorn sculpins, which they gulp down whole. Turnstones walk about, turning over small stones and rockweed with their bills and grabbing the creatures living underneath before they can scurry away. Common snipe probe deep into the soft mud for worms and other

Greater yellowlegs in salt-marsh slough with staghorn sculpin fry

organisms. With just the tips of their bills they can sense these burrowing organisms, and they can raise and curve the upper bill, while it is still deep in the mud, in order to seize their prey.

RUFOUS HUMMINGBIRD

Rufous hummingbirds leave their winter home in Mexico in late February to early March and begin arriving in Southeast Alaska by mid April. The brightly colored males arrive first and begin their courtship displays as soon as the females arrive. After courtship and mating, the male leaves the nesting and rearing of young up to the female. The female aggressively defends the nesting site, attacking with vigor any person, animal, or bird that ventures near.

Most female and young rufous hummingbirds don't leave Southeast Alaska for their southern wintering grounds until August, although by late June most males have already gone. However, some linger on even into winter, because of the availability of sugar water feeders. The survival of these lingerers is doubtful; hence it is a good idea to stop feeding them sometime in August.

The rufous is the only common nesting hummingbird in Alaska, although one other species, the Anna's hummingbird, occasionally ventures up to Southeast and may nest here. The Anna's can be distinguished from the rufous by the lack of any reddish coloration on its back, belly, or tail. Also, the male Anna's is the only hummingbird with rose-red color on its crown.

Rufous hummingbird. Tail fanning is an aggressive display.

Adult male rufous hummingbirds have a brilliant iridescent orange-red throat called a gorget. The color in this gorget is structural, like that of a rainbow or a blue sky, rather than pigmentary, like that of a red shirt, hence its light-refractive iridescence.

Hummingbirds have the highest metabolic rate of any warm-blooded vertebrate in the world except possibly some species of shrews. Because of this, they must feed or refuel almost continuously all day to remain alive. However, they cannot eat enough by day to survive the night at their daytime metabolic rate. To survive the cool nights in Southeast Alaska, they become torpid, a state of reduced body temperature and metabolism that uses energy 20 times slower than normal sleep.

Many flowers depend on hummingbirds for pollination. These flowers typically produce little or no scent (which would attract insects), have projecting stamens and pistils that touch the crown of the visiting hummingbird, and lack the landing platforms needed by bees. In addition, they are usually red (a color that bees cannot perceive) and hold large quantities of nectar at the base of a long tube. Flowers thus structured specifically to attract birds as pollinating agents are termed "ornithophilous."

In Southeast Alaska, only the western columbine and four species of Indian paintbrush have floral characteristics associated with hummingbird pollination. The rufous hummingbird probably invaded Alaska fairly recently, and the spread of most of these hummingbird-adapted flowers has lagged behind that of the birds. The distribution of western columbine in Alaska, however, closely coincides with that of the rufous hummingbird.

Upon arrival in Southeast Alaska, the rufous must obtain nectar from flowers adapted for insect pollination, such as blueberries, salmonberries, and rusty menziesia, because only near the end of their nesting season is there a significant bloom of flowers adapted for hummingbird pollination.

To obtain nectar from flowers, the rufous has a very long and specially adapted tongue. This tongue is split at the end, and each half forms a curled trough. Through capillary action the nectar is carried into these troughs, and the bird then retracts its tongue to swallow the nectar. If you carefully watch a hummer at your feeder, you can see its tongue rapidly darting in and out. In addition to flower nectar, hummingbirds capture and eat tiny insects, which provide them with a needed source of protein.

STELLER'S JAY

Steller's jays are found in western North America from the Kenai Peninsula in Alaska south through Mexico to Nicaragua. Throughout this range they are typically birds of the mountain and coastal coniferous forests. In Southeast Alaska they are a common year-round resident and, because of their affinity for bird feeders, are well known.

The first European record of the

Steller's jay

BIRDBRAINS

Have you ever raised binoculars to study a passing "hawk," then sheepishly lowered them, muttering "Oh, it's just a raven"? Many perceive ravens and their kin as scroungers or even pests, less worthy of attention than proud raptors or dressy warblers. It wasn't always this way. The Tlingit and other original peoples of the Northwest Coast recognize the deep intelligence and profound ecological importance of ravens and their smaller relatives the crows, magpies, and jays. The Native sense of humor and sophisticated mythology accord Raven a sort of hobo's dignity. He is a creature to be reckoned with—the world is Raven's playroom, and every other creature is Raven's toy. The raven's ubiquity is eerie—he uproots mountaineers' snow caches on the ice field, drops from mossy hemlocks onto deer hunters' leavings, surveys for roadkills and Big Macs from power poles, and strides confidently down the sidewalk.

Ravens and crows offer evidence—somewhat rare in nature—that curiosity pays. Most birds and mammals mind their own business, behaving in relatively predictable ways, with a narrow range of forage and cover preferences. Ravens, however, use every unsubmerged community in Southeast Alaska. Northwestern crows are beach-oriented, but penetrate into each nearby blowdown and alder tangle and blueberry thicket. What do crows seek there? Often they may simply be "prospecting."

An intertidal ecologist might envy a crow flock's collective knowledge of its territory. A flock contains about 50 birds, many with over a decade's experience in place, passing on each discovery to precocious offspring. No shell or washed-up fish skeleton escapes their attention.

You learn a lot from watching crows. Once, scoping a pair of crows digging in a hummock of foxtail barley, we found them plucking horsefly pupae from their cases. We hadn't realized these flies breed in the intertidal. Crows also excavate hiding sand lances from 4-inch-deep pits, to the puzzlement and admiration of nearby gulls. Both crows and ravens fly up from rocky beaches to drop mussels, smashing them open, but ravens are most apt to improvise on this theme, being known to yank down pies cooling on second-story windowsills (the ultimate shellfish?). They've even been seen flying with toxic-skinned boreal toads. Whether they drop and eat them is uncertain. Maybe it's just Raven's idea of a good joke on the toad.

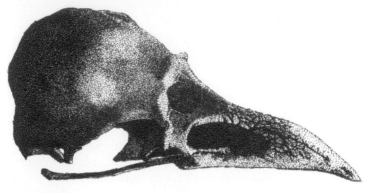

Raven skull

species was an individual shot along the coast of Alaska by Georg Wilhelm Steller, a German zoologist and member of Vitus Bering's Arctic expedition in 1741. Both common and scientific names *(Cyanocitta stelleri)* reflect Steller's discovery. The Steller's jay belongs to the family Corvidae, which is thought to include some of the most intelligent birds in the world, an intelligence reflected in their social behavior, voice, and food-gathering abilities.

Near nesting sites, jays are territorial and maintain territory mostly by vocal communication. A simple "Too-leet" call tells others to leave the area. Calling saves energy by avoiding physical confrontations.

Beyond the immediate nesting territory, Steller's jays frequently travel about in small groups. Within these groups, they help each other mob predators and dominate bird feeders. Each group usually has a pecking order, and a bird's status and dominance can change by mating with a bird of a higher status. For instance, the union of a high-ranking female and a low-ranking male results in the "husband" taking on the status of his "wife."

Other vocalizations of Steller's jays also indicate their intelligence. For example, they are known for their ability to mimic the voice of other species. The "Tee-ar" call is a perfect imitation of the red-tailed hawk. We have noted this call is frequently given by a jay flying to a feeder occupied by other species. As would be expected, the other birds at the feeder quickly disperse. We have also heard them give a close imitation of a bald eagle.

The sex of jays can sometimes be told by their voice. A mechanical-sounding "rattle" is given by females, whereas only males give a high, muted whistle, usually on one pitch. The most unusual sound they make is their "whisper song." This song is surprisingly musical and consists of a medley of whistled and gurgled notes interspersed with snapping or popping sounds run together. The male's "whisper song" is given in early spring to court the female.

AMERICAN DIPPER

The American dipper is a permanent resident of most of Alaska. It is especially common in Southeast, where most streams support one or more pairs. These birds walk and feed underwater, sing in midwinter, and sometimes build their nests behind waterfalls.

The official common name for this bird comes from the habit of bending its legs so its body moves up and down in a dipping motion. This dipping is most frequent when it is disturbed or closely approached. They rarely "dip" when feeding or resting. Other names are water ouzel and Anaruk Kiviruk, an Eskimo name that translates as "old woman sunk."

In search of aquatic insects, dippers walk underwater against a strong current and swim from one place to another. They walk by grasping stones with their long toes and by keeping their heads down, so the pressure of the running water helps force them against the bed of the stream. Underwater photography has revealed they also use their wings to propel themselves.

Dippers have several anatomical adaptations that help them underwater. These adaptations include nasal flaps to prevent water from entering the nostrils, a large uropygial preen gland that produces oil for waterproofing their feathers, muscular modifications to aid in the swimming motions of their wings, and probably the ability to see as well underwater as above.

Dippers are well insulated to withstand icy streams and Alaskan winters. Their plumage is unusually dense, and they possess more contour feathers than most other perching birds. Most important, their very heavy coat of down between the feather tracts is similar to that of

American dipper

ducks and other waterfowl. This excellent insulation enables them to maintain a normal body temperature at air temperatures as low as 40 degrees below zero, with less than a threefold increase in metabolism.

Dippers' circulatory systems are also well adapted to underwater dives. Experiments have shown they can decrease their blood supply to nonvital tissues and organs during diving. Also, they can store more oxygen in their blood than most nondiving birds. This all helps to provide the oxygen needed by the central nervous system and heart while underwater.

The American dipper is highly territorial even during winter. Spring and summer territories may include over a half-mile of stream, while winter territories usually average 1000 feet or less. During extreme cold, dippers may be forced into the intertidal areas of streams or along saltwater beaches because their normal habitat ices over.

Like other songbirds, the American dipper declares or "stakes out" its territory by singing. Territorial singing during winter, however, is quite unusual for any songbird in Alaska, and the dipper could be considered almost unique in this respect. Its song, among the most melodious of any songbird's, is difficult to describe but sounds somewhat like a long rendition of some of the best notes of the thrushes and wrens. It is especially delightful to hear during the otherwise almost silent winter. We once timed a dipper's midwinter song that lasted for a full 15 minutes.

FISH

CHAPTER 4

Southeast Alaska has thousands of freshwater lakes, ponds, rivers, and streams. About 15,500 miles of shoreline break up the marine waters into a myriad of fiords, channels, lagoons, bays, and open ocean (p. 85). Together, our fresh and salt waters support millions of fish, including nearly 300 species representing about 65 families.

In contrast to other states and countries, the fish in most parts of Southeast Alaska still live in a relatively pristine and pollution-free environment. Our rivers are mostly free of dams and discharges by large industries so detrimental to fish elsewhere. Our towns and cities are small and usually not located along major fish-producing rivers. Yet, wherever people have concentrated, damage to fish habitat has occurred. Channelization of streams and the destruction and alteration of wetlands are commonplace in and near most of our towns and cities. Clearcut logging to streambanks without provision of protective buffer strips has damaged fish habitat throughout the region, and extensive

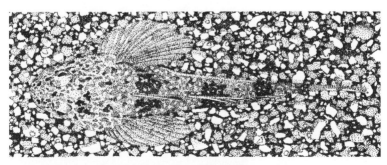

Pacific staghorn sculpin juvenile in salt-marsh slough

damage to fish habitat in Washington and British Columbia has reduced the numbers of salmon migrating to and through Southeast waters. For instance, the multiple dams on the Columbia River decimated chinook salmon populations that once fed in the inside and offshore waters of Southeast Alaska.

Most of our fish are native. Only 2 exotic (nonnative) freshwater species (Arctic grayling and brook charr) and 1 more or less marine species (American shad) have been introduced. Both freshwater species were introduced into a variety of waters but appear to have established a foothold only in lakes barren of other species. American shad were introduced from the Atlantic coast to the Sacramento River in California around 1870. The fish rapidly spread to other rivers as well as at sea, reaching Alaska by 1904. A few Atlantic salmon have been recently caught by commercial fishermen in Southeast. These salmon

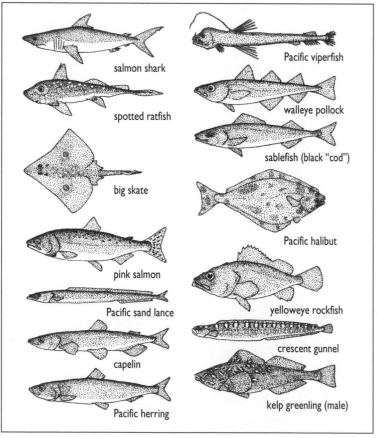

Selected Common Fish of Southeast Alaska

had apparently escaped from fish-farming pens in British Columbia. Although native to Southeast Alaska, rainbow trout have also been successfully stocked in a few barren lakes throughout the region.

FRESHWATER AND ANADROMOUS FISH—Salmon, trout, charr, stickleback, and sculpin complete the list for most of Southeast Alaska's fresh waters. In freshwater systems with sea access, sculpin and stickleback may be the only true year-round residents.

For anadromous salmonids (salmon, trout, and charr), whose life cycles occur in both salt and fresh waters, the ocean provides the bountiful food necessary for rapid growth. Many spend two or more years feeding at sea (chinook, sockeye, chum, steelhead); others spend between 1 and 2 years at sea (pink and coho) or only a few weeks or months (Dolly Varden and cutthroat). In the winter most salmon, except some kings, leave our inside waters for the food-rich areas in the Gulf of Alaska.

Lakes and streams blocked to migrating fish usually contain resident Dolly Varden and sometimes cutthroat trout. Here their growth is quite slow. The fish in streams seldom grow longer than 7 inches and in lakes seldom longer than a foot (see exceptions under "Cutthroat Trout"). The slow growth of the fish in our freshwater lakes and streams is related to cold waters and the nutrient-poor soils of the surrounding coniferous forests.

MARINE FISH—In contrast to our fresh waters, the marine waters of Southeast Alaska, including the eastern Gulf of Alaska, contain hundreds of fish species. The most common are flatfish (flathead sole, rock sole, yellowfin sole, arrowtooth flounder, Pacific halibut), cod

Starry flounder

(Pacific cod, walleye pollock), rockfish (Pacific ocean perch, rougheye rockfish, yelloweye rockfish, dusky rockfish, silvergray rockfish), sculpins (great sculpin, spinyhead sculpin, buffalo sculpin), skates, sablefish, herring, smelt, salmon, charr, Pacific sand lance, and threespine stickleback. Other common marine fish include eelpouts, snailfish, poachers, pricklebacks, gunnels, ronquils, kelp greenlings, wolf-eel, prowfish, and tube-snouts.

Southeast Alaska has about 9 of the 30 or so shark species found on the west coast of North America; the salmon shark is probably our most common and most voracious. These fast swimmers grow to a length of about 10 feet. In the Gulf of Alaska they eat salmon, often destroying those caught in nets as well as damaging the nets themselves. The legendary white shark occasionally migrates to Southeast, where it has been seen most often off the west coast of Prince of Wales Island. The relatively small (2 to 4 feet) spiny dogfish can be common in certain areas of Southeast. Fishermen should be cautious with these fish, as they have mildly toxic fin spines and can also inflict severe bites.

At least 8 species of skate occur in Southeast. These flattened fish have enlarged pectoral fins that act like wings, which propel them as if they were slowly flying through the water. They are bottom dwellers and take in water for respiration through openings called spiracles, located on their topsides, rather than through their mouths, like most other fish. The Aleutian and Alaska skates are common in the Gulf of Alaska off Southeast. Most skates attain 2 to 4 feet in length, but one species, the big skate, may reach up to 8 feet.

Another common, unusual-looking marine fish is the curious and oddly named spotted ratfish, unmistakable with its rather large head resembling that of a rabbit. It has a venomous dorsal-fin spine that can cause a painful, though not fatal, wound.

Southeast Alaska marine waters abound with huge schools of small, slim, silvery fish, often seen breaking the water's surface when pursued by predators. Many people use the misnomer needlefish, a family of fish occurring farther south. The species most often seen here are Pacific sand lance, Pacific herring, and capelin. Collectively, these fish form the most important component of the diet of most salmon, trout, and charr while they are at sea. Many other creatures also rely on these fish as a food source. Pacific herring support a multimillion-dollar commercial fishery. They are used for bait and cut into fillets for human consumption. Herring eggs (roe) are considered a delicacy in Japan, where they command a high price.

In the depths of our marine waters live some very bizarre-looking fish. In general, these deep-sea fishes have light organs called photophores, and some have large mouths with numerous long, fanglike teeth. The purpose of their photophores is not well known, but they may be used for recognition, especially at night or in the dark depths of the sea. They may also serve to illuminate their surroundings or attract food. The small Pacific viperfish (to 10 inches) has huge fangs protruding from its mouth. One of the largest deep-sea fish in our region is the long and slender longnose lancetfish, which may reach almost 7 feet in length. It has a large, sail-like dorsal fin, long daggerlike teeth in the roof of its mouth, and is hermaphroditic (bisexual). The daggertooth, northern pearleye, northern lampfish, and barreleye are other bizarre fish that only researchers, using mid- to deep-water trawls, are apt to see alive. Most of the rest of us can only marvel at them preserved for study in museum jars.

Four members of the cod family—Pacific cod, Pacific tomcod, walleye pollock, and Pacific hake—occur in Southeast Alaska marine waters. The Pacific cod is of major commercial importance along the North Pacific coast, where it is marketed for the fresh and frozen market and made into fish sticks. Walleye pollock and Pacific hake are also important commercial species harvested by both domestic and foreign fisheries. Walleye pollock are used to make the popular imitation crab (surimi), and since its use, the commercial harvests of pollock have increased considerably. A cod look-alike is the commercially important sablefish, or black cod, caught in trawls, in traps, and on longlines.

Flatfish, including flounders, sole, turbot, and Pacific halibut, are abundant in Southeast waters. These unique fish start out life with their eyes on either side of their head, but as they grow, one eye eventually migrates to the other side of the head. This allows the fish to lie flat on the ocean bottom, some completely buried and hidden, with just their eyes exposed. Many regard the Pacific halibut as our finest fish for eating. As a result they are heavily sought by both commercial and sport fishermen. Halibut are among the larger species of fish in our waters, and females often exceed 100 pounds (one 500-pound halibut was caught near Petersburg).

We have around 31 species of rockfish in our marine waters. Known for their tasty flesh, rockfish are basslike in appearance, with somewhat compressed bodies and large mouths. Most adults range from 1 to 2 feet in length. One, the rougheye rockfish, may grow to 3 feet and live up to 140 years. Most rockfish are among the longest-lived of all fish, and several species have a maximum age of over 60. As their name implies, many live in reefs and rocky areas. Some species are attracted to old shipwrecks, where they live their entire lives.

A search of our rocky intertidal waters usually reveals pricklebacks and gunnels. There are numerous species of these eel-like fishes, often erroneously called blennies, which do not occur in our region. Small sculpins are often seen darting this way and that in shallow tide pools.

We may never see many of the numerous other groups of marine fish occurring in our waters. We know little about many of their life histories; new species are no doubt out there waiting to be discovered.

DOLLY VARDEN CHARR

Dolly Varden charr live in some of the most beautiful waters in the world. Imagine a long, winding fiord bordered by snowcapped mountains, cliffs with waterfalls cascading to the salt water's edge, a river teeming with Pacific salmon, which snakes its way up the valley through ancient forests of Sitka spruce and western hemlock—this is a typical home of the Dolly Varden charr in Southeast Alaska.

Dolly Varden charr fingerling

Walking up one of these streams, you begin to see the almost-motionless, well-camouflaged schools of Dolly Varden. Occasionally an individual fish darts out of the school to grab something. Each pool of significant size seems to have a school of about 50 to 100 charr. Most seem to be waiting patiently for something to happen. Some wait for spawning to begin from 1 to 3 months after they entered the stream. Others, for no apparent reason, leave the stream for the ocean, then enter another stream a few miles down the coast. In the riffles between the pools, each pair of spawning salmon seems to have a small number of Dolly Varden in close attendance. These charr wait for the numerous salmon eggs that are knocked out of the gravel during the salmon's nest-building activities. They gorge themselves on these nutritious eggs until they are quite rotund.

In the streams' side channels, undercut bank areas, quiet shallow-water areas, and side tributaries, you see many small Dolly Varden ranging from 1 to 5 inches in length. They are the progeny of Dolly Varden that have previously spawned in the stream. Most occupy territories, and some viciously defend them from other Dolly Varden and other species such as young coho salmon.

Continuing to walk along the stream, you begin to realize that Dolly Varden occupy almost all available habitats, in such a great variety of sizes, and exhibiting so many different types of behavior, that you suspect great complexities must exist in their life cycles.

One of these complexities is migration. Each fall in Southeast Alaska, thousands of Dolly Varden migrate from the sea into lakes,

BOUNTIES ON DOLLY VARDEN

A bounty program destroyed more than 6 million Alaskan Dolly Varden between 1921 and 1940. This program, administered by the U.S. Bureau of Fisheries, was done because Dolly Varden were then thought to be a serious predator on salmon young and eggs. Bounties ranged from 2½ to 5 cents per Dolly Varden tail.

In 1939, almost 20 years after the bounty program was instigated, biologists were called in to investigate its effectiveness. What they found revealed that the bounty program was one of the greatest boondoggles in the history of Alaskan fisheries. They discovered that many, and in some instances the majority, of tails turned in for bounty were from rainbow trout and salmon, the very species they were attempting to save. For instance, in the U.S. Bureau of Fisheries office in Yakutat, of 20,000 tails examined by biologists, 3760 were from rainbows, 14,200 from coho salmon, but only 2040 from Dolly Varden.

Since the early 1940s, numerous studies have been done to determine whether or not Dolly Varden were a serious predator on salmon young and eggs. These studies showed not only that they were not harming salmon populations, but that Dolly Varden may actually benefit them. For example, Dolly Varden eat drifting salmon eggs dug up by the nest-building activities of salmon. These eggs, if not eaten, eventually die and develop fungus, possibly infecting healthy live eggs and yolk-sac fry in the gravel. Another possible benefit is that while in lakes, Dolly Varden feed heavily on, and may help control, freshwater snails that are an intermediate host of a parasite infecting the eyes of coho and sockeye salmon young, eventually causing blindness. Even the competition for space, which seems to occur with Dolly Varden and more serious salmon young predators, such as cutthroat trout, may play a role in reducing overall predation of salmon young by all species of fish.

where they spend the winter. Most have never been in lakes before, and come from the numerous small-to-medium-sized streams that intersect our shorelines. This run of Dolly Varden into lakes also includes fish that originated in a particular lake system, fish that completed spawning in other streams along the coast, and immature fish on their second or third annual trip from the sea.

In spring all Dolly Varden leave their overwintering lakes and migrate to sea. The mature fish then continue, via salt water, directly to the mouth of their home stream, the one in which they hatched, and enter it to spawn. The immatures, which usually number in the thousands from each lake, move apparently at random between lakes and streams, and between streams, making the fish appear more abundant than they really are and creating a manager's nightmare.

Most streams in Southeast Alaska serve as both spawning grounds for adults and early rearing habitat for their young. Although some large rivers such as the Taku, Stikine, and Chilkat are used by Dolly Varden in winter, they usually do not overwinter in streams without lakes.

It is uncertain whether Dolly Varden can overwinter at sea. Bob Armstrong's tagging showed that most, perhaps all, winter only in fresh water. Attempts in Norway to rear Arctic charr (a close relative) year round in salt water failed; all the fish died. Perhaps Dolly Varden cannot tolerate seawater for extended periods.

CUTTHROAT TROUT

Throughout their range cutthroat trout, like the canary in the mine, are sensitive indicators of environmental change. Once native cutthroat trout were in great abundance throughout the west, but now, except for places like Yellowstone Lake and River in Yellowstone National Park, many populations have vanished. Widespread introductions of exotic (nonnative) races of rainbow trout and brook charr and a host of other human changes to the environment caused their demise.

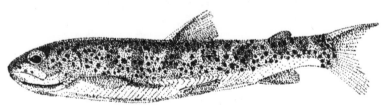

Cutthroat trout fingerling

In Southeast Alaska we are still blessed with some pristine environment. In addition, the Alaska Department of Fish and Game now prohibits introductions of exotic species of fish. Thus many "pure" populations of cutthroat, our most beautiful and abundant trout, can be found (p. 187). They may be sea-run (anadromous), may spend their entire life in a lake-stream system, or may reside only in streams.

Sea-run cutthroat are usually associated with lakes and a few of the larger, slow-moving rivers. Most of these anadromous populations are found south of Frederick Sound. Each year the fish go to sea in May and June and return to fresh water in September and October. In Southeast Alaska, approximately 2500 freshwater systems contain sea-run salmon, trout, or charr, but only 88 watersheds contain significant numbers of sea-run cutthroat trout. A good run of sea-run cutthroat may be about 3000 fish, and of these, only about 300 to 400 may be maturing females that will spawn the following spring. In addition, the fish are relatively slow growing, taking about 5 to 6 years to reach a length of 10 to 12 inches. These factors make our sea-run cutthroat trout very sensitive to overharvest.

Resident cutthroat trout are found in most landlocked lakes at the lower elevations in Southeast Alaska. In a few of these systems, you may find the large, trophy-sized cutthroat trout of 3 to 8 pounds. In contrast, most sea-run cutthroat seldom exceed 1 to 2 pounds. Some lake-resident cutthroat grow large because they prey heavily on small kokanee (landlocked sockeye salmon), and they are longer-lived than sea-run individuals. Lake residents may live up to 19 years, whereas few sea-run individuals live beyond 8 years. Other resident cutthroat have evolved ways to live their entire lives in streams so small you can easily step over them. Since these fish reach a length of only a few inches, they are ignored by most anglers.

THE FRESHWATER LIFE OF COHO SALMON

In Southeast, most adult coho salmon leave the sea and begin entering their spawning streams and rivers between July and November. The young hatch from their eggs in early spring and remain protected in the gravel of streambeds, nourished by absorbing the material in their yolk sacs. Most emerge from the gravel during May and June.

The freshwater life of these young coho may last only a few days

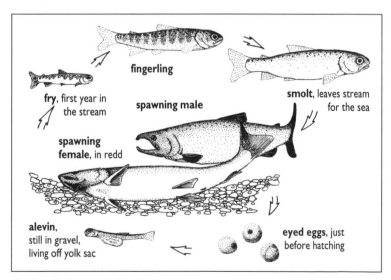

fingerling

fry, first year in the stream

spawning male

smolt, leaves stream for the sea

spawning female, in redd

alevin, still in gravel, living off yolk sac

eyed eggs, just before hatching

Coho Salmon Life Cycle

or weeks, or may last from 1 to 5 years. During this time, the young coho can be found in almost all bodies of water accessible to them. They may live in streams, glacial rivers, beaver ponds, lakes, side sloughs, and even intertidal portions of some streams.

Those living in streams usually set up territories, chasing and nipping at other fish in order to defend the most favorable feeding areas. Since most of their food comes from insects drifting in the currents, certain areas of a stream are more productive than others. In contrast, coho living in still waters such as ponds, lakes, and sloughs may not defend territories. In these situations, the food may appear from almost any direction, so territorial behavior would be of little advantage.

WINTER SURVIVAL TACTICS

In Southeast, fish are not subject to the extensive freezing waters that occur in the more northern areas of Alaska. Nevertheless, significant migrations and behavior changes prepare them for winter. For instance, most salmon, except some kings, leave our inside waters for the more food-rich areas in the Gulf of Alaska. Dolly Varden and cutthroat trout migrate from the sea and into lakes and deeper portions of large rivers. Young salmon, trout, and charr living in streams make significant moves before winter to avoid areas that freeze. Pacific sand lance bury themselves and rest in the sand during the winter period of low food supplies.

At Hood Bay Creek on Admiralty Island, Bob Armstrong observed large schools of young Dolly Varden and coho salmon moving upstream in the fall. His subsequent studies showed that these fish were seeking spring areas near the headwaters of the stream. During extreme periods of cold, these springs were the only significant ice-free areas in the stream.

At Lake Eva on Baranof Island, about 100,000 Dolly Varden and 2000 cutthroat trout entered the lake before winter during one study of these fish. In our Southeast lakes the water temperature may be only slightly above freezing in winter; hence the fishes' metabolic rate and resulting food requirements are less than if they remained in the warmer salt water. In lakes there are no currents to swim against, and they are usually covered with ice, so no predators can get to the fish. One fall, Bob marked all the Dolly Varden entering Lake Eva. The following spring he counted 94 percent of these marked fish leaving the lake, an amazing overwinter survival.

Streams have a certain carrying capacity (total number of fish the stream will support) for coho young. When this limit is reached, thousands of excess coho young may migrate to sea within days or weeks after emerging from the gravel. These very young fish eventually perish at sea because they have not developed the physiological and behavioral processes that would allow them to grow and develop normally in the ocean. These processes require 1 to 4 years in fresh water, at which time the coho successfully migrate to sea as smolts.

Some fisheries biologists believe that these excess coho young are driven to sea by individuals that have already established territories. In Alaska competition for territories may be high because a large proportion of a population of young coho remains in fresh water for at least 2 years before going to sea. In other Pacific Coast states and British Columbia, most coho young go to sea as year-old smolts, reducing competition for territories among those remaining in the streams.

Research at the Auke Bay Biological Laboratory in Juneau has revealed that many coho young move into the intertidal portions of streams where territorial fish like older coho and Dolly Varden young do not live. In summer these areas are generally warmer and have much more food, mainly small crustaceans called isopods and amphipods, than the areas of streams above tidal influence. Researchers found the coho young grow faster in these warmer, food-rich areas and then move upstream in the fall, when water temperatures drop.

Most research into the early life history of coho salmon points to one common denominator, the overall importance of small streams and tributaries to the maintenance of their populations. One study showed that during periods of flooding, coho young moved into side tributaries to escape the tremendous velocities of water in the main stem of the river. Another study revealed that coho young moved into spring-fed tributaries and portions of streams with upwelling groundwater for the winter. Since spring-fed areas are warmer in winter, the coho could avoid the severe icing elsewhere in the watershed. In a study of the streams in Juneau, biologists found that some of the smallest streams contained unusually high numbers of young coho.

Protection of these small streams is difficult, and development has harmed coho habitat. Channelization of intertidal portions of streams for flood control and to protect airports renders these areas much less productive as coho habitat. Urban development often eliminates the streamside vegetation and canopy of smaller streams.

The removal of coniferous trees along streams by logging and other activities can be detrimental to young coho in ways that are not obvious. For example, trees that fall naturally into streams provide excellent cover, creating pools and velocity shelters for young coho in streams that otherwise plunge rapidly from the mountains to the sea.

When trees are removed from stream banks, the natural cycle of decay and replacement of an important form of coho salmon habitat is lost.

THREESPINE STICKLEBACK

Threespine stickleback are widely distributed in Southeast Alaska and are particularly abundant in lakes, ponds, slow-moving streams, and estuaries containing emergent vegetation. Two forms of threespine stickleback occur in Southeast—a marine form and a freshwater one.

The marine form lives in the sea for most of its life, migrating into fresh water or estuaries in spring to breed. In early autumn the off-spring and adults leave the streams and estuaries and move out into salt water. Some remain near shore through the winter, and others move out to open sea for considerable distances. Large numbers of threespine sticklebacks, for example, have been taken at the water surface up to 496 miles from shore in the Gulf of Alaska. The marine form probably

---

NEST-BUILDING MALE STICKLEBACKS

A male stickleback builds a nest by sucking up sand or mud and depositing it away from the construction site. In the resulting depression, he glues together pieces of vegetation with mucus secreted by his kidneys, until a dome-shaped structure is formed. He then wiggles into the structure to form a tunnel. He defends the nest by viciously attacking any other colored male that swims near.

When a female whose belly bulges conspicuously with eggs approaches, the male courts her with a zigzag swimming motion while retreating toward the nest. He repeats these move-ments until the female follows him to the nest, where he points out the entrance with his snout. If the female likes the nest, she will wiggle into the tunnel and eventually deposit between 50 and 100 eggs. At once, the male enters the nest and sheds sperm over them. He may repeat this courtship with several females until the nest becomes stuffed with eggs.

The male cares for the fertilized eggs and the young. At frequent intervals he fans the nest with his large pectoral fins, creating a flow of water that helps improve the supply of oxygen to the eggs. The eggs hatch in about 2 weeks, and as the young begin emerging from the nest, the male darts about catching them in his mouth and spitting them back into the nest. About 10 days after hatching, the young begin to disperse, and the male no longer attempts to retrieve them.

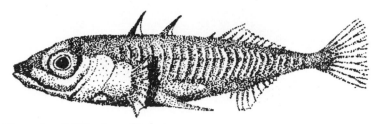

Threespine stickleback, marine form

lives only one year, and is best distinguished by numerous (22 to 37) bony plates along its sides and by its bright silver color.

The freshwater form remains in streams, lakes, and ponds throughout its lifespan of about 2 years. This form is best distinguished by only a few (0 to 9) bony plates on its sides and an olive color mottled with indistinct bars.

The males of both forms become brilliantly colored at breeding time, making them one of the most attractive of the small fishes residing in our waters. Colors include a blue or green eye, bright red or orange underparts, a red lining to the mouth, and translucent silver scales on the back.

With a small hand seine we can often capture hundreds of these little fish in only a few minutes. Other fish and birds take advantage of the stickleback's amazing abundance and availability. We find them to be an important food of cutthroat trout and Dolly Varden charr. Also, we often see Arctic terns, mergansers, and great blue herons feeding heavily on them.

SCULPINS

Sculpins are bottom-dwelling fish that include several species which scoot about the rocks and sit propped up on their large pectoral fins. Marine species live in tide pools or in shallow or deep marine waters, and freshwater species live in lakes, rivers, and streams. Most species range in length from 2 to 10 inches, but a few, such as the great sculpin, may reach a length of 2½ feet. They have various names but are most often called sculpins, Irish lords, and sometimes bullheads. Southeast Alaska has about 43 species.

Sculpins are among the most abundant fishes in Alaska. In a study of the coastrange sculpin, estimates reached 10,000 per half-mile in 1 Southeast Alaskan stream. Along the Beaufort Sea coast in Northern Alaska, more than 69 percent of all fish were estimated to be fourhorn sculpins. Pacific staghorn sculpins seem to be everywhere in Southeast marine and tidal waters. At least fishermen seem to catch them more frequently than any other species of fish, especially if their bait nears the bottom.

Sculpins have some of the most unusual habits of any Alaskan

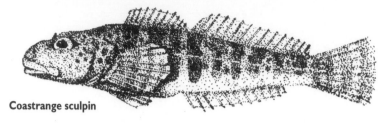

Coastrange sculpin

fish. For instance, the Pacific staghorn sculpin hums when under stress. Attempt to take one from your hook and you may feel the vibration from its humming. In territorial defense, the male fourhorn sculpin also produces a low-pitched humming sound with a frequency of about 125 cycles per second. One species, the tiny grunt sculpin, obtains its name from the half-grunting, half-hissing sound it makes when removed from the water.

Male sculpins may carry territoriality and defense of nesting sites to an extreme. The slimy sculpin "barks" at an opponent by quickly opening and closing its large mouth. "Barking" is usually followed by a quick dart at the opponent and by fighting. In contrast to most fishes, in which territorial behavior is mostly ritual, the loser of a fight between two male slimy sculpins may be killed.

Female sculpins usually lay their adhesive eggs in clumps attached to the surface or underside of rocks. Males of many sculpin species guard the eggs, sometimes keeping them clean by fanning them with alternate movements of their large pectoral fins, and by removing debris and dead eggs in their mouths. Males may be so attentive to their duties that they do not feed until the eggs have hatched.

Sculpins benefit some other fish and birds by providing food. In Southeast Alaska, the abundance of young Pacific staghorn sculpins in the shallow intertidal areas makes them easy prey for greater yellowlegs, great blue herons, Arctic terns, and common mergansers. Sculpins are also a potentially good source of food for humans. The staghorn sculpins' abundance, ease of capture in shallow waters, relatively large size (up to 18 inches), and edibility make them an excellent survival food for those stranded along Southeast Alaska's coastal waters. Foragers should be aware, however, that the eggs of this fish are poisonous.

PACIFIC SAND LANCE

Pacific sand lance are small (6 to 8 inches), thin, silver-sided fish. They have a long pointed snout, projecting lower jaw, and no paired ventral fins. They are present in a variety of habitats, including offshore waters, tidal channels, and along sandy beaches, where they typically form dense schools and burrow in sand and fine gravel.

This little fish is among the most important in our marine waters, since most fish-eating birds, mammals, and other fish feed on them.

When the food habits of fish and sea birds are studied, the sand lance usually shows up as the major food item. For example, they were the most important fish in the diet of troll-caught pink, coho, and chinook salmon in Washington's Strait of Juan de Fuca, and an important food of seaward migrant sockeye salmon in Bristol Bay. Sand lance were found to be the most important fish in the diet of marbled murrelets during nesting season and a major component of the food supply of kittiwakes, murres, and puffins. In fact, research has revealed that the abundance of sand lance makes a major difference in the success or failure of the reproduction of nesting sea birds at Cape Lisburne and Cape Thompson in western Alaska. Studies also indicate that sand lance may be important food for seals, halibut, cod, Dolly Varden, and even herring, which feed on their larvae. They are also an excellent fish for human consumption.

Sand lance do not have a swim bladder, and they sink to the bottom unless they make continuous undulating movements. To conserve energy and escape from most predators, sand lance bury themselves completely in the sand at night, and are reported to spend most of the winter months resting in the substrate. This behavior enables the fish to efficiently use the fat reserves acquired the previous summer to maintain their metabolism and to allow their gonads to mature. Remaining buried and inactive in a relatively predator-free environment at a time when food supplies, such as zooplankton, are much reduced is a highly successful survival adaptation.

Look for sand lance along sandy beaches and sandy intertidal sloughs at or near low tide. Often their presence is revealed by the feeding frenzies of gulls, terns, and bald eagles. The larger gulls usually alight on the water, then jab for the sand lances, while the Arctic terns and smaller Bonaparte's gulls hover and then plunge after their prey. Eagles may swoop and take them from the water in their talons or stand alongside a water-filled pocket in the sand, waiting patiently for a sand lance to emerge. On occasion we have observed up to 85 eagles standing in a group and gorging themselves on sand lance. By watching through a spotting scope, we have seen sand lance popping out of the sand all around the feeding eagles, with hundreds of the fish lying on the beach. This concentrated feeding by so many predators apparently panics and eventually exhausts the sand lance.

Watching sand lance is fun. When startled, they may dive headfirst into the sand. Then, apparently by wiggling upward in an arc, they

Pacific sand lance

may poke their heads out of the sand to look around (p. 187). If you move suddenly, they wiggle backward into the sand until they are completely covered. Sometimes as you walk about in the shallows, they panic and squirt out of the sand, madly rush about, then dive back in. If you grab one, hang on—upon escaping, they instantly disappear into the sand.

We could find only one study on sand lance from Southeast Alaska. It indicated that the fish may choose only very select areas for burrowing. Since they spend such long periods within the sand, it is essential that the substrate be well supplied with oxygen. We have found concentrations of sand lance buried where the substrate almost seemed to be in suspension. Identification and protection of their burrowing areas may be essential for the future maintenance of these important little fish.

INVERTEBRATES

• • •

CHAPTER 5

The invertebrate fauna of Southeast Alaska is abundant and diverse, but we will mention here only some of the more interesting forms we have encountered. Most of the research on invertebrates has emphasized relatively few commercially important species, and the vast majority of our invertebrates are poorly known scientifically. The abundance of Alaska's biting insects is legendary, however, and a full account of these alone would fill several volumes.

We eat some of the invertebrates of Southeast Alaska. There are both commercial and sport fisheries for a wide variety of our marine invertebrates. Commercial fisheries take tanner crab, golden king crab, spot prawns, pink or other species of shrimp, pinto abalone, geoducks, sea cucumbers, and sea urchins. The last two groups find an eager market in Japan.

Sport fishermen set pots for red king crab, Dungeness crab, and shrimp, while divers take pinto abalone, scallops, and some sea cucumbers. Some steamer and butter clams are harvested despite the ever-present danger of paralytic shellfish poisoning, while some people harvest chitons. A few people collect limpets, which make excellent hors d'oeuvres.

Most of our invertebrates, of course, are not so tasty. One of our most impressive invertebrates is the banana slug, an enormous terrestrial

Fragile test (hard covering) of the green sea urchin, with spines fallen off.

BUT CAN YOU SLICE THEM ON CORNFLAKES?

Students can ask peculiar questions. One of the most outlandish we ever heard came from a young man who, with a look of fascinated disgust, was watching an enormous banana slug rasp methodically at the cap of a king bolete mushroom. Suddenly he looked up and queried, "Are banana slugs edible?" After emitting an insuppressable guffaw, one of us advised, "Sure, but you have to peel them first!"

Boat-backed ground beetle, an eater of slugs and snails, on little shaggy moss.

mollusk whose color pattern of yellow or olive with blackish blotches is responsible for its common name. This animal is an herbivore and is often seen grazing on mushrooms and sometimes on devil's club leaves, if a nearby lady fern frond offers access. At Ward Cove, near Ketchikan, we have seen albino (pure white) specimens, and after a rain these ghostly slugs slither through the forest. Albino banana slugs occur in other parts of Southeast Alaska as well.

One of the most common beetles in the forest is the half-inch-long lacewinged beetle, a scavenger on decaying vegetation. Its all-red, matte-finish color contrasts strikingly with the dark green foliage it frequents. We also have many large purplish-black ground beetles of the family Carabidae, carnivores which may attack and devour slugs and other prey.

Butterflies are uncommon here—they simply cannot cope with our abundant rainfall. We do have at least 1 bumblebee, however, seen in habitats ranging from sea level to the alpine.

We also have many gall-forming insects, such as those species that form the tiny galls on blueberry stems, or the midges (tiny flies) that make the roselike deformities on Barclay willows.

Many of our most notorious insects also belong to the order Diptera, whose members have but a single pair of wings. In addition to the black-and-yellow-banded hover flies, which hang like miniature helicopters over flowers, and the fragile crane flies with their almost impossibly long legs, we have many species of mosquitoes, black flies, "no-see-ums," deer flies, and horse flies, invertebrates that eat us.

Culiseta alaskaensis is a large, slow-flying mosquito with spotted wings. After spending the winter in a protected spot such as a crack in the bark of a tree, the female emerges in early spring and seeks a blood meal as a prerequisite to the development of her eggs, which are laid on the surface of small ponds having lots of emergent vegetation. Somewhat later in the spring, smaller, fast-flying mosquitoes of the genus *Aedes* appear. They overwintered as eggs laid the previous fall and spent the early part of spring going through larval and pupal stages in fresh water.

Among other cues, such as odor and carbon dioxide emission, mosquitoes find their warm-blooded prey by sensing the heat given off by their victim's body, and we have found that there's nothing like a strenuous hike in the mountains to attract mosquitoes.

Black flies are small humpbacked flies with very short antennae. The females are vicious biters, slicing small chunks of skin from the victim and then lapping up the blood that trickles from the wound. Their larval stages are aquatic. "No-see-ums" (but "bite-um-like-hell") are tiny biting midges. They are easily identified by their minute size; often they are seen only when a glint of light betrays their tiny wings. Their bites are annoying but usually lead only to small reddish inflammations on the skin. Again, the larvae are aquatic, being restricted to running waters.

Both deer flies and horse flies are in the same family (Tabanidae). These are very large flies, and once again the females are bloodsucking (males feed on flowers). Deer flies are smaller, brownish, and have

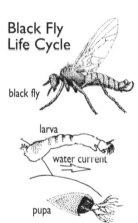

Black Fly Life Cycle

black fly

larva

water current

pupa

YES, ICE WORMS REALLY EXIST.

Ice worms were first discovered in 1887 on Muir Glacier in Glacier Bay National Park and Preserve. They are segmented worms, annelids, which include earthworms. Ice worms range from about a half-inch to a little over 1 inch long. Most live within the irregularities of glaciers caused by melting that takes place along ice crystals. Most species are nocturnal; at dusk they move to the surface of the glacier, where they feed on the ever-present algae that wash into the drainage furrows.

dark spots on their wings, while horse flies are enormous blackish flies that usually have clear wings. At least one species has bright green eyes. The only kind thing we can say about deer and horse flies is that after landing on their victim, they take so long to get ready to bite that we have ample time for a well-aimed swat.

Because many of these blood-feeding insects have aquatic larvae, they are important in freshwater food chains and help support fish populations and, in turn, fish-eating birds and mammals.

Many Alaskan terrestrial insects have ingenious adaptations enabling them to survive cold winters and thrive despite the shortened growing season. They bask in the early morning sunshine until their bodies warm up, or loiter in bowl-shaped blossoms, which shelter them from cold winds. They may overwinter as eggs, larvae, pupae, or adults, often having glycerol-like antifreeze compounds in their tissues to prevent freezing. Finally, in many species individuals may survive for more than 1 year, rather than racing through the entire life cycle in a single season.

In striking contrast to terrestrial insects, which tend to "shut down" during winter, a majority of aquatic insects are active, growing, and abundant all winter. They thrive because of the insulating properties of water and because aquatic insects are cool-adapted, meaning that they have evolved a biochemistry and enzymes that continue operating at temperatures near 0 degrees C. At cold temperatures (0 to

TAKING A CRANE FLY CENSUS

A highlight of our summer of 1988 was a visit by Drs. Irwin and Fenja Brodo of Ottawa, Canada, who came to Juneau to offer classes in lichen biology and entomology, respectively, at the University of Alaska Southeast. We knew that Fenja's expertise lay with crane flies, and, eager to interest her in our insect fauna, we told her that we had seen large crane flies with spotted wings and small ones with clear wings. "So we have at least 2 species!" we exulted. "I'll just take my net and see what I can find," she returned. Just before the Brodos left several weeks later, we asked Fenja how she liked our crane flies. "Just fine," she replied with a noticeable twinkle in her eye. "Your insect fauna here is very rich. I think you probably have at least 200 species of crane flies!"

5 degrees C), some species temporarily slow down or stop growing, although they remain active. Others, however, continue growing even at 0 degrees C.

MUSSELS

The blue bay mussel forms extensive beds in the upper mid-intertidal zone in Southeast Alaska. Blue bay mussels grow to 3 inches long and have relatively thin, smooth shells. In most individuals the shell is blue-black, which permit the maximum absorption of heat from the sun, but some are chestnut brown.

The blue bay mussel attaches to rocks and other hard objects by a cluster of exceptionally strong strands called byssal (rhymes with "whistle") threads. To form these golden threads, the mussel uses its foot, a narrow orange structure which it can protrude from between its shells. The mussel first attaches its foot to a rock, to the shell of another mussel, or to a piling. Then, using a special gland, it secretes a solution of structural proteins and enzymes through a groove along the lower edge of its foot. When the foot finally pulls away from the attachment point, the byssal thread is left. Dozens of these threads anchor the mussel. In quiet muddy bays, the preferred habitat of the blue bay mussel, entire beds may be formed by mussels attaching only to each other, and rocks may be almost entirely absent. These beds form shelters for innumerable tiny marine creatures which live between the mussels and among the byssal threads.

The blue bay mussel spawns in the spring in Southeast Alaska. Eggs and sperm are simply shed into the sea, where fertilization and early development take place. Soon a tiny creature called a veliger larva is formed. On its head end, the veliger has a looped band of cells carrying cilia, minute whiplike structures that beat in a coordinated fashion to propel the animal through the water. The ciliated cells also direct a current of water down to the mouth, where the veliger removes tiny unicellular algae called phytoplankton from the water and swallows them. The veliger floats in the sea for several weeks, feeding on the dilute soup of phytoplankton that blooms in response to increasing daylight hours of spring.

Eventually the veliger settles out of the plankton and selects a piece of real estate where it will become an adult mussel. By this time, it has secreted a minute, glassy double shell and is capable of crawling over the surface of rocks. At this stage, it is called a plantigrade. If the plantigrade is unable to find a suitable surface, it may swim up into the water again and drift farther. The drifting plantigrade may even secrete its first byssal threads, which stream out behind it, increasing its flotation and thus enabling even the weakest currents to carry it. Eventually, however, the plantigrade settles out, often on such filamentous objects as finely branched seaweeds or the byssal threads of established individuals. The settled plantigrade secretes its own threads, but for some time is able to break them and move around, to avoid being smothered by accumulating sediments. This mobility is probably one reason for the blue bay mussel's abundance in quiet waters. The settlement of young mussels is highly variable from one year to the next.

After settlement, the young mussels feed in a manner quite different from that of the planktonic stages. Each mussel opens its two shells slightly and draws a current of water through its delicate gills.

Blue bay mussels feeding

Phytoplankton and other organic materials (especially detritus from decomposing kelps) stick to the mucus coating the gills. Again, ciliated cells guide the trapped food toward the mouth, where it is swallowed. This type of feeding is called filter feeding because food is essentially strained out of the seawater. Food particles as fine as 0.00002 inch in diameter are removed. Among the many kinds of phytoplankton which may be caught are those which cause paralytic shellfish poisoning, and since these organisms are so common in Southeast Alaska, mussels should not be eaten here. (Even mussels farmed in Puget Sound must be continually tested for contaminated individuals.)

In nature, many animals eat mussels. Birds such as the northwestern crow pick up mussels, fly into the air, and drop them onto the rocks below to break them open. Scoters swallow mussels whole and crush them in their gizzards. Both river otters and sea otters eat them, and even black bears forage in the intertidal for mussels. All of these predators are susceptible to paralytic shellfish poisoning.

Crabs also eat mussels, chipping away at the shells with their heavy pincers, and many species of sea star also eat mussels by pulling the shells apart. Mussels torn off the rocks by wave action also may be caught by the tentacles of large anemones lurking in deeper waters.

THE MUSSEL'S REVENGE—Several species of marine snails eat mussels by first boring a hole in their shells. Locally, the wrinkled whelk and the file dogwinkle remove numerous mussels from the population every year. But unlike other fixed marine invertebrates, such as oysters, the beleaguered mussel can to some extent defend itself. It can attach new byssal threads to the shell of the rasping predator and then anchor the snail either to the rock or to the shells of other mussels. The attacked mussel then hunkers down, and the predatory snail is unable to rasp effectively. Snails anchored in this fashion may starve and die.

Blue bay mussels that successfully avoid all these predators may live for only about 3 years, but in nature entire beds of mussels are often obliterated by storms, only to be replaced by recruitment of young another season.

CLAMS

Steamer and butter clams are 2 of the most abundant species of shellfish found on protected intertidal beaches throughout Southeast Alaska. The steamer, or littleneck clam as it is often called, has short siphons ("little necks") and therefore lives only 1 to 3 inches beneath the surface. Butter clams can burrow as much as 14 inches deep because they have much longer siphons.

Both steamer and butter clams are common to abundant in muddy sand mixed with gravel, although butter clams are also found in mud alone. Steamers tend to live slightly higher on the beach (up into the lower mid-intertidal zone just below the beds of mussels and brown rockweed), while butters extend from the lower intertidal to almost 100-foot depths.

These 2 species of clam are easily distinguished by their shells. The shell of a steamer clam is moderately heavy, up to 2 inches long and whitish to tan, often with brown tepeelike markings in juveniles. The shells are marked externally with fine concentric growth lines that intersect delicate radial lines. The dark elastic hinge, which opens the shells when the clam relaxes its muscles, is somewhat hidden between the two shells and is not conspicuous externally.

In contrast, the heavy shells of butter clams are up to 5 inches long and are basically grayish white, although the shells of individuals living in mud low in oxygen and high in iron sulfide will be blackened. Externally, butter clams have only fine concentric growth lines; radial lines are completely lacking. The hinge ligament of butter clams is well developed and externally conspicuous.

In Alaska, steamer clams require fully 8 years to reach a harvestable size. By comparison, steamers in southern British Columbia require only 3 years. This dramatic difference in growth rates probably results from the colder temperatures of Alaskan waters. Comparable information on butter clams is not available, but we do know

Steamer clam

that they can live 20 years or more in Alaskan waters, and it is probable that they, too, have a slow growth rate. These slower growth rates are of direct economic importance because often such animals produce fewer offspring annually, and hence are more susceptible to being locally exterminated if commercial harvesting is established.

Among the most important predators of clams are various species of sea stars. In Southeast Alaska, the common mottled sea star finds steamer clams easy prey, while the larger butter clams are often taken by the many-armed sunflower sea star. In either case, the sea star digs the clam from its burrow, fastens dozens of tiny suction cups (called tube feet) to the shells, and then exerts enormous force to pull the shells apart. Even if the shells gape only a fraction of an inch, that is enough, for the sea star then everts its stomach through its mouth, located on the underside of its body, and slides its delicate stomach tissues through this narrow slit to begin digesting the tissues of the clam. Eventually, enough of the clam's muscles are digested that the shells can no longer be held closed, and the sea star makes quick work of its exhausted prey.

Other important predators of clams include such large snails as moon snails and their close relative, the Arctic natica. These snails can drill a small round hole in one shell of a clam and then stick their feeding organs through it to rasp at the soft tissues within.

Of course, humans are important predators, too. Both

Northwest neptune snail, a predator of clams.

PARALYTIC SHELLFISH POISONING (PSP)

Symptoms of PSP include initially a tingling sensation around the mouth and lips, which may spread to general paralysis, respiratory failure, and death in susceptible individuals. There is no antidote for PSP, but stricken individuals are given oxygen until their paralysis wears off.

PSP is caused by toxins that accumulate in the digestive glands and, often, in the siphons of clams as they feed by straining microscopic plants from seawater. The toxins are produced by a species of microscopic alga (called a dinoflagellate) which grows in seawater. Resting stages, or cysts, of dinoflagellates occur in marine mud. At some unknown environmental cue they hatch, and the resultant swimming stage may multiply at staggering rates to produce a "bloom" of the species. Feeding clams or mussels then strain these swimming stages from the water. The consumed PSP toxins are harmless to clams and mussels, but can be passed on to other animals which prey on them. Invertebrate predators like moon snails are likewise unharmed and can carry even higher concentrations of PSP than the clams they eat. One group of marine invertebrates that never carry PSP are grazers of algae, such as limpets. Cooking and freezing do not lower toxin levels.

Some species of dinoflagellate contain a red pigment, and when they bloom they can actually turn the water reddish, producing the "red tide" that strikes various parts of our coast each year. From the vantage point of 39,000 feet in a commercial jetliner, we have seen the tongues of red tide sweeping along the coast and penetrating into inlets and bays. Red tides do not necessarily indicate contaminated shellfish, however, since some species of dinoflagellates do not form the toxins associated with PSP. On the other hand, some species (such as *Alexandrium catenella* on our coast) are so toxic that they can poison shellfish even when their populations are too low to cause a red tide noticeable to the eye.

Clams from Porpoise Island near Glacier Bay have proven toxic every time they have been tested, and the poison (called saxitoxin) from these clams was used by the U.S. military in World War II.

Alexandrium catenella, a toxic dinoflagellate in plankton.

species of clam are prized edibles. But because of periodic blooms of toxic phytoplankton, it is dangerous to eat any clam harvested in Southeast Alaska, even when the consumer has ready access to hospital care. To eat clams while boating or camping far from medical assistance is to play Russian roulette, Southeast Alaskan style.

While it is true that spring and summer are the most dangerous times for eating clams, even winter clamming is risky because the toxins can remain in the tissues of the clams up to 2 years after the original contamination occurred. Removing the siphons may help, but there can still be enough poison in the contaminated digestive glands to cause a severe problem.

To be safe, your best bet is to get your clams at the grocery store. Commercial canners must test their harvested clams regularly to detect any that carry dangerous levels of toxins, but such complex laboratory testing procedures are expensive and not available to the general public.

ACORN BARNACLES

Acorn barnacles are the small, whitish volcano-shaped creatures that live permanently attached to hard surfaces such as rocks and boat hulls. When exposed by a receding tide, they close their plates and wait. When the tide returns, they open the 2 pairs of tiny plates at the top of the "volcano," extend 6 pairs of feathery appendages called cirri, and in effect comb their dinner from the water, extracting tiny drifting animals (zooplankton), microscopic algae (phytoplankton), or edible organic particles. This food is then removed from the cirri and, with the aid of various mouthparts, is transferred to the mouth and swallowed.

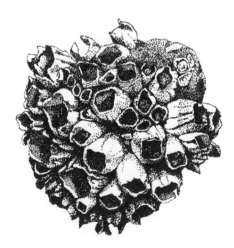

The common acorn barnacle leaves a white scar on the rock when it breaks off.

In Southeast Alaska we have 5 species of acorn barnacle living intertidally. Highest on the shore is a tiny species with brownish plates, the little brown barnacle. This species is more resistant to exposure than the others and can live where the sea covers it less frequently. Adult little brown barnacles rarely exceed a quarter of an inch in diameter.

A little lower on the shore live 2 species rather similar in appearance; both have smooth white plates and reach about

half an inch or so in diameter. One of these, the common acorn barnacle, leaves a white scar on the rock when the individual is broken off,
while the other, the northern rock barnacle, leaves no scar. Both species
may be abundant down into the middle intertidal area, which is often
marked by the development of extensive mussel beds.

Somewhat below the common acorn barnacle and the northern
rock barnacle, one may find the thatched barnacle, which grows much
larger (perhaps 2 inches across the base) and has outer plates decorated
with distinctive downward-pointing spines.

In the very lowest part of the intertidal zone, one may encounter
Balanus crenatus. Like the common acorn barnacle, it has a smooth
white shell and leaves a scar when broken off the rock, but it grows
much larger and has a relatively small opening to its "volcano." *B. crenatus* is really a subtidal species and is not common intertidally.

Because of their calcified plates, barnacles were originally thought
to be mollusks related to clams and snails, but a careful study of their
life history soon revealed that they are true crustaceans, related to crabs,
lobsters, and their kin. They brood fertilized eggs in a space between the
body tissues and the shell until a distinctive stage called the nauplius is
reached. The nauplius is shaped something like a rutabaga with horns
and has 3 pairs of appendages for locomotion.

An adult barnacle will brood from 3000 larvae (in the little brown
barnacle) to 10 times that number in the common acorn barnacle, and
undoubtedly even more in larger species. Each species of barnacle will
produce pulses of nauplii through the spring, and in many cases they
are released during a plankton bloom, which ensures that plenty of food
is available.

The nauplius drifts, feeds, and molts in the plankton for a varying
amount of time until a new stage, the cypris, is formed. The cypris has a
bivalved (double) shell like a clam and 6 pairs of swimming legs on the
front part of the body. The cypris, which does not feed, may be eaten
by juvenile salmon.

The cypris stage eventually settles out of the water and selects a
spot on which to become an adult barnacle. In accomplishing this, it
attaches to a rock with one antennule and "tastes" the rock with the
other. If the spot is satisfactory, the cypris then glues itself down permanently, using cement glands in its antennules, and within a few hours
changes radically into a miniature adult. These newly settled adults are
only a millimeter or two in diameter and are quite translucent, but they
are shaped like fully formed acorn barnacles. Feeding commences soon
thereafter, since the thoracic appendages of the former cypris have
become the feeding cirri of the adult.

Acorn barnacles are a staple in the diet of drilling snails, such as
species of *Nucella*, and are the sole food of both the green ribbon worm

and the rough-mantled sea slug. Some species of sea star also find barnacles delectable. All of these animals either drill holes in the shells of the barnacle or pull the plates apart to expose the soft and nutritious tissues within. Barnacles may also be eaten by the larval stages of flies in the Dryomyzidae family.

How do acorn barnacles reproduce? Most other directly attached marine invertebrates solve the problems imposed by a lack of mobility by simply releasing eggs and sperm into the water, where fertilization can occur. Barnacles, faced with the same problem of being literally glued to the spot, have solved the problem of how to court fair lady by evolving what must be proportionally the longest sex organs of any animals. They are also hermaphroditic. This means that any individual barnacle can mate with any neighbor, since they are all both male and female at the same time.

COMPETITION AND SURVIVAL—Although it seems odd to think of fixed-in-place organisms as possessing survival and combative behavior, in fact the acorn barnacle has such skills. As it feeds and grows, it may encounter other individuals either of its own kind or of another species. If it encounters many others of its own species, each individual tends to grow taller and narrower. If the growing barnacle encounters individuals of another species, however, then an intense competition for space may ensue, with one species characteristically bulldozing, growing over, or crushing the other species off the rock. In this manner, for example, the common acorn barnacle routinely removes lower individuals of the little brown barnacle from the rock.

DRAGONFLIES AND DAMSELFLIES

Dragonflies and damselflies belong to the order Odonata, a word derived from two Greek words meaning "toothed jaws." Although they do not sting or bite humans, they are real dragons to other insects. Damselflies are recognized by their similar fore and hind wings, which are held erect at rest, and by their widely separated eyes. Dragonflies' hind wings are wider at the base than their fore wings, and both pairs of wings are held outstretched at rest. Their eyes are also closer together than those of damselflies.

Larval stages of dragonflies and damselflies are abundant in Southeast Alaska in small, shallow lakes or ponds with the aquatic vegetation that provides dissolved oxygen, shelter, and food for the insects on which dragonflies and damselflies feed. Adult dragonflies (p. 187) and damselflies are well equipped for their role as voracious predators. Among insects they are masters of flight and have impressive eyesight.

Most insects raise and lower their wings by muscles attached inside the body. The contraction of these muscles changes the shape of

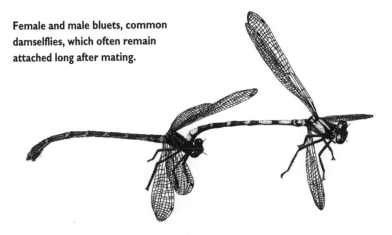

Female and male bluets, common damselflies, which often remain attached long after mating.

the body, thereby causing the wings to lever up and down simultaneously. In dragonflies and damselflies, however, special groups of muscles are attached directly to the wings. This enables the insect to move each of its 4 wings independently, resulting in great agility. In pursuit of their prey they can fly backward, or suddenly stop and turn while in rapid forward flight. A big dragonfly may reach a speed of 60 miles per hour. Furthermore, they can easily sneak up on prey because their flight is noiseless; since their wingbeats are slow, they do not produce a hum. Only when zooming through dense vegetation do they alert us by the rattling of their wings against the leaves.

The iridescent eyes of dragonflies and damselflies are composed of up to 30,000 small facets covering almost the entire side of the face and giving them an enormous visual field. Their heads are also exceptionally movable, and a complex system of joints in the neck enables them to maintain a precise focus on their prey, even while being buffeted by the wind. They can also see at night and can hunt in almost complete darkness, although they are most active in sunshine.

Dragonflies and damselflies feed on a variety of other insects. The smaller damselflies may snatch aphids and mosquitoes from the foliage as they flit by. The large dragonflies often chase larger insects such as moths. Their long legs are specially adapted for seizing prey because they are situated far forward and are armed with spines, forming a basket that enables the dragonfly to capture and hold its prey in flight.

The larval stage of a dragonfly is called a naiad. Naiads live in freshwater pools, where they are fearsome predators which capture insects and even small fish by firing a huge lower lip at their prey with lightning speed (p. 188). The adult or winged form lives less than 5 weeks, whereas the naiad stage may survive as long as 4 years.

Dragonflies and damselflies mate in flight. The male curls the tip of his abdomen forward and deposits a sperm packet in a chamber below his second abdominal segment. Then, while still in flight, the male clasps the female by the neck with special claspers located at the tip of his abdomen, and the female picks up the sperm packet with the tip of her abdomen. Later she deposits fertilized eggs in or close to water. Many damselflies remain joined even after they have mated, and you can often see them flying about in pairs with the male in the lead.

CADDISFLIES

Adult caddisflies are slender, dull-colored, mothlike insects belonging to the order Trichoptera. They have 4 somewhat transparent wings (p. 188), which they fold tentlike above their body when resting. They remain hidden during the day, waiting for evening to conduct their rather clumsy, reeling flights. In Southeast Alaska the adults are best seen during September and October, when they are attracted like moths to outside lights at night.

The mouth structure of adult caddisflies is best suited for lapping, so they cannot bite you. In fact, many adults do not feed at all, since their only activity is mating. Their mating flights or nuptial dances are enchanting to watch. Often they circle with whirring wings just slightly above the water surface, paddling vigorously with their middle legs, the female in front and the male in hot pursuit. Other species may dance vertically in the air with their long antennae diverging.

Caddisfly Life Cycle

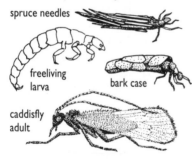

spruce needles

freeliving larva

bark case

caddisfly adult

Caddisfly adult and various larvae

Caddisfly larva in case made of sand grains. A mason could be proud of a chimney this well crafted.

Throughout spring, summer, and fall, adult caddisflies emerge from the water and mate, and the females lay their eggs near or in water. These soon hatch into larvae, which live in streams, lakes, and ponds from winter to summer and provide important food for Dolly Varden charr and cutthroat trout.

Each larva may build a case or house. A caddisfly larva makes a house by spinning an open tube, using a silken thread that flows from its mouth. It manipulates this thread with specially adapted forelegs. Most species then use

A CADDISFLY SURVEY

A survey of Southeast Alaska caddisflies was conducted by Richard Vineyard between 1978 and 1980. He collected 1004 individuals and found 74 species representing 41 genera and 11 families. Most types of caddisflies described above were found, including many case-making species, the predaceous free-living forms, and members of the bizarre net-spinning caddisfly family. Vineyard speculated that as of 1980 only about 60 or 70 percent of the species living in our area had been identified.

sticky silk to glue grains of sand or pebbles, bits of wood, or parts of plants to the outside of the case to enhance its camouflage.

If you look carefully along the shallow margins of a stream, you may see these tiny houses and the protruding, caterpillarlike forepart and 6 tiny legs of the little inhabitant, as it pulls its house along. The whitish caddisfly larvae hide their soft bodies inside their houses, which camouflage them and protect them from predators. The cases also provide ballast and streamlining to help prevent the larvae from being washed away by swift currents. The case can also help the young caddisfly extract oxygen from the water, since the larva undulates continuously within it, bringing a steady current of fresh water across the filamentous gills on the abdominal segments.

A unique group of these insects belongs to the net-spinning caddisflies (Hydropsychidae family). These larvae build miniature retreats out of bits of debris attached permanently to small stones or sticks along the stream bottom. Each retreat looks like a small mountain tent, higher at one end and tapering sharply to the lower end. At the high end of its retreat, on the downstream side, the larva builds an elegant silk net complete with silk "guy wires," and uses it to strain algae and small invertebrates from the water. Spiderlike, the larva waits in its retreat for food to become entangled in the net, then extracts it with special brushes on its forelegs.

Not all caddisfly larvae construct homes. Many members of the Rhyacophilidae family (primitive caddisflies), for example, do not make cases. These larvae are predators that eat other insects and even each other, so perhaps carrying a tube of stones or sticks would hinder their predaceous activities. When full-grown, a caddisfly larva makes a cocoon within which it becomes a resting stage, or pupa. When its wings are fully developed, the pupa cuts its way out of the cocoon and swims to the water surface, where it crawls out on a rock or stick. The adult eventually bursts open the pupal skin and flies away. Mating flights begin and the cycle is repeated.

BUTTERFLIES

Despite the seemingly hostile Alaskan climate, more than 75 species of butterflies have been found throughout the state. According to Dr. Kenelm Philip of the University of Alaska in Fairbanks, our butterflies survive the winter cold by 2 strategies. Some use the insulating qualities of snow to protect them from extreme temperatures, while others living in areas with little snow contain natural "antifreeze" chemicals in their bodies. Because interior Alaska gets more summer sun than Southeast, it has far more butterfly species, in spite of its more severe winters.

Butterflies go through 4 stages of life: egg, larva, pupa, and adult. Their eggs, which are about the size of a pinhead, are deposited by the female, usually on the underside of a leaf. Each female butterfly may lay up to 500 eggs during her rather brief adult life.

The eggs eventually hatch into larvae, the familiar caterpillars, which feed almost constantly on the leaves of whatever plant is their specialized food. Usually this is a flowering plant or tree,

Mourning cloak.
These butterflies are more
common during relatively dry summers.

which they recognize by its aromatic oils. Butterfly larvae appear never to eat ferns or mosses. Caterpillars are extraordinarily specific in their feeding habits, and each species will usually feed only on a small number of closely related plant species. If a suitable food plant is not available, the caterpillar will starve to death rather than eat something else.

The caterpillar grows rapidly and molts several times until it finally produces a pupa or chrysalis. The pupa is immobile and neither eats nor drinks; its mouth and anus are both sealed over. While in the pupal stage, the butterfly reorganizes itself into a winged adult. When this process is complete, the chrysalis splits open and a fully formed adult butterfly emerges. Eventually the butterfly flies off to mate, and the cycle is repeated.

SOUTHEAST TOUGH ON BUTTERFLIES—Adult butterflies need warmth and sunshine, hence our often cool and cloudy summers don't support a large and diverse butterfly fauna. We have identified only 5 species of butterflies in Southeast Alaska, although we suspect a few more exist. At least 3 species—the red admiral, the painted lady, and the tiger swallowtail—are occasional migrants to our region. Another, the mourning cloak, appears during our rare periods of extended sunny weather.

The most common and obvious species found here is the mustard white (p. 188). These delicate butterflies have wings mostly white on top and cream-colored to yellowish underneath. The veins on their wings may have light to heavy gray-olive or brown scaling, which has earned them the alternative common name "veined white."

Although the adults seem to feed on a wide variety of flowers, mustard whites lay their eggs on members of the mustard family only. They may have 2 broods within the year, and adults emerge in May to early June and again in August. Their eggs are laid singly, usually on the underside of a leaf. The caterpillars are forest green in color, with darker or yellowish back and side stripes. They are solitary and well camouflaged on the green leaf.

Mustard white butterflies are not considered pests of the garden. In fact, their caterpillars feed on plants considered weeds by most gardeners. They are beneficial as pollinators of flowers and as a thing of beauty to watch in our otherwise butterfly-poor environment. They are of no value to insect-eating birds, as both their pigments and body fluids are toxic.

PSEUDOSCORPIONS

Beachcombing between tidelines is a popular activity with residents of Southeast Alaska, who take advantage of the extreme low tides of spring to treat their lingering cabin fever. One fascinating animal, the pseudoscorpion, can be found by diligent searching beneath rocks in the upper intertidal barnacle zone near freshwater streams.

"Pseudoscorpion" means "false scorpion," appropriate because these animals look like miniature scorpions, but without the long tail and terminal sting. Like scorpions, spiders, and mites, pseudoscorpions are arachnids, or arthropods with 4 pairs of walking legs. Intertidal arachnids are extremely rare, making our local pseudoscorpion almost unique.

What tiny creatures! Most species of pseudoscorpion are less than a third of an inch long, and the local intertidal species *(Halobisium occidentale)* is one of the largest. *Halobisium* is a glossy chestnut brown.

Pseudoscorpions have *two* body regions. The front region carries a pair of biting jaws, a pair of pincers, and 4 pairs of walking legs. The tiny jaws are used for tearing holes in the flesh of prey species, often mites or other minute arthropods. The large pincers are used to capture and manipulate prey, build nests, hold a mate, and fight. When a pseudoscorpion walks forward slowly, it holds these pincers out in front, in a manner suggestive of a flamenco dancer using castanets. Tiny bristles on

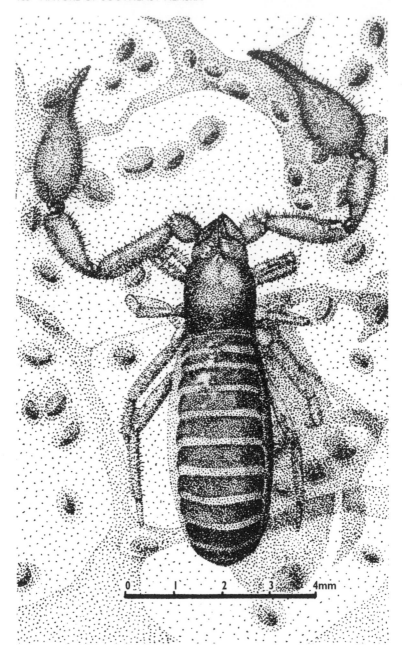

Pseudoscorpion on intertidal rock with freshly colonized baby barnacles. Large white patches are scars where common acorn barnacles have peeled off.

the pincers are thought to detect the vibrations of moving prey. In some species, the pincers carry poison glands and may secrete a poison, or perhaps an anesthetic, to immobilize the prey. The 4 pairs of walking legs are armed with claws, which help the pseudoscorpion cling to rough surfaces. The hind region of the body bears no appendages and is composed of 12 distinct segments.

In feeding, pseudoscorpions inject large quantities of digestive juices into the body of their prey, wait several minutes for these juices to decompose the prey's flesh, and then simply suck out the body contents. When they have finished, only the indigestible hard outer cuticle of the prey remains. Like some other species of carnivores, pseudoscorpions feed infrequently and can withstand several weeks or months of starvation. Pseudoscorpions have no particular enemies, but they may be eaten by centipedes, spiders, beetles, or even birds.

Pseudoscorpion reproduction is fascinating. Females, which are usually somewhat larger than males, can store male sperm for months or even years. For this reason, transfer of sperm from males to females need occur only infrequently. Mature sperm are packaged by males into complicated and delicate structures called spermatophores.

Sperm transfer occurs by a bewildering variety of techniques in different species of pseudoscorpion, and may or may not involve mating. In the latter method, the male deposits spermatophores on the ground and hopes that one will be discovered by a receptive female and taken up into her seminal receptacle. To prevent females from taking up

CRAB-SPIDERS

Our local crab-spider is also called the goldenrod or flower spider because of its habit of lurking on flowers, waiting for prey. The females, about a third of an inch long, are twice the size of males and either ghostly white or butter yellow, with a broad, brick-red stripe down each side of the abdomen. Individuals can change color slowly, and it is reported that white spiders placed on goldenrod flowers turned yellow in about 11 days. The adaptive value of this color change is that the spiders find camouflage in white flowers early in the season and then transfer to yellow flowers which may be more abundant later in summer. A crab-spider holds its crablike front legs outstretched, waiting for an insect to visit the flower on which it sits. The spider's venom is highly toxic to flies or even bees much larger than itself, and such insects are grabbed, bitten, paralyzed, and eaten with dispatch (p. 188).

stale spermatophores, males routinely destroy old ones. This method of sperm transfer is successful only in gregarious species, where the chance of a female finding fresh spermatophores is high.

Sperm transfer by mating is much more interesting. Usually the male grasps the female's pincers with his own, and the pair execute an elaborate mating dance, the choreography varying from species to species. At one point in this dance, the male slyly deposits a fresh spermatophore on the ground, and then in subsequent steps, he maneuvers the female to position her directly over the spermatophore so that she can take it up. The entire dance may last up to an hour, depending on the species. This second method of sperm transfer reduces spermatophore wastage and, since spermatophores must remain moist, makes the animals less dependent on environmental humidity.

The mated female then builds a nest of silk, which she spins from glands near her mouth. She ties bits of wood and perhaps sand grains together, lines the entire structure with more silk, then retreats into the completed nest and lays her fertilized eggs. The developing eggs are carried in a special brood pouch attached to the underside of her hind region, where they are nourished by secretions of the mother's genital openings. In 4 or 5 weeks the eggs hatch; in some species this is effected by use of a sawlike hatching organ. The mother, who stopped feeding while brooding, can now leave the nest to feed, but her hatchlings stay in the nest until their soft outer layer hardens for protection.

Most species of pseudoscorpion reproduce in the spring or summer, and can produce several broods per season. Some species live 3 or 4 years.

FUNGI AND LICHENS

CHAPTER 6

Recognizing that fungi are neither plants nor animals, biologists have split them off into their own taxonomic kingdom. Like some of the primitive terrestrial plants, such as mosses and ferns, fungi reproduce by releasing prodigious numbers of unicellular microscopic spores. When a spore germinates under favorable conditions, it produces minute threadlike growths called hyphae. After the hyphae of one individual have grown for a while, they may fuse with those of another, eventually producing the fruiting bodies we call bracket fungi, coral fungi, and many more familiar cap-and-stalk mushrooms.

Our familiarity with the fungi of Southeast Alaska increases each year. We have seen, identified, and in most cases photographed some 230 species, classified by the microscopic structures on which they produce their spores. One is a zygomycete (related to bread molds); about 20 are ascomycetes (cup fungi, morels, and their relatives); 200 are basidiomycetes, including well over 100 mushrooms with the familiar gill structure on their cap undersides; and 10 are slime molds. None of these species is endemic to Southeast Alaska, which is not surprising in view of the ease with which the microscopic spores are spread by wind or water. Southeast Alaska has a rich and varied fungal flora, which we attribute to our abundance of wood and other organic materials and to the wet climate. Our list of 230 probably includes just a small fraction of the total number of fungal species occurring here.

Our growing knowledge of these fungi has heightened our pleasure in hiking and other outdoor activities. When the fungus season starts each summer (or spring, for a few species), old friends are greeted with delight, while unknown species are carefully collected and taken home to be compared with the many descriptions in our personal libraries and, perhaps, eventually added triumphantly to our list.

Many of the ascomycetes can lichenize; that is, individual species which cannot thrive on their own can associate with a particular species of terrestrial alga to make what we call a lichen. Lichens grow on rocks, on soil, and on trees and shrubs. Those growing on other plants are called epiphytic and abound in Southeast Alaska's heavy rainfall.

FOREST MUSHROOMS

Every year, late in the summer and throughout fall, mushrooms burst forth in our forests with an overwhelming diversity of shape, texture, color, and odor. Tiers of orange and yellow chicken mushrooms troop up the trunks of dead conifers (p. 189), while an unusual resinous fragrance cloaks the plush, deep blue-violet caps of the violet cort (p. 189) on the ground below, and the haunting odor of Amaretto liqueur leads the delighted hiker to the tawny almond waxy cap nestling in a carpet of moss, its thick, snow-white gills suspended beneath a rosy-tan cap.

It is tempting to conclude that this rich diversity of mushrooms is

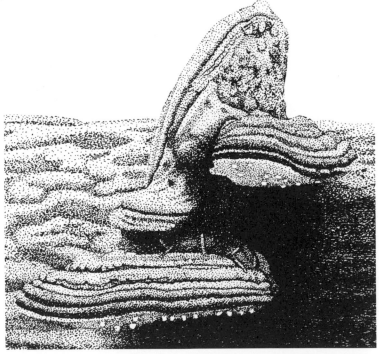

The red-belted polypore, locally called bearbread, forms horizontally oriented conks on spruce and hemlock. If the tree falls, new conk growth is reoriented to let the spores fall vertically. Annual growth layers, 6 on this specimen, reveal how long the tree has been down.

designed purely for our own pleasures, both visual and gastronomic. But recently, scientists unraveling the intricate forest fabric have found mushrooms (and their other fungal relatives) to be links between forest plants and small rodents, such as squirrels and voles.

Forest fungi can have 1 of 3 possible life-styles. They may be saprophytic, parasitic, and symbiotic or mycorrhizal. Saprophytic fungi decompose already dead wood and other organic material. Parasitic fungi attack and injure or kill living organisms. Mycorrhizal fungi establish intimate and mutually beneficial relationships with the roots of forest trees, shrubs, and other vascular plants.

SAPROPHYTES—For a long time we have appreciated the importance of fungi to decomposition in the forest. The chicken mushroom, for example, grows as a tangled mat of hyphae within the rotting wood of a dead tree. The hyphae grow only at their tips, secreting digestive enzymes into the wood. The fungus resorbs some of the resulting decomposed nutrients, such as simple sugars and amino acids, but releases most eventually to be washed into the surrounding soil, where they become a vital stimulus for the growth of green plants. This type of fungal nutrition leads to the typical fruiting bodies of the chicken mushroom on the outside of the tree. These fruiting bodies release millions of spores, which can carry on the life cycle of the fungus by germinating on other dead trees.

PARASITES—A parasitic fungus—such as the multilayered dye polypore, which attacks the living roots of Sitka spruce trees, or the honey mushroom, which attacks many kinds of forest trees and is particularly common on alders in our area—is also composed of hyphae which spread within the wood of the tree, but the difference here is that parasites can attack living and apparently healthy trees and seriously injure or kill them.

MYCORRHIZAE—Other species of fungi, however, are incompetent as saprophytes or parasites and instead obtain most of their organic nourishment by infecting the roots of forest plants, an association that scientists call mycorrhizal (literally, mycorrhizae means "fungus-roots"). A wide variety of forest trees, shrubs, herbs, and other plants carry mycorrhizae on and within their roots.

The host plants transfer organic compounds such as sugars, amino acids, and vitamins into the dependent fungus, and, as it turns out, the fungi are not ungrateful boarders. Thanks to their finely divided hyphae, mycorrhizal fungi can extend into the soil from the host roots, picking up large quantities of water and such essential nutrients as phosphorus, nitrogen, potassium, and calcium, which they then pump into the roots of their host plant. Most forest trees and many other plants simply will not grow without their fungal assistants. Conifers infected with mycorrhizae are twice as drought-resistant as uninfected trees, and seedlings of most trees die unless they are infected by mycorrhizae in their first year of growth. Fungal growth is equally dependent on the trees; mycorrhizal fungi growing in a clear-cut area will not bear fruit and may eventually die.

The complexity of the interdependence between a host plant and its mycorrhizal fungus has intrigued and amazed scientists. Mycorrhizal fungi produce hormones that both stimulate the production of new root tips by the host plant and augment the normal life span of these roots. Mycorrhizae also protect the delicate roots from invasion by disease-causing microbes such as water molds, secreting antibiotics into the soil around the roots. Mycorrhizae help aerate the soil and increase its water retention, both essential for plant health. To return the favor, fungal growth is attracted to and enhanced by substances released from the tips of healthy plant roots.

The importance of mycorrhizae associated with forest trees has been underscored by the recent discovery that water and nutrients can pass among trees using their linking mycorrhizae in a manner analogous to an interstate highway system. Some researchers even speculate that an individual tree placed temporarily at a disadvantage by shading can receive "care packages" from other nearby trees situated more favorably. Such cooperative behavior among trees was heretofore largely unsuspected. It has been recently discovered that mycorrhizal fungi are themselves infected with nitrogen-fixing bacteria. These bacteria absorb organic nutrients from the fungi and in turn fix nitrogen, which can then stimulate the growth of the fungus and, ultimately, the growth of the host tree.

ABOVEGROUND AND UNDERGROUND FUNGI—Mycorrhizal fungi can be divided into 2 kinds, depending on whether their fruiting bodies are produced aboveground (epigeous species) or underground (hypogeous species).

Examples of epigeous mycorrhizal fungi found in Southeast Alaska fill a good-sized field guide. Members of the bolete, waxy cap, gomphidius, russula, chanterelle, and hedgehog families, plus species in the nearly ubiquitous genera *Amanita, Armillaria, Cortinarius, Hebeloma, Inocybe, Laccaria, Ramaria, Rozites, Tricholoma,* and many others are mycorrhizal fungi producing fruiting bodies above ground.

Spores of such species are formed on the sides of gills or fleshy spines, or within tubes, and are discharged into the air for dispersal. The fruiting bodies of these species take up moisture rapidly after a substantial rainfall and seem to burst through the soil, where they mature quickly and release their spores. In Southeast Alaska, northern red-backed voles feed heavily on epigeous mushrooms, and red squirrels often cut off mature mushrooms and carry them up into the trees, where they lodge them in branch crotches. Although these fungi have little fat, and hence lag far behind seeds and nuts in caloric value, they are rich sources of B vitamins and also contain valuable concentrations of minerals.

Hypogeous fungi, which fruit underground, locally include the false truffle. Their fruiting bodies resemble small potatoes. An outer layer forms a roughly spherical structure enclosing masses of spores. As the spores slowly mature, the fruiting body develops and gives off highly specific and aromatic odors. These odors attract small rodents, such as red-backed voles, red squirrels, and northern flying squirrels, which dig up the fruiting bodies and eat them. The protective outer layer of the fruiting body is digested in passing through the intestinal tract of the squirrel or vole, but the spores are deposited unharmed in the animal's droppings. Red-backed voles drop about 200 fecal pellets per day, each containing about 300,000 fungal spores. In this fashion, the hypogeous

IDENTITIES REVEALED

We have known for years that certain species of fungus fruit in association with certain species of forest plants, and we have assumed that this indicates a mycorrhizal relationship. In the tangle of delicate soil hyphae, however, specific connections between a given mushroom and its host plant are impossible to trace, and until recently we had no way of knowing for sure which fungus was associated with which plant. An exciting breakthrough has come from the research of Drs. Caroline Bledsoe and Joseph Ammirati and their colleagues at the University of Washington in Seattle. These workers have successfully removed the genetic material (DNA) from mycorrhizal hyphae, digested it with special enzymes to break it up into characteristic fragments, and then separated these fragments using a technique called chromatography. By comparing the chromatograms obtained in this manner with chromatograms of DNA extracted from known species of mushrooms, these workers have been able to determine the identity of the mycorrhizal hyphae. This key piece of work will unlock many secrets of the specific associations among species of fungi and plants in nature, and will undoubtedly lead to such practical applications as the enhancement of reforestation programs.

fungus is dispersed throughout the forest. In Southeast Alaska, several species of false truffles of the genus *Rhizopogon* occur with conifers.

This assemblage of plants, mycorrhizal fungi, bacteria, and forest rodents is more complex than biologists appreciated at first glance. For example, some species of mycorrhizal fungus can associate with a wide variety of plants. Examples of such species include the fly agaric, the king bolete, the common laccaria, and the chanterelle. Other species may be restricted to a single host; for example, suillus is mycorrhizal only on the shore pine. Furthermore, forest trees often require infection by different species of mycorrhizal fungi at different stages in their life cycle, or may be infected by many species simultaneously.

AMANITA MUSHROOMS

Summer's end is always accompanied by monsoonlike rains throughout Southeast Alaska, and suddenly the forests are decorated with mushrooms of a bewildering variety and number. Many of us take great delight in collecting mushrooms to add interest and flavor to various dishes, but indiscriminate collecting is dangerous because numerous poisonous species also occur in our area. Some, however, are easy to recognize. Two particularly interesting local species that can cause violent reactions are the panther mushroom and the fly agaric.

PANTHER MUSHROOM—
The panther (*Amanita pantherina*) is almost as deadly as its name suggests, but it is, fortunately, not too common. It usually grows in small groups on the ground under conifers or in forests of mixed conifers and deciduous trees. The cap of the panther is up to 7 inches in diameter; it is a distinctive smoky yellowish brown and is covered with numerous large, white, conical scales (p. 189). The cap is spherical or convex when young but flattens with age. Like many other amanitas, it has closely set, chalky-white gills, a white stem carrying a well-developed skirtlike veil, and a large white cup, or volva, at the base.

"There's no such thing as a toadstool."
Fly agaric and boreal toad.

LIFE-THREATENING TOXINS

Since almost all species of *Amanita* are known or suspected of being poisonous, it is essential to learn to recognize
and avoid them. Any mushroom with white, flaky scales on the
cap, a well-developed ring on the stem (caution: the ring may
have dropped to the ground on older specimens), and a cuplike
volva at the base should not be tasted. Very young specimens of
Amanita can outwardly resemble the highly edible puffball, so it
is best to slice all putative puffballs in half vertically; true puffballs are structureless inside, while young *Amanita* will show
features of the developing cap, gills, and volva.

The principal toxins present in the fly agaric are ibotenic
acid and muscimol. Symptoms usually appear within an hour of
consumption and include excitement, confusion, profuse sweat-
ing, severe hallucinations, and delirium lasting 4 hours or
longer, followed by a comalike sleep and, usually, recovery
within 24 hours. There is, however, at least one record of a
death caused by consumption of the fly agaric. Also, repeated
use may result in damage to the liver. It is suspected that different geographic races of the mushroom, and perhaps even individual mushrooms, vary in the amounts or proportions of the
toxins that they contain. Therefore, those who eat this mushroom in order to distort their perceptions are courting disaster.

If you suspect that you may have eaten a poisonous mushroom, induce vomiting and call a physician or poison control
center immediately.

The panther contains high amounts of the toxin muscarine,
which slows the pulse and can result in death if enough has been consumed. Atropine, a drug isolated from nightshades, is used as an antidote. The panther also contains the toxins ibotenic acid and muscimol,
which result in diarrhea, vomiting, and severe hallucinations. This is
definitely a species to avoid!

FLY AGARIC—The fly agaric (*Amanita muscaria*) resembles the panther
but has a scarlet cap (which may fade to pale orange with age) and has
flattened rather than conical scales. The fly agaric is the toadstool of
fairy tales and also the hallucinogenic species which has figured so
prominently in the folklore of Asia, Europe, and North America. Native
peoples have used the fly agaric for centuries as a ritual hallucinogen. It
was believed that eating this mushroom permitted a tribal shaman to
communicate directly with his spirit guides. Even earlier, around 2000 B.C.,

the Aryan civilization worshipped the fly agaric as the god Soma.

SPLASH CUPS

Splash cups are ingenious devices developed by both fungi and plants. They use the kinetic energy of falling raindrops to disperse seeds or spores, or in some cases to assist pollination or fertilization.

Typically, a splash cup is an elastic, thimble-shaped fruiting structure between a quarter and a half inch across the open top, with sloping inner surfaces. These features enable the cup to extract the maximum amount of kinetic energy from falling raindrops, which scatter its mature seeds or spores. Splash cups always mature in a vertical position in order to catch rain.

BIRD'S NEST FUNGI—Probably the best examples of splash cups are found in a small group of unusual fungi called bird's nest fungi.

Like many other fungi, the major part of the body of a bird's nest fungus is composed of a mass of fine hyphae, the white threads that grow within the fibers of old wood and decompose it. When environmental conditions are right, the fungus may produce the characteristic fruiting structures responsible for its common name. Tiny buttons grow on the surface of the rotting wood, enlarging to about the size and shape of small thimbles. At maturity, a thin membrane over the surface of the thimble ruptures to reveal numerous "eggs" within the "nest." Each of these eggs, or peridioles, contains masses of spores. The peridioles are actually lentil-shaped, but within the thimble, they look like tiny eggs in the nest of some miniature bird.

Common gel bird's nest. "Eggs" or peridioles are ejected by the impact of a raindrop in the cup.

COMMON GEL BIRD'S NEST—In Southeast Alaska we have found two species of bird's nest fungus, the common gel bird's nest and the white-egg bird's nest. In the common gel bird's nest, the peridioles lie free within a gelatinous material in the nest (p. 189). When a large raindrop or a drop of water from the vegetation above the nest hits the opening, the force of the water is redirected upward and outward, causing a peridiole to be splashed as much as several inches away from

SPLASH CUP MECHANICS IN PLANTS

Good examples of splash cups which disperse seeds are seen in the fruiting structures of the flowering plants known as the alpine mitrewort and the swamp gentian. The alpine mitrewort is a saxifrage found in the subalpine meadows of Southeast Alaska. At maturity, its fruit is cup-shaped and open at the top, the tiny seeds lying loosely within. The swamp gentian can be found in muskegs from sea level to subalpine zones and usually blooms in mid to late summer.

Flowers with small, cup-shaped blossoms, such as buttercups and anemones, can also use the force of raindrops to splash pollen from the ripe stamens to the receptive female structures of the blossom, thus assuring that seeds will be produced.

Mosses, too, form splash cups at one stage in their life cycle, but here it is sperm cells that are splashed into receptive female cups where fertilization occurs. The splash cups of mosses are composed of tight circles of special broad, overlapping leaflike structures.

Some species of liverworts, which are moss relatives, also form splash cups on the upper surface of the flattened plant body, or thallus. For example, the common liverwort found in disturbed habitats in Southeast Alaska (*Marchantia polymorpha*) forms splash cups throughout most of the year. These tiny, bright green cups, called gemmae cups in liverworts, contain lentil-shaped fragments (gemmae) which bud asexually off the parent's body and which can grow into a new thallus when splashed onto receptive soil.

the parent nest. Biologists think that the peridiole later weathers to release its spores, which can then germinate and grow as hyphae down into the wood, to continue the rotting process. This species is particularly common on old dead canes of salmonberry and thimbleberry and is easily recognized because the gray to tan nest is fuzzy on the outside.

WHITE-EGG BIRD'S NEST—In the white-egg bird's nest, the nest is a rich brown and has walls with smooth external surfaces. Each peridiole is attached to the wall of the fruiting cup by an elastic anchoring thread fastened to a small knob on its undersurface. This anchoring thread probably aids in ejecting the peridiole, possibly by acting as a spring to amplify the kinetic force of the raindrop. At any rate, the anchoring thread tears off at the base and dangles behind the soaring peridiole. When the thread encounters stems of vegetation, or even hairs on stems or leaves, it clings fast and wraps around them, securing the peridiole. Biologists are not sure what advantage accrues from attachment to living vegetation, but in some species it is known that when peridioles are eaten accidentally by herbivores, they can then be easily dispersed to another area and deposited in the natural fertilizer of the animal's dung.

SLIME MOLDS

Slime molds are bizarre "creatures" generally regarded as primitive forms of life only tenuously related to other fungi. In fact, some scientists think slime molds may be equally related to amoebas, which are single-celled animals. Slime molds may, in fact, form a kind of "missing link" between fungi and primitive animals. Slime molds have remarkable life histories. At one point in its life cycle, each individual slime is represented by many thousands of scattered cells that crawl through the forest in amoeboid fashion. Stimulated by some unknown environmental cue (possibly heavy summer rains), some cells secrete a chemical signal that attracts other amoeboid cells.

The attracted cells slowly aggregate and fuse into a large and often colorful slimy mass, giving rise to a "blob" technically called a plasmodium. The plasmodium often persists for many days and may ooze slowly over the forest floor or climb up onto vegetation.

This slimy mass is the spore-forming stage in the slime mold's life cycle. Microscopic spores are formed by the millions all over the surface of the slime, often causing it to harden and change color. The spores are thought to be dispersed on air currents or perhaps by adhering to the feet of ground-feeding birds such as thrushes. Under the right environmental conditions, each spore can germinate to release a single amoeboid cell, thus completing the slime mold's life cycle.

Slime molds feed on the bacteria so abundant in the forest. As the plasmodium creeps along over mosses and other vegetation, or within rotting logs, it engulfs and digests bacteria. Many amoebas show the same kind of feeding behavior, giving rise to the theory that the slime mold is a link between fungal and animal life forms.

In Southeast Alaska, slime molds are quite common in our forests in midsummer. Two species we have often encountered are the coral slime and the scrambled-egg slime.

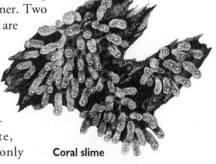

CORAL SLIME—The plasmodium of the coral slime is always found on rotting wood. It is composed of masses of minute, translucent whitish stalks, each only

Coral slime

about a quarter of an inch long. Spores form on the outer surfaces of these tiny stalks. A log covered with coral slime looks as if it has a heavy coating of frost, which is, of course, entirely inconsistent with summertime temperatures. The coral slime may form small patches a few inches across, or it may cover several square feet. This species is very delicate, and we have seen it only on vertical or shaded wood surfaces.

SCRAMBLED-EGG SLIME—The plasmodium of the bizarre scrambled-egg slime looks as if someone has dumped the contents of a frying pan unceremoniously onto the ground (p. 190). The scrambled-egg slime, which forms irregular cushions up to 8 inches or so in diameter, has a whitish, somewhat translucent base (the "egg white"), upon which is heaped a fluffy mound of bright yellow tissue (the "yolk"). The yellow part is capable of forming spores on its surface, and as it does so it hardens and turns first dirty yellow and then charcoal gray.

Slime molds are not known to be edible, and indeed we know of no one, ourselves included, willing to try eating one.

LICHENS

Our coastal rainforests seem almost constantly drenched in fine cold rain or blanketed in a thick layer of winter snow, making them ideal habitats for a wide variety of lichens.

A lichen is an intimate association between 2 unrelated organisms,

---

ALIEN LIFE FORMS?

The spring of 1973 was particularly rainy in the eastern United States and throughout this area people reported finding weird bloblike creatures apparently growing in their backyards. One terrified woman reported that an original blob seemed to have been obliterated by heavy rains, but when she searched again, she discovered 3 more had appeared in its place! Some blobs were red and pulsating and were reported to climb telephone poles.

Newspaper journalists speculated that the blobs were either mutant microbes in the process of taking over the earth or that they were creatures from another planet sent to conquer the human race. This brouhaha was finally resolved when a prominent mycologist (scientist who studies fungi) identified the "blobs" as slime molds, which, while usually not well known to the layman, nevertheless have an established track record in the annals of science.

1 a species of fungus and the other a species of alga. The fungus constitutes most of the lichen's bulk; it forms the "house," so to speak. Nestled within the fungal house are clusters of algal cells. Like all algal cells, those of the lichen contain chlorophyll and hence can make food with the assistance of light. The algal contribution, then, is to keep the lichen larder filled.

At the latest count, nearly 40 genera of terrestrial algae are involved in forming lichens, and thousands of species of fungi may lichenize. Within any given species of lichen, however, only 1 particular species of fungus and 1 alga are involved. But many lichens also contain a species of blue-green bacterium, making these forms an assemblage of 3 different species.

This raises an interesting point—what is a "species" of lichen, when it actually consists of 2 or more unrelated organisms? Lichens are given generic and specific names, just as if they were actually single organisms, but we must remember that a "species" of lichen is not a species in the same sense as a species of tree.

Their sheer abundance in the forest suggests that lichens are probably crucial to that community, but few ecological studies of lichens have been done. It is certain, however, that after glaciers have receded, lichens are important in the early formation of soils.

Some lichens can fix nitrogen, taking nitrogen gas from the atmosphere and forming nitrate fertilizers with it. Excess nitrates leach into the soil around these lichens and enrich it, enhancing the growth of other plants. This nitrogen fixation is especially important in the nutrient cycling within old-growth forests, where nitrogen-fixing alders have long been shaded out.

Arboreal lichens, which grow on trees, do not parasitize them, but take advantage of the increased light levels above the more darkened forest floor, although some species can smother bark lenticels (openings that permit gas exchange) and can penetrate and damage bark. On the other hand, arboreal lichens may shade older needles of conifers, causing them to drop prematurely. This benefits the tree because old needles

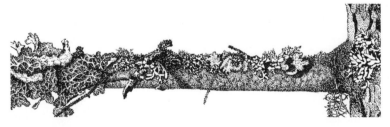

Lichens high in a Sitka spruce. Lungwort at left, old man's beard at base of branch, and inflated lichen on the trunk.

shaded by new growth cannot make as much food as the younger needles near the tips of branches.

Some forest creatures eat lichens. The northern flying squirrel, a nocturnal species not often seen, depends on arboreal lichens for the major part of its diet, and Sitka black-tailed deer in winter often eat masses of lichens that have blown down onto the forest floor.

Lichens are sensitive to the quality of the air and indicate air pollution if they are absent from otherwise appropriate habitats. Trees near pulp mills, for example, are often relatively devoid of lichens. The sulfur dioxide in the smoke from such mills oxidizes the chlorophyll in the algal cells of lichens and kills them. The soil beneath affected trees may not be as rich because of the absence of nitrogen-fixing lichens above.

LICHEN FORMS— Lichens have 3 growth forms. Crustose lichens adhere tightly to rock or wood and resemble a coat of paint. If you try to pry a crustose lichen from its substrate, it crumbles. One easily recognized crustose lichen in Southeast Alaska is the heath lichen, a blue-green form that grows mostly on well-rotted wood in the forest.

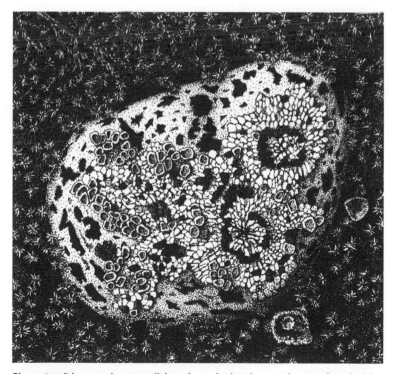

Placopsis gelida, a semicrustose lichen that colonizes bare rock soon after glacial retreat. At lower right are pixie cup lichens.

Because it usually grows on vertical surfaces, heath lichen may require well-drained conditions. We have often seen this rapidly growing lichen overgrowing neighboring mosses and leafy liverworts. When reproductively mature, heath lichen is covered with smooth pink bumps.

Foliose lichens are flat and leafy. They adhere much less to the substrate and can either be lifted off with your fingers or pried off with a knife blade. Foliose lichens may grow on rocks, trees, or soil, or among mosses and other plants on the ground. The upper surface of a foliose lichen is usually a markedly different color from its lower surface. In addition, the lower surface may bear rhizines, short rootlike structures serving to anchor the lichen onto its substrate. Dog lichen is a local foliose lichen abundant on the ground in coniferous forests.

Fruticose lichens have erect stems, which are often elaborately branched. Some arboreal fruticose lichens are hairlike and hang beneath the branches of trees. The so-called reindeer "moss," a common local ground-dwelling fruticose lichen, is not a moss at all. Branched and white, it grows on the ground in open areas and is usually abundant on rubble near glaciers. This lichen made headlines as a vector for radioactive isotopes. When atmospheric nuclear testing led to the fallout of radioactive elements over the North American and European Arctic, these radioactive atoms were taken up by the reindeer moss and transferred to caribou, which feed on it, and further to Native peoples, who eat caribou. The ability of this lichen to take up radioactive isotopes led to the Nuclear Test Ban Treaty of 1963, something politicians had previously failed to achieve.

OLD MAN'S BEARD LICHENS

Coniferous trees, especially those near muskegs, are so heavily decorated with long, draping strands of pale lichens that they seem prepared for Christmas year round. These lichens are commonly called "old man's beard," and the most common in our area is *Alectoria sarmentosa*, which hangs in large, pale, grayish green clumps. Lichens of the genus *Alectoria* are so abundant in our coastal forest that 1 acre may contain nearly 1½ tons dry weight. If you tease apart the numerous strands of a clump, you discover that this organism is highly branched and that most branches are roughly the same diameter. If you break a strand and examine the broken end with a small magnifying glass or field lens, you will see that it is filled with cottony material, giving it a solid appearance.

Another common old man's beard lichen found hanging from the branches of conifers is *Usnea*. You can distinguish specimens of *Usnea* from *Alectoria* by examining the cut end of a broken strand. *Usnea* usually contains a distinct solid central cord within each main branch,

Continued on page 193

▲ The black oystercatcher, an inhabitant of small rocky islands throughout Southeast and the mainland coast of Glacier Bay.

▲ Female blue grouse in subalpine meadow.

▲ The northern saw-whet owl.

▲ Arctic terns feeding coho fingerling to their young.

▲ Greater yellowlegs with young in muskeg.

▲ **Marbled murrelet on nest** (Alaska Dept. Fish & Game, J. Hughes, S. Quinlan)

▲ **Bald eagle in a sideslip, a common maneuver when diving after fish.**

▲ **Tufted puffins can be seen in Glacier Bay and on Saint Lazaria Island near Sitka.** (C. O'Clair)

▲ **Rufous hummingbird feeds on early blueberry nectar.**

▼ **Female northern harriers fighting over food.**

▼ **Spotted sandpiper on nest under Nootka lupine.**

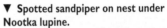

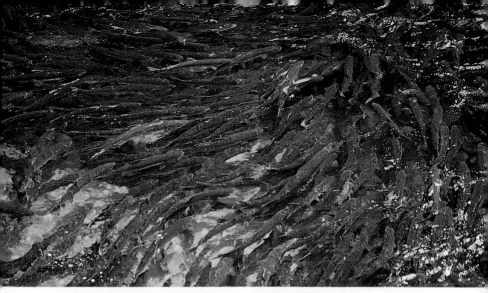

▲ Pink salmon swarm up **Anan Creek** near **Wrangell** to spawn. (J. Hyde)

▲ Pacific sand lance pokes its head tentatively out of the sand.

▲ A dragonfly, in search of insects to eat, cruises past a common marestail.

▼ Sea-run cutthroat trout in Southeast take about 5 to 6 years to reach a length of 10 to 12 inches.

▲ Aquatic dragonfly larva pursues threespine stickleback.

▲ Water striders are common on muskeg ponds.

▲ The goldenrod spider sits on flowers or other vegetation and grabs insects with its crablike front legs.

▶ An adult caddisfly on the cap of a small forest mushroom.

▼ Mustard white butterfly flits past northern yarrow.

▲ This panther mushroom is identified as a member of the Amanita family by the white scales on the cap, crowded white gills, skirtlike veil, and cup-shaped volva at the base of the stem.

▲ Shelves of the chicken mushroom troop up the trunk of an old-growth conifer.

▲ Two violet corts in the moss beside a stream.

◄ Thimbles of common gel bird's nest fungus sprout from a dead twig on the forest floor.

▲ Scrambled-egg slime, like other slime molds, consumes bacteria, pollen, spores, and detritus on mosses and other forest floor plants.

▲ Old man's beard lichen is an important winter food for Sitka black-tailed deer.

▼ Several species of lichens vie for space on an exposed alpine boulder.

▲ Bunchberry is found in Southeast's forests and muskegs.

▲ Sticky hairs on a long-leaf sundew trap flies.

▲ Purple mountain saxifrage is one of the earliest blooming spring flowers in Southeast.

▲ Pinesap, a plant without chlorophyll, produces ghostly flowers.

▲ Tiny beetles on the spadix of yellow skunk-cabbage are thought to be important in pollination.

▲ The calypso orchid is found in the heavy needle litter beneath Sitka spruce trees.

▲ One of the most toxic plants in North America, Southeast's baneberry produces poisonous red berries.

▲ Sea milkwort

▲ Dainty twin blossoms of fern-leaf goldthread

▼ Nutritious leaves of devil's club are protected by long, brittle spines.

Beard Lichens

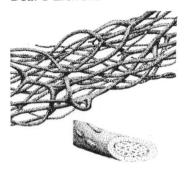

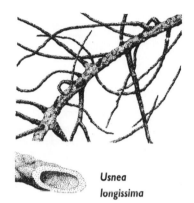

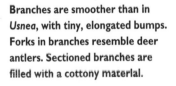

Alectoria
sarmentosa

Usnea
longissima

Branches are smoother than in
Usnea, with tiny, elongated bumps.
Forks in branches resemble deer
antlers. Sectioned branches are
filled with a cottony material.

Main branch is lumpy or wrinkled,
shedding the greenish cortex,
which remains on the side
branches. Sectioned branches are
hollow, sometimes containing a
central cord.

which is absent in *Alectoria*. *Usnea longissima* has main strands up to 8
feet long, each carrying numerous short lateral branches called fibrils
(p. 190). The effect is similar to a popular type of Christmas garland.
Usnea filipendula is firmly affixed to its host tree via a blackened base,
rather than being merely draped over the branches of the tree like the
other species of old man's beard. Both species of *Usnea* are similar to
Alectoria in color. Other species of arboreal lichens closely related to the
foregoing species belong to the genus *Bryoria*. These kinds are easiest to
recognize because they are a rich chocolate brown. *Bryoria* are most
common on shore pines in our muskegs.

   In the summer of 1988, Dr. Irwin R. Brodo of the Canadian
Museum of Nature collected lichens around Juneau and Sitka. In a
muskeg at about 1000 feet on Douglas Island, he discovered large
patches of yet another kind of old man's beard lichen, *Bryocaulon pseu-*
dosatoanum. This lichen is easily recognized because the long, branched
strands are deep wine-red and glossy. This lichen probably occurs
throughout Southeast Alaska in similar habitats, since Brodo had previously collected it on the Queen Charlotte Islands.

   A local study of a semitame Sitka black-tailed deer revealed that it
actively sought both *Usnea* and *Alectoria,* which it ate wherever winter
storms had blown them from the canopy down onto shrubs or the
forest floor.

PLANTS
...
CHAPTER 7

A perusal of the distributional maps in Hulten's *Flora of Alaska* reveals that over 900 species of vascular plants (ferns and their allies, conifers, and flowering plants) occur in Southeast Alaska. Of these, about 50 species occur primarily farther north of our area and reach the southern limit of their distribution in Southeast. Among them, the more conspicuous species are the wild iris, the shrubs bearberry, soapberry, and Beauverd spiraea as well as many arctic flowers. Another 60 or so species occur mostly to the south of Southeast Alaska, reaching the northern limits of their distribution within our area. In this group are Pacific yew, sword-fern, western bracken fern, Pacific silver fir, western red cedar, red alder, dwarf mistletoe, Douglas spiraea, black twinberry, snowberry, red huckleberry, salal, Douglas maple, thimbleberry, and many flowering herbs. The other 800 or so species occur both north and south of our area. There are no well-documented records of any species of vascular plant endemic to Southeast Alaska. Since most of our area was glaciated less than 14,000 years ago, perhaps there has not been sufficient time for endemic species to evolve. Indeed, 145 species or varieties have been successfully introduced into Southeast Alaska since the first Russian contact.

Plants include algae (which most contemporary botanists place in a separate kingdom, Protista), liverworts and mosses (bryophytes), ferns and their allies (club-mosses, spike-mosses, horsetails, and quillworts), conifers (the only gymnosperms represented in our area), and flowering plants (angiosperms).

ALGAE—These plants live in marine, freshwater, or terrestrial habitats and can be either microscopic or macroscopic in size. Microscopic species include such unicellular forms as desmids, diatoms, and dinoflagellates. Most of these tiny algae are planktonic and form the phytoplankton (phyto = plant) which "blooms" in both fresh and marine waters in spring and early summer. Phytoplankton, along with macroalgae, contributes to the producer level in aquatic food chains; in marine waters, for example, many species of phytoplankton are grazed by such herbivores as copepods and larvae of many bottom-dwelling (benthic) invertebrates, or are filtered from the water by clams and other animals. Copepods and filter-feeders are then consumed by carnivores such as fish and sea stars. Several species of microscopic marine algae, among them the dinoflagellate *Alexandrium catenella*, form blooms called red tides; poisons contained within these algae are accumulated by herbivores, making some, such as clams and mussels, toxic to carnivorous vertebrates, including people. Some microscopic terrestrial algae can enter into special partnerships with certain fungi to form lichens.

SEAWEEDS—Macroscopic algae include the red, brown, and green seaweeds so characteristic of our rocky marine intertidal and shallow subtidal coastlines. These algae are part of the producer level of marine food chains; in addition, dead algal bodies break down to help form the detritus that is the pre-ferred food of many species of benthic marine invertebrates—mussels, *Macoma* clams, and seg-mented worms (Polychaeta). Some species of macroalgae form such luxuriant growths— offshore kelp beds for example—that they attenuate wave action and help protect our intertidal communities from storm damage. These beds also form structurally diverse habitats important to many species of fish and crustaceans. Some seaweeds are important substrates for herring roe, and most are both nutritious and edible by people and could add significantly to our future diets. Already many Southeast Alaskan gardeners have discovered that seaweeds are an excellent organic fertilizer.

Ribbon kelp, a common edible seaweed on rocks at about the zero-foot tide level.

MOSSES—Many kinds of mosses and liverworts (bryophytes), being partial to wet climates, flourish in Southeast Alaska. Not only does their reproduction depend on water, but the outer layer of their bodies lacks the protective waxy cuticle that, in vascular plants, helps keep delicate tissues from drying out. Like fungi, they reproduce by wind-dispersed microscopic spores; the species found in Southeast Alaska are also found throughout most of the Pacific Northwest. Mosses and liverworts are abundant in all habitats, from just above the high tideline up into the alpine, and many species are found in ponds, streams, and muskegs. The latter habitat, in particular, is home to at least a dozen different species of *Sphagnum* (peat moss). Forest bryophytes also prosper on the ground, on rotting logs, and in shrubs and trees. The total number of bryophytes in Southeast Alaska easily exceeds 300 species.

FERNS—The ferns and their allies are present in suitable habitats throughout our area. All 27 species of ferns found in Southeast Alaska

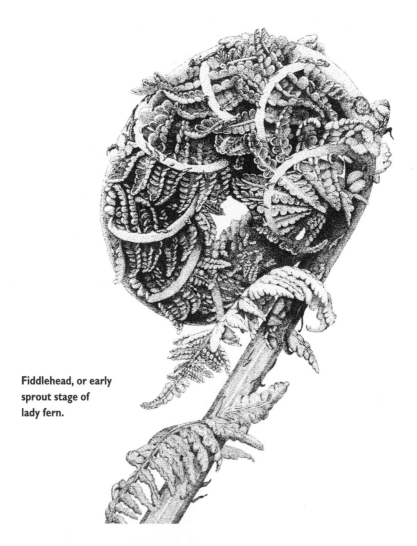

Fiddlehead, or early sprout stage of lady fern.

are terrestrial species; water ferns and tree ferns do not occur here. The maidenhair fern, lady fern, oakfern, and spinulose shield-fern are deciduous species, with the leaves (fronds) dying off at the end of each growing season, while sword-fern, holly-fern, deer fern, and parsley fern are evergreen. Many species make fiddleheads in the spring, and some are harvested by people. Some 8 species of club-mosses occur in Southeast Alaska; all are slow-growing, evergreen, and terrestrial. Our 8 species of horsetail grow in wet meadows, stream margins, ditches and

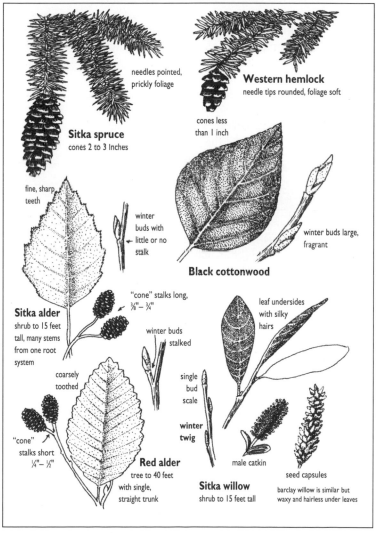

needles pointed, prickly foliage

Western hemlock
needle tips rounded, foliage soft

cones less than 1 inch

Sitka spruce
cones 2 to 3 inches

fine, sharp teeth

winter buds with little or no stalk

winter buds large, fragrant

Black cottonwood

"cone" stalks long, ⅜" – ¾"

leaf undersides with silky hairs

Sitka alder
shrub to 15 feet tall, many stems from one root system

winter buds stalked

coarsely toothed

single bud scale

winter twig

"cone" stalks short ¼" – ½"

Red alder
tree to 40 feet with single, straight trunk

male catkin

seed capsules

Sitka willow
shrub to 15 feet tall

barclay willow is similar but waxy and hairless under leaves

Common Trees and Tall Shrubs of Southeast Alaska

disturbed soils. The little-known quillworts, perennial fern relatives, have been found in the shallows of Auke Lake in Juneau.

CONIFERS—Only some 10 species of conifers (gymnosperms) occur in Southeast Alaska, but several are exceedingly abundant and form the evergreen forests that define our area. The decomposition of their dead needles acidifies the shallow soil and helps determine what other plants can grow here. Forests also stabilize the water table, preventing excessive runoff and erosion. Conifers are typically wind-pollinated, and their winged seeds in most cases are also dispersed by wind.

FLOWERING PLANTS—Hundreds of species of flowering herbs, shrubs, and trees occur in Southeast Alaska. Many depend on wind to carry their pollen and seeds, while some are pollinated by birds or insects, and some produce succulent fruits such as berries to entice birds and mammals to disperse their seeds. Flowering-plant families that do particularly well in Southeast Alaska include sedges (Cyperaceae), grasses (Poaceae), and heathers (Ericaceae), the first 2 probably because they are wind-pollinated and the latter because they thrive in the acidic conditions found in forest soils and muskeg waters.

FOREST MOSSES

Despite their small size and often inconspicuous growth habits, mosses are important members of forest communities in Southeast Alaska. In the rain-drenched coastal forests, hundreds of different species of mosses luxuriate, carpeting the forest floor, fallen logs, living tree trunks and branches, and stream banks.

Although the nutrient-energy content of moss tissues is almost 80 percent as high as that typical of flowering plants, they are relatively indigestible thanks to their high content of cellulose and ligninlike compounds, also abundant in wood. On the other hand, mosses are rich in polyunsaturated fatty acids, which would be beneficial in the diets of mammals. Two compounds in mosses—benzyl benzoate and oxalic acid—are toxic to some insects and mites, so these invertebrates don't eat much moss. Most birds and mammals are likewise thought not to eat mosses—except incidentally, while eating other plants. We've found only one published record of intentional moss consumption by any of the vertebrates of Southeast Alaska—the bog lemming. And indeed we once examined a dead bog lemming whose mouth was full of well-chewed moss. The most common use of moss by Southeast birds and small mammals is for nest linings.

One invertebrate that is able to live almost exclusively on mosses is the microscopic water bear, a distant relative of insects. These minute animals are only about 1 millimeter long and have 4 pairs of legs armed

Sphagnum girgensohnii,
**the first species of
peat moss to appear in
the forest understory.
Its role in habitat
evolution in the
temperate rainforest
has aroused much
controversy.**

with sharp claws for clinging tightly to the tiny plants upon which they feed. The water bear uses sharp stylets to pierce individual cells of the moss plant and suck out the contents, leaving behind the indigestible cell walls.

Mosses are not consumed by people, but they are a possible source of potent therapeutic drugs. One study of mosses and some of their close relatives showed that 56 percent of the species tested contained effective antibacterial compounds; 1 species contained chemicals that inhibited the growth of fungi.

The value of mosses to a forest community involves far more than their worth as food and as a potential source of drugs. Thick beds of moss absorb and retain rainwater together with its precious cargo of dissolved nutrients (such as phosphorus and nitrates). Without mosses, much of this water would be lost to streams. The moss carpet prevents soil erosion and moistens an underlying network of tree roots which would otherwise dry out during summer warm spells.

All healthy soil contains nitrogen-fixing bacteria unless it is waterlogged. These bacteria may be free-living in the soil or associated with the roots of such plants as legumes, alders, and Drummond mountain avens. Nitrogen-fixing bacteria grow best when the soil is buffered between certain moderate pH values. Such buffering of soil acidity is another service of mosses.

Finally, and perhaps most important, mosses are highly productive—they grow rapidly. For example, a recent study conducted in the black spruce forests in the interior of Alaska showed that the total growth of mosses was 3 times (by weight) the total growth of the tree foliage! Obviously, any scheme attempting to describe the cycling of vital nutrients in such a forest must account for the primary role of mosses if it is to be accurate.

ADAPTATIONS OF ALPINE PLANTS

Midsummer lures us up into the lush subalpine meadows and alpine tundra that carpet our mountains above the timberline. While enjoying the wonderful profusion of wildflowers growing there, one can easily observe some of the special adaptations that enable plants to live in this harshest of our habitats.

Lichens, of course, are admirably suited to the highest alpine areas because they can live where there is no soil at all, obtaining their minerals from rainwater (p. 190).

What soils do exist in the alpine are thin, acidic, and low in nutrients, because water from rainfall and snow melt leaches out minerals. Plants tolerant of such poor soils, such as lupines and heathers, do well in the alpine. Lupines not only thrive in but also actually enrich poor soils because their root nodules contain nitrogen-fixing bacteria. The excess nitrates they create then seep out into the soil to increase its fertility and make it more hospitable toward other species.

Alpine azalea, arctic willow, and reindeer "moss," actually a lichen, on a crack in bedrock.

HEATHERS—Heathers are abundant in the alpine, not only because they are able to thrive in acidic soils of poor quality, but also because they can readily tolerate a lack of water. At first it seems a contradiction to think of any habitat in Southeast Alaska as being dry, but in the alpine, most of the water present is frozen for much of the year and hence unavailable to plants. During summer dry spells the thin alpine soils dry out rapidly.

Heathers are well adapted to dry conditions, as they have thick leaves heavily coated with protective waxes, and undercurled edges providing additional protection to their lower surfaces. The microscopic air holes (stomata) with which plants respire are located on the undersides of their leaves. If these holes are sheltered from the direct wind, the leaves lose water less rapidly. Alpine heathers found in Southeast Alaska are the starry cassiope and Mertens' cassiope, both of which have tiny, white, bell-shaped blossoms, and yellow mountain-heather, which has pale yellow lantern-shaped flowers.

Some plant species adapt to the alpine by growing slowly. If an individual can live for many years, then during a particularly harsh summer it can forgo growth, waiting for better conditions to return. The map lichen, for example, can live an enormously long time and grows extremely slowly.

On the other hand, if the effective growing season in a summer is only 2 to 3 months long, a good adaptation is the ability to grow very rapidly, completing the entire life cycle as fast as possible in order to form and disperse seeds before the first frost. Perennial plants are well adapted to do this. They can store much nourishment in their underground structures, and thus as soon as the snows melt back, they can sprout and flower rapidly. A particularly good example of this strategy is the Cooley buttercup, which blooms in June at the edge of melting snowbanks. Annual plants, on the other hand, do poorly in the alpine because they must start from seed each year, and just 1 bad year can wipe them out entirely.

While the wind-pollinated grasses and sedges do well in the alpine, wind scour is a force with which to be reckoned. Many plants try to avoid wind scour by growing as low as possible, and cushion growth forms are hence in vogue in the alpine. The moss campion, for example, may be a foot in diameter and less than an inch high. This cushion-shaped growth form is so effective at avoiding wind that air temperatures within the cushion can be as much as 40 degrees F higher than the air several inches above the plant. The delightful wedge-leaf primrose is another species that huddles close to the ground to avoid wind. The extreme case of ground-hugging among the heather family is the alpine azalea, which creeps over rocks on the most exposed and bitter ridge tops.

Many plants that do stick up into the wind protect themselves by wearing fur coats. The woolly hawkweed, a close relative of dandelions, has long hairs on its stems, leaves, and around the bases of its flowers. These hairs insulate against cold and prevent rapid water loss.

In adopting dwarfed dimensions, however, alpine plants have run into some problems. Insect pollinators require flowers of adequate size to attract their attention and support their weight. For this reason, many dwarfed alpine plants retain normal-sized flowers, which then look out of scale with the rest of the plant. Good local examples of apparently outsized flowers are the mountain harebell, an alpine representative of the bluebell family, and the beautiful purple mountain saxifrage (p. 191).

Excessive sunlight can also be a problem in the alpine, where the air is thinner and less polluted than at sea level. Tender new growth is especially sensitive to ultraviolet rays, and many alpine plants protect their rapidly growing parts with anthocyanins, red pigments that can screen out the harmful, highest-energy wavelengths of sunlight.

The alpine flowering season is shorter than at sea level, and many insects need temperatures above 45 degrees F to fly and pollinate. Plants attract these often-sluggish pollinators with the largest and most colorful flowers possible. The narcissus-flowered anemone and mountain marsh-marigold have huge white blossoms with yellow centers that contrast strikingly with their dark green foliage. The arctic cinquefoil and caltha-leaf avens both have large, bright yellow blossoms.

Flowers may further enhance their attractiveness to pollinators by their strong perfume. The Jeffrey shooting-star and the arctic sweet coltsfoot are 2 alpine flowers that give off a strong perfume when ripe for pollination.

Because seed reproduction is difficult in the short, cool alpine summer, many plants spread vegetatively. The luetkea, or partridge foot as it is often called, is a member of the rose family which can send out runners much like those of strawberry plants. At intervals along these runners, new shoots sprout upward. The alpine bistort, which may also be found at sea level, has tiny bulblets located on its stem immediately below its white flowers. These bulblets can drop off the parent plant, take root, and give rise to completely independent offspring.

STRATEGIES FOR PLANT DISPERSAL

Unlike most animals, plants stay put where they originate. This usually works fine until time for reproduction, when seeds must somehow travel. To see whether plant dispersal strategies differed between the natural communities of Southeast Alaska, we compared forest to open beach meadow communities at Eagle River, northwest of Juneau. We listed the most common vascular plants in these communities according

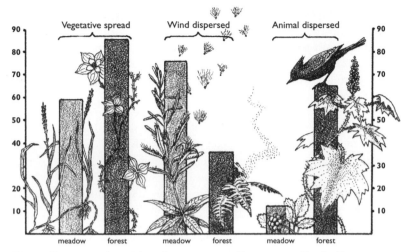

Plant Dispersal in Meadow versus Forest at Eagle River

to how they colonize new ground. In the following comparisons, the 17 most abundant species in each community are considered.

VEGETATIVE SPREAD—Many plants partially avoid the problems of seed production by simply extending a network of stems and runners into nearby terrain either above or just below the ground surface. This strategy is more common in the forest (86 percent) than in the meadow (59 percent). In the more stable forest understory, dim light provides little energy for flowering and fruiting. Plants spreading vegetatively can grow into new areas, reserving their relatively "expensive" seeds for colonizing more remote sites like clearcuts and new windthrow gaps.

DISTRIBUTION BY WIND—The majority of the open-meadow plants rely on wind to disperse their seed (76 percent of meadow species versus 36 percent of forest species). Very little breeze occurs in the forest understory; there, most airborne seeds and spores are nearly microscopic, easily lifting free to take advantage of the slightest air movement.

DISPERSAL BY ANIMALS—While some plants produce seeds with burrs or sticky coverings in order to hitchhike on the coats of mammals and feathers of birds, this strategy is less common in Southeast Alaska than elsewhere. Our most successful animal-dispersed plants are those

Seed head and hooked seed of large-leaf avens. This hitchhiker on fur and pant legs is common along trails and sidewalks.

which produce fleshy fruits like berries. Berries are offerings to birds and mammals, who repay this gift by eating and distributing seeds. Here we find the most striking differences between the 2 communities at Eagle River. Only 12 percent of the common meadow species produce berries, but in the forest 65 percent of the common understory plants are berry producers.

The seeds of forest plants are, on average, heavier than those of plants in more open communities. In the dark understory, a seed needs more nutrient reserves to sustain the germinating plant until it can begin gathering and producing its own food. But a heavy seed is a burden when it comes to dispersal, so most successful forest understory plants enclose their seeds in edible berries. This allows for heavier, nutrient-rich seeds without sacrificing mobility.

BERRIES: HOW TO BE OBVIOUS—A berry wants to be eaten, quite the opposite condition from that faced by nearly all other animals and plants, even the rest of the plant on which the berry grows. While everything else is hiding, running away, trying to taste terrible, or wearing armor or spines, a berry tries to be as delicious and noticeable and available as possible.

A berry faces its own unique set of problems. It is a lavish expenditure, and it is immobile. In addition, once a plant fruits in the forest, it may take up to 5 years for it to accumulate enough energy to fruit again. So its berry should grow where the odds are good that it will be found by some creature who spends lots of time in places where that berry would like to have its seeds excreted. And it should avoid being eaten until its seeds are viable; it should stay green and bitter and cathartic until ripe.

It's also a good idea for a ripe berry to be red, a beacon color for birds and primates (including humans) but not visible to insects. In general, flowers love insects (as pollinators), but berries fear them (as seed predators). This is why so few local wildflowers and so many local berries are red. The obvious exception—blueberry—is also the Southeast Alaskan fruit most frequently infested by insect larvae. This may not be a coincidence.

While everything else is competing to survive intact, the berry is competing to be eaten. There are many ways to hide, or be speedy, or be indigestible, but only a few ways to be obvious. Odor is one, but birds have a poor sense of smell. Wiggling around is another, but plants aren't very good at that. A berry can only hang out in public places and be colorful. Thus, while there are quite a few specialists at cracking the intricate defenses of the hiders and runners and armor wearers (woodpeckers tweezering larvae from bark, deer digesting twigs), anything can eat a berry, and almost everything does!

In the tropics, different berry-producing species ripen at different times throughout the year, which reduces competition, yet sustains high populations of berry eaters year round. In Southeast Alaska, where fruits can ripen only between midsummer and late fall, plants have less choice. But there is still clearly a partitioning of ripening seasons, between early fruiters like salmonberry and late fruiters like highbush

THE BEAR SCAT PROJECT

In October 1984 we made a detailed map of the tree trunks, shrubs, and windthrow tangles in a small plot of old-growth forest at Eagle River Scout Camp near Juneau. While applying the finishing touches to this map, we noticed a fresh bear scat composed mostly of blueberries, and included its location on the map. Already, heavy fall rains were dissolving the mashed blueberries into the moss and litter. By marking the site, however, we could return at intervals to see what happened there.

By September 1985, the material of the dropping had washed away, but a plate-sized circle of blackened mosses revealed where it had been. As if to remove any doubt, a small fragment of garbage bag lay in the center—the bear had likely been "Hefty," a local yearling excessively fond of plastic. Rimming the circle was a fairy ring of *Cortinarius* mushrooms. But the most exciting discovery was 150 tiny sprouts of blueberry inside the ring! Obviously, they had germinated from the abundant seeds contained in the bear scat.

We revisited the site in October 1987. Nothing showed where the scat had been. Green mosses had moved back into the circle, and the fairy ring was gone. It hadn't been an auspicious site for blueberries, either—thick, interlocking hemlock canopies passed little light. But 5 of the original 150 blueberry plants had survived and entered the young seedling stage, still less than an inch tall, with minuscule, toothed, evergreen leaves.

These young leathery-leaved blueberries are tenacious. They may endure for years under poor light conditions, prostrate and inconspicuous, waiting for their luck to change. Maybe our next big windstorm will open a space in the canopy and give the go-ahead to 1 of Hefty's sprouts. Our forest is a collaboration of animals and fungi and green things, and every square foot has a history as intriguing as the spot we had chosen to mark.

6mm

7 mm

A forest collaboration—brown bear, varied thrush, and red huckleberry.
Clockwise from top: **mature autumn branch, young creeping evergreen plant,**
berry chewed by deer mouse, and second-year sprout.

cranberry. And some berries persist in winter, like those of mountain ash, a favorite of grosbeaks, and deerberry, under the snowpack with the hungry voles.

Berries ripening too early or too late face problems. In midsummer most birds are still in their breeding territories, too sedentary to be good seed distributors. In addition, most breeding birds forage for insects, as berries aren't often fed to nestlings, who need diets higher in protein. Similarly, it doesn't pay to ripen so late that only winter-resident birds (and denned bears) remain. The ripening of most temperate-zone berries is timed to fall migration, when southbound birds are plundering the forest in search of quick energy.

BERRIES AND GAPS—Everyone who gathers berries knows that more fruit is produced on forest fringes and under well-lit windthrow gaps than beneath dense, interlocking tree canopies. More energy is available to plants in sunny locations. But there may be more to this story. Recent studies in eastern deciduous forests have shown that there are greater rates of fruit removal under canopy gaps than under closed-canopy forests. Berries are offered "where they know they are wanted." And if birds forage selectively in gaps, they certainly distribute seed selectively there as well.

In our forests, Pacific red elderberry is a good example of this process. Young plants are very common on the root masses of recently downed trees, but rare under closed canopies. Red elderberry is a common food of birds such as varied thrushes, American robins, and Steller's jays, all of which favor the edges of forest openings. Birds and mammals that are "faithful" to specific habitat types help, by their seed dispersal, to maintain the distinctiveness of those habitats.

FERNS

Ferns display a remarkable anatomical diversity, from tiny floating aquatic forms measuring a fraction of an inch in diameter to giant tree ferns, which may be dozens of feet tall. Of the 12,000 or so different species of ferns presently living in the world (many more are known only from the fossil record), about two-thirds are restricted to the tropics. The great success of ferns in tropical forests is due to abundant rainfall, and that is probably why they are also such successful members of our coniferous forests here in Southeast Alaska.

Woodland ferns display a continuum of growth forms ranging from broadly scattered fronds (leaves) as in oakferns, through more closely grouped fronds, as in parsley fern or licorice fern, to fronds that are tightly clustered into a circle or rosette, as in sword-fern or holly-fern. Regardless of the arrangement of the fronds, every species of forest fern has a perennial underground stem, or rhizome, which interconnects the fronds. The difference between a scattered growth form and a rosette, therefore, is simply the relative length of the rhizome. This means that when you see numerous fern fronds scattered over a large area in the forest, you are not looking at many separate plants, but rather at a single plant (or a few plants) of truly impressive dimensions. So even in Southeast Alaska, ferns may rival small trees in size.

NORTHERN BEECH-FERN—A good local example of the type with scattered leaves is the beech-fern, which does not grow well in dense shade. It is more commonly found in open areas at edges or gaps in our coniferous forests. The deciduous fronds are about 20 inches long, but at least half of this length is due to the long leaf stem (also called a stipe or petiole). The blade of each frond is cut into numerous pairs of finger-shaped lateral branches called pinnae, which form an elongated triangle because the lower pinnae are the longest. The blade of the frond is held at 90 degrees to the stipe, and droops so that the endmost tip is brought downward toward the ground, and the basal pinnae are actually often uppermost. This unusual orientation may help the fern shed rainwater. The basal pair of pinnae are fused at their midribs only, so when the frond is held with the tip of the blade pointing upward, the basal pair of pinnae droop noticeably with respect to the others. This one feature permits instant identification of beech-fern, since no other species has it.

Beech-fern

Each of the small round structures (sori) found on the undersurfaces of beech-fern pinnae contains clusters of tiny organs (sporangia), which in turn contain developing spores. As the spores mature, the sori darken. When the spores are ripe and the environmental conditions agreeable, the spore-bearing structures split open, and many thousands of microscopic spores are released and carried by the wind far from the parent plant.

DEER FERN—The rosette type of growth form is clearly seen in the deer fern, which is commonest in the high montane forests in northern Southeast but grows abundantly to sea level in places like southern Baranof Island. In deer fern the underground rhizome is greatly abbreviated, and from it arise two very different kinds of fronds. Present year round are the numerous vegetative fronds, which form a distinct rosette that lies rather flat on the ground. These coarse and shiny vegetative fronds are up to 30 inches long and carry as many as 70 pairs of lateral branches, the pinnae. The vegetative fronds are widest midway from base to tip, and are sterile because they lack sori.

The deer fern also produces fertile fronds in summer, in the center of the vegetative rosette. Fewer in number than the sterile fronds and more nearly erect in posture, they have gracefully drooping tips and are up to 3 feet long. The pinnae of the fertile fronds are similar to those of the vegetative fronds but much narrower. On their undersurfaces the fertile pinnae bear 2 continuous rows of sori where spores develop. Each row of sori is covered and protected by a conspicuous membrane, which is attached along the outer margin of the pinna but is free along its centrally directed edge. Around Juneau, the spores of deer fern do not ripen until September or October, depending on the altitude of the plant. In late fall the fertile fronds are shed, while the vegetative ones persist through the winter beneath the snow. In the spring, the sterile fronds of previous growing seasons are augmented by the growth of additional ones, which are added to the center of the thickening rosette.

YELLOW SKUNK-CABBAGE

In late February or early March, before the winter snows have completely melted, the first leaf of yellow skunk-cabbage pokes up through mucky soil in the forest. A member of the arum family (Araceae), it is a distant cousin of lilies, sedges, and grasses.

Spring spathe, nipped by deer at ground level when young, still bears evidence of grazing.

This first bright butter-yellow leaf is called the spathe and forms an erect sheathing enclosure for the thick, fleshy floral spike, or spadix, within. It has been suggested that the generic name, *Lysichitum*, which may be translated as "loose tunic," refers to this yellow spathe. In boggy forests one can often find hundreds of these gleaming yellow spathes rising out of the black muck; the first harbingers of spring, they almost seem to be candles

Mature leaves of skunk-cabbage are eaten by deer, beginning in mid July.

lighting the forest in preparation for the pageant that is to follow.

The central spadix is about 15 or 20 inches long and is composed of a thick, solid, basal stem supporting a yellowish club-shaped spike. Toward the end of March, the hundreds of tiny flowers on the spadix begin to bloom, their anthers splitting longitudinally to release copious clouds of pale yellow pollen. At this time one can find dozens of tiny beetles both on the surface of the spadix and basally where the spathe clasps it tightly (p. 191). These beetles may be eating the pollen, and they could be important in this plant's pollination; this relationship

A MATTER OF TASTE

Despite the cabbagelike texture of skunk-cabbage leaves, they are inedible to humans because their tissues contain long sharp crystals of calcium oxalate. Even a nibble, especially of the young shoots, embeds these crystals in the tongue and gums and causes extreme irritation. But bears, geese, and deer seem oblivious to them. Bears dig up the thick underground parts, and mature plants are staple food for nesting Vancouver Canada geese. Skunk-cabbage is one of the highest-quality plants available to Sitka black-tailed deer, eaten in early spring when other forage is in low supply and when deer are in the poorest condition of the year. In April we've seen places where nearly every spathe was clipped off at ground level. This doesn't seem to hurt the plant. A month later the only evidence of grazing will be a slight wrinkling of the giant leaf tip. Skunk-cabbages may live for 70 years, 10 times longer than the deer which prune them each spring. As other young and tender plants become available, skunk-cabbages are ignored for a time, but between mid July and October, the mature leaves are again eaten by deer.

Native peoples used to roast the roots to destroy the calcium oxalate, after which they could be ground into a flour. The leaves were used to wrap salmon before baking and to line berry baskets and steaming pits.

needs to be studied further. During this time of pollen production the plant releases the odor responsible for its common name, although in all fairness we should note that many people find its odor neither skunklike nor objectionable.

At the time of flowering, the plant's first green leaves also rise above the mud. These leaves are inrolled, forming thick spears, which push up and then unfold into huge elliptical fans perhaps 4 or even 5 feet long. The fact that these leaves are so long delayed past the appearance of the spathe and spadix tells us that these latter structures are produced entirely from compounds manufactured the previous season and stored underground in the thick roots. Green leaf production continues throughout summer, until as many as 30 huge leaves are present in an immense cluster. They are now making materials for next year's reproductive parts to be stored in the thickening underground parts over winter.

By late summer, the ripened spadix droops to the ground and the seeds begin to separate and fall onto the mud. Although seeds may germinate to give rise to new skunk-cabbage plants, probably most of them are consumed by such opportunists as Steller's jays.

ORCHID STRATEGIES

Orchids are surely among the most beautiful of all flowers. Most of the 17,000 or so species in the orchid family are found in lush tropical rainforests, where they are typically epiphytic—that is, they grow on other plants in a nonparasitic manner in order to take advantage of the increased light found above the forest floor. In North America, only about 140 species of orchids occur, and most are terrestrial rather than epiphytic. About 16 species are found in rainy Southeast Alaska, and most of these huddle inconspicuously in our wet meadows and muskegs. The fairy slipper or calypso orchid (p. 192) is an exception; it has large pink and purple blossoms. It is found in the heavy needle litter beneath Sitka spruce trees, especially on small islands, but many have been picked, and it is now quite rare around our towns.

Orchid flowers are typically complex in structure and often flamboyant in color. Many are exquisitely perfumed as well. Searching from the outside of the blossom toward the center, one finds 3 sepals, 3 petals, 2 stamens, and a single pistil (female part). The sepals are often highly colored and petal-like in appearance. The lowermost petal, the lip, is usually broadly expanded and especially colorful; it functions as a landing platform for an insect pollinator. The stamens are completely fused with the style of the pistil to produce a structure called the column. Two masses of sticky pollen, called pollinia, and the equally sticky female stigma are found at the end of the column.

Many orchids are specifically shaped, colored, and scented to attract a single species of insect. When the insect lands and attempts to feed, the pollinia become stuck to the top of its head or thorax. When this insect visits another blossom of the same species, the pollinia are transferred to the stigma of that flower, thus effecting pollination.

In North America, orchids having small whitish or greenish flowers are usually pollinated by male mosquitoes, which visit the blossoms to feed on nectar. These orchids either lack detectable fragrance or emit only a faint perfume. Orchids that are white and emit a heavy perfume are typically moth-pollinated.

After pollination, the seeds within the ovary mature. In orchids, the seeds are extremely small and numerous (over 3 million seeds have been counted in a single ovary). After all the machinations involved in getting pollen transferred, the orchid is content to let the seeds be dispersed by the vagaries of the wind. Orchid seeds are so tiny that there is no room for any of the baggage (stored food reserves) present in most other kinds of seeds. For this reason, germinating orchid seeds must immediately set up an intimate relationship with a particular species of fungus in order to survive.

This orchid–fungus relationship is said to be mycorrhizal. The delicate strands of fungal tissue (hyphae) penetrate into the growing orchid and soon pump in water and nutrients from the surrounding soil. Without this fungal pump the orchid could not survive. Orchids transplanted from the wild will languish in your garden, unless you also transfer a backhoe-load of fungus-laced soil with them. In some species it appears that the orchid seed refuses even to germinate unless penetrated and chemically coaxed by fungal hyphae.

LOCAL ORCHIDS—Looking at 3 terrestrial local orchids, we can speculate about their mycorrhizal relationships. Menzies' rattlesnake plantain (which is not a plantain at all but an orchid) bears a basal rosette of lustrous evergreen leaves. Although the plant is probably associated with a fungus, apparently it achieves a good measure of independence and can at least make its own food via photosynthesis.

The fairy slipper orchid has but a single small basal leaf per plant and is probably more nutritionally dependent on its root fungi than is rattlesnake plantain. It is possible that as the fungus "digests" dead organic matter in the soil, part of the resulting nutrients are passed along to the orchid as a bonus.

Of all the local orchids, coral-roots are the most heavily dependent on their mycorrhizae. Coral-roots get their name because their underground parts look like knobby pieces of branched coral. In fact, these are not roots at all but underground stems, or rhizomes. Coral-roots have actually lost all vestige of roots and are utterly dependent on their mycorrhizae, which plug right into the rhizomes. Mertens' coral-root has lost all its chlorophyll and cannot photosynthesize. The erstwhile green leaves have been reduced to purplish scales. Lacking green leaves, individual stems of coral-roots can readily live in shady places and can grow in dense clumps rather than spaced well apart to obtain sufficient light.

Menzies' rattlesnake "plantain," actually an orchid. A male *Aedes* mosquito's head is buried in the faintly fragrant lowermost blossom.

Comparing these 3 species of orchids, we may see a progression from partial to complete dependence on mycorrhizae. It appears that some orchids are perhaps "burning their bridges" by becoming utterly dependent on certain fungi, unable to survive on their own. This may explain why so many species of orchids are so rare, and possibly why orchids produce so many millions of minute seeds to be scattered at the mercy of the wind—if enough seeds are sent forth, maybe at least one will find some hyphae of the right kind of fungus.

DWARF MISTLETOE

Dwarf mistletoes are fascinating flowering plants that parasitize trees in the pine family, including pines, Douglas fir, true firs, spruces, hemlocks, and larches. In western North America, dwarf mistletoes are serious forest pests because they can reduce tree growth and predispose their hosts to attack by insects and fungi, which leads to increased mortality. Heavily infected trees may have their cone crop reduced by 75 percent or more.

Dwarf mistletoes probably originated in Northeast Asia and spread to North America across the Bering land bridge during the last glaciation. Once in North America, dwarf mistletoes found a great variety of possible host species and so evolved into many different species, each rather specialized in its host preference. Today there are about 40 species of dwarf mistletoe worldwide, three-quarters of which occur in western North America.

In Southeast Alaska there is only 1 species of dwarf mistletoe. It occurs primarily on western hemlock from Haines southward, and seems most abundant at lower elevations. Dwarf mistletoe is a long-lived parasite. It requires at least 5 years from the time of infection until the dwarf mistletoe plants mature, producing a new generation of leafless but reproductively mature aerial shoots outside the host tissues. These shoots are about 1 to 4 inches high.

In dwarf mistletoes, male and female plants are separate. The flowers are minute—less than an eighth of an inch across—and so reduced in structure as to be hardly recognizable. The male flower has 3 tiny "petals," each fused with a stamen so that the pollen sacs erupt through the surface of the petal. Pollen ripens in late August or early September. We do not understand completely how female flowers receive this pollen, but both wind and insects probably act as vectors.

Small berrylike fruits, each containing a single seed, ripen slowly on female plants. In our local dwarf mistletoe, fruit ripening requires about 13 months and usually concludes in September to October. At that time, sudden cold weather can trigger the explosive release of the seed. Hydraulic pressure builds up beneath the seeds, and they are shot away at speeds up to 60 miles an hour. Often they travel 40 feet or more from the parent tree. Each seed is covered with a sticky coating enabling it to adhere to almost anything it strikes. Many seeds are trapped by overlying host branches, intensifying the infestation of that host. The vast majority fall to the ground and perish, but some land on nearby trees and spread the disease. Dwarf mistletoe can spread in this manner through a forest at the snail's pace of 1 to 2 feet per year.

Although the dwarf mistletoes first entered our continent near today's Bering Sea, our local species apparently colonized Southeast Alaska from a source about 1000 miles to the south during the last 10,000 or 12,000 years. This spread into Southeast is equivalent to an annual rate of some 500 or more feet, greatly exceeding the 1 to 2 feet per year estimated from the method of seed dispersal described above, and hints that other mechanisms may be involved.

Seeds mature in the fall when most birds are migrating south, which wouldn't seem to explain mistletoe's northward movement. But several birds, among them the Steller's jay, overwinter in Southeast Alaska, and the random movements of these birds could assist the gradual northward spread of dwarf mistletoe. In fact, seeds of dwarf mistletoes have been found on the feathers of Steller's jays. The jay may preen these sticky seeds out with its bill and then wipe them against a branch, where they can germinate. Jays love to perch in tree crowns, and parasites established there not only are best situated for further dispersal, but also damage the most actively growing part of the tree.

Dwarf mistletoe seeds have also been found in the feathers of warblers, juncos, red crossbills, and robins and in the fur of red and flying squirrels. Birds and squirrels often build their nests in branches misshapen by dwarf mistletoe infestation, where they may frequently encounter seeds. One study showed seeds stuck to the fur or feathers of up to 20 percent of the mammals and birds examined, and radio-tracked birds moved repeatedly between infected and healthy trees.

Seeds stuck to hemlock needles loosen in the rain and either wash to the ground and die, or slide to the base of the needle, where they contact exceptionally thin bark and germinate. Seeds and seedlings of dwarf mistletoes apparently contain enough food reserves to survive the few months which pass

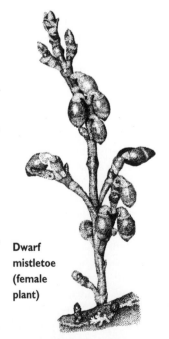

Dwarf mistletoe (female plant)

before they can penetrate this thin bark and begin to parasitize their new host.

Within the bark of the host branch, the roots of the dwarf mistletoe spread through those tissues (called phloem) which conduct foods manufactured by the host tree, pirating and absorbing them. The parasite also sends sinker roots deeper into the branch to penetrate other specialized tissues (called xylem) conducting water and minerals upward into the tree, robbing the host of even its raw materials. Because dwarf mistletoe plants do not manufacture much of their own food, they lack their own phloem tissues.

As the parasite grows, the host branch swells, and additional nutrients are brought to the site, which further favors the growth of the dwarf mistletoe. Its growth also interferes with the normal activity of the host hormones, which may radically alter the regular pattern of branching within the infected region, creating large, bizarrely branched structures known as witches' brooms.

Witches' brooms continue to enlarge in size and may survive more than 70 years. The age of brooms can be determined by cutting the infected branch through the center and counting the distorted rings of wood laid down since the infection began. Brooms that eventually become shaded by continued upward growth of the host may die and be removed by natural self-pruning. Rodents such as porcupines and squirrels also are somehow attracted to the swollen branches of these brooms; they chew on them and can girdle and kill them.

Our dwarf mistletoe occurs as far south as central California, where its preferred host is mountain hemlock rather than western hemlock. This switch in preference with latitude is only one of the many mysteries surrounding the biology of this intriguing plant. It is also unknown why levels of infestation are lower in Southeast than farther south, and why dwarf mistletoe does not accompany hemlock throughout its range almost to Kodiak Island.

FERN-LEAF GOLDTHREAD

Fern-leaf goldthread is another harbinger of spring in Southeast Alaska; it seems the plant can hardly wait for the snow to melt before the stems begin to push up from soft mossy beds in the forest or at the edges of bogs. Early April in Ketchikan or mid-April in Juneau is not too early to begin searching at sea level for blooms of this diminutive member of the buttercup family. At higher elevations fern-leaf goldthread may bloom several weeks later.

Every stem supports 2 or sometimes 3 of the most exquisite blossoms, each on its own side-branch, or pedicel. To most of its admirers, these blossoms look "decidedly unbuttercuppy," as a friend of ours once proclaimed. The 5 to 8 white sepals are about half an inch long and

The football-shaped seeds of fern-leaf goldthread roll down one at a time into the opening of the pod, to be "fired" by a raindrop or a passing animal. Only when the seeds mature do the canoelike pods split at the "bow" and droop slightly, permitting dispersal.

almost threadlike. They are strongly reflexed, or arched backward away from the center of the blossom, and somewhat resemble comet tails (p. 192). The petals equal the sepals in number, but each has a kneelike swollen region close to the base.

There are usually 13 to 17 stamens arranged in 2 or 3 whorls; the outer whorl of some half-dozen stamens matures and releases its pollen first. In the center of the blossom lie 5 to 12 unfused pistils (one of the characteristics that assign this species to the buttercup family); if you use a hand lens to check on the maturation of this blossom over a few weeks, you can watch the ripening ovaries swell and move outward as the little stem beneath each pistil lengthens, until finally the entire fruiting structure resembles a pair of uncovered parasols.

Digging in the soil beneath the stem will reveal the thin, bright yellow roots which are responsible for half of the common name of this plant. The leaves, attached at the base of the flower stalk, account both for the first half of its common name and for the specific name *asplenifolia*, which means "having leaves like those of *Asplenium*"—a genus of fern with rather highly subdivided leaves. The evergreen leaves of the fern-leaf goldthread have blades about 4 inches long and are indeed much subdivided. They are surprisingly firm-textured and are so shiny on their upper surfaces that they appear to have been shellacked. The ultimate leaf segments are sharply toothed. Fern-leaf goldthread leaves are evergreen, and are winter forage for Sitka black-tailed deer.

Fern-leaf goldthread takes much longer than bunchberry and five-leaf bramble to colonize forests after glacial retreat. It's especially common in streamside old growth with a high percentage of spruce and lots of devil's club.

POISONOUS PLANTS

Early sprout and flower buds of baneberry

BANEBERRY—This handsome member of the often-toxic buttercup family prefers moist areas. Often found at the edges of our coniferous forests or along roadsides where more light penetrates, it is usually 2 feet high but occasionally reaches 4 feet. The soft, thin leaves are mottled green and divided into as many as 9 smaller sections; they have deeply toothed margins and veins which stand out in sharp relief below. The stems are never reddish, like those of the somewhat similar goatsbeard.

By late May or early June a congested cluster of tiny white flowers appears on a long stem at the top of the plant. Each flower has 5 white, well-separated petals. Like other buttercup species, the baneberry's sepals fall off as soon as the flowers open and hence are often not seen. The numerous stamens protrude well beyond the blossoms, giving the entire flower arrangement the appearance of a short bottle brush. In the center of each flower is a single pistil with a barrel-shaped green ovary surmounted by a large glandular stigma.

In August the ripening ovaries swell into glossy scarlet berries, each slightly less than half an inch in diameter (p. 192). Rarely, plants bearing pure white berries are found in our region.

Consumption of these enticing fruits is dangerous, as it can result in severe gastrointestinal sickness and even respiratory paralysis, hence the significance of this plant's common name. The poison, protoanemonin, is closely related chemically to other toxins found in different species of the buttercup family. Children should be taught to recognize and avoid the plants.

WATER HEMLOCK—This common local member of the parsley family may rank as the most virulently poisonous plant in all of North America. Since many other members of the parsley family in Southeast Alaska are both abundant and edible, it is especially important to be able to recognize water hemlock.

Water hemlock prefers wet places and is common in many freshwater marshes, along the edges of slow-moving streams and roadside ditches, and more rarely along the shoreward edges of our marine wetlands. A rather slender plant, it often reaches a height of 5 or 6 feet.

Water hemlock leaves are divided into many leaflets having rather sharply toothed margins. A distinctive feature of this species is its veining. Many of the leaf veins run out to the notches between teeth rather than to their tips, as in other parsleys. The bases of the leaf stems do not carry large sheaths, as do cow parsnip and bent-leaved angelica.

In midsummer each water hemlock plant carries a large umbrella of tiny white flowers. The umbrella, which may be supported by as many as 3 dozen spokes, is not as flat-topped as that of cow parsnip; the individual sections of the flowering head of the water hemlock are well rounded. These flowers may emit a somewhat musty fragrance.

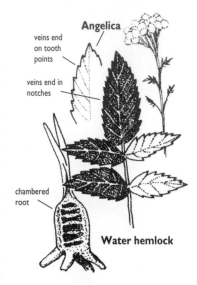

Comparison of leaf veining may help to distinguish the common angelica (upper left) from the deadly water hemlock.

Water hemlock is supported by a large underground taproot, where the poison, cicutoxin, is concentrated. This part of the plant is most frequently responsible for human poisonings; a single mouthful may be fatal. The early leaves and stems growing from the taproot also contain highly concentrated poison. Although it becomes somewhat diluted with further growth, the entire plant should be considered highly dangerous.

Internally, the root of water hemlock is divided into a series of very regular chambers separated by complete partitions. Other local members of the parsley family may also have a somewhat hollow structure to their taproots, but these spaces are not as regular or as numerous as those of water hemlock. Even the roots of edible plants in this family are scarcely gourmet eating and should be reserved for survival situations, or left to bears, who better appreciate their taste.

CARNIVOROUS PLANTS

The comedy *Little Shop of Horrors* has many scenes dominated by Audrey II, a sort of bloodsucking cabbage (Audrey I is the human heroine of the play). While bloodsucking plants exist only in the imaginations of playwrights, carnivorous plants that eat entire animals are found throughout much of our state. The carnivorous plants occurring in Southeast Alaska are butterworts (Lentibulariaceae family, closely related to the Indian paintbrushes) and sundews (Droseraceae family, which has no really close kin).

BUTTERWORTS—Bog violets, as butterworts are sometimes called, grow in the drier parts of muskegs or on wet, acidic meadows. They also frequent the damp margins of ponds in recently deglaciated valleys. The species most encountered in Southeast Alaska is the common butterwort. We also have the hairy butterwort, so tiny (only 1 to 1½ inches high) that it is often overlooked.

Common butterwort, with flies stuck to the leaves.

Each butterwort has a rosette of thick yellowish green leaves that lies rather flat against the surface of the ground. These leaves secrete a greasy or sticky material over their upper surfaces, and any insects landing or crawling on them become stuck fast. Digestive enzymes are secreted, and the prey is consumed. If you examine the upper surfaces of the butterwort leaves, you will see numerous tiny corpses in various stages of digestion.

Butterworts flower in summer, when a single deep-blue blossom with a backward-directed spur and a thatch of thick white hairs in its throat is produced on a stem rising perhaps 6 inches above the dangerous leaf rosette. The blossom is held high above the leaves; it would be disadvantageous for the plant to trap and eat its own pollinators.

SUNDEWS—These *Drosera* species (Greek for "dewy") are also found in muskegs and wet meadows. There are 2 species in Southeast Alaska, the round-leaf sundew and the long-leaf sundew. Both have a cluster of long-stemmed leaves, and the 2 are distinguished by their rounded or elongated shapes. Both species of sundew bloom in early summer. The dainty white blossoms develop at the tops of leafless stems, and the flowers open only during bright sunshine.

In both species, the sundew leaves are covered with a liberal supply of stalked red glands. These glands secrete glistening droplets of thick glue. Any tiny animal that contacts these glands is held fast (p.191). The stalked glands bend inward with their captive toward the center of the leaf, where digestive enzymes are released.

Our 2 species of sundew seem to have different "fishing" strategies. The round-leaf sundew is found in drier parts of muskegs and holds its leaves rather flat against the ground. This growth habit likely helps it catch tiny spiders and crawling insects. The long-leaf sundew, on the other hand, lives around the edges of small pools in the muskeg and holds its leaves more vertically, probably to capture the mosquitoes and gnats that hover about the water.

One interesting question about carnivorous plants is whether they really depend on chance encounters. It has been suggested that they secrete sugars or other substances to attract potential prey, but this idea has not been supported by any field experiments or observations.

But why go to all this trouble in the first place? After all, sundews and butterworts are all green plants with a good supply of chlorophyll, and all are capable of making their own food with the help of sunlight. It turns out that most carnivorous plants live in highly acidic conditions, and in such areas many nutrients, such as nitrogen and phosphorus, are in limited supply. Animals are concentrated packages of a wide variety of nutrients, including nitrogen and phosphorus, and so by eating them, carnivorous plants are able to compete successfully in what might otherwise be marginal habitat.

DEVIL'S CLUB

The ginseng family is a small group of about 70 genera containing 700 species of primarily tropical woody shrubs and lianas (woody vines). Our forest shrub called devil's club is the only member of this family occurring in Southeast Alaska.

Devil's club prefers the rich and moist but well-drained soil of stream and river banks and steep talus slopes, where it often forms an almost impenetrable understory. The roots of devil's club seem to require good lateral movement of soil water, rather than the standing water tolerated by species such as yellow skunk-cabbage.

The generic name of devil's club is partly derived from hoplon, a Greek word meaning "weapon." Its generic and common names are highly appropriate, for not only the stems but also the petioles (leaf stalks) and even the undersides of the leaf veins are armed with brittle,

Overwintering stem of devil's club with next year's bud at top. Leaf scars at nodes on base and midstem show 2 years' growth.

yellowish brown spines up to half an inch long. When you brush against this plant carelessly, these spines break off and penetrate your skin. If the spines are not extracted, they may fester for days. People who are allergic to substances on these spines have especially inflamed reactions. Bushwhacking in Southeast entails learning how to weave unpricked between the stems and leaves.

Why is this plant so heavily armed? The leaves of devil's club are particularly nutritious (rich in protein), and if they weren't so well protected, they might be the preferred food of many forest herbivores.

Each devil's club has several coarse and flexible pithy stems that may rise to about 7 feet or droop to the ground and then turn up at their tips. These prickly stems persist over winter. By mid-May, buds on the tips of these stems swell and open, releasing several large leaves that expand to 18 inches across. While still young and tender these green shoots can be cooked and eaten as a vegetable; they are also sometimes browsed by Sitka black-tailed deer and banana slugs.

The blade of each leaf is shallowly cut into 5 to 9 lobes, each of which is marginally toothed around a single central drip point, which helps the leaf shed rain easily (p. 192). These long-stemmed leaves spread out in a nonoverlapping array to catch the maximum amount of light filtering down to them in the dense forest. The leaves, light green in summer, briefly turn lemon yellow before being shed in the fall.

The flower cluster of devil's club appears in June. Clumps of small, greenish white flowers are supported by a common central stem; the entire inflorescence may be up to a foot tall. By late summer the ovaries of these flowers have ripened into glossy scarlet berries. Despite their enticing appearance, these berries consist of little but a thin skin and meager pulp enclosing 2 huge seeds. They're considered inedible. Brown bears, hermit thrushes, and red squirrels eat devil's club berries, however, apparently with no ill effects.

BUNCHBERRY

Bunchberry is a highly attractive trailing forest and muskeg plant, a miniature member of the dogwood family. In the forest, bunchberry seeds germinate only in places where light can penetrate. In darker places bunchberry propagates by means of a rhizome, or underground stem, forming large beds of genetically identical shoots.

From these underground stems, sterile and fertile shoots are produced, about 5 inches high. The vegetative, sterile shoot bears 4 large leaves which form a circle at the tip of the stem. The fertile shoot carries 6 leaves terminally and will produce flowers and fruit.

In late May the flowers of bunchberry begin to develop. At this time, the fertile shoots have 2 large and 4 much smaller leaves. Between the developing flowers and the 6 green leaves is a circle of 4 large, white modified leaves called bracts. Early in the season these bracts are smaller and greenish, but by the time the flowers are ready to open, they are much larger and are snowy white (like those of some species of ornamental dogwood). Since the developing flowers are dark purplish, the white bracts contrast with the dark green foliage, perhaps making them more easily seen by future pollinators.

The center of the bunchberry "flower" is actually a cluster of many tiny blossoms (p. 191). On each of these tiny flowers, 1 petal out of 4 bears a long bayonetlike spine on its tip. Before the blossom opens, these spines stick upward, forming a spiny carpet over the surface of the flower buds. When the blossoms finally open, the petals bend strongly backward away from their centers, and the spines rotate downward and are no longer visible—a unique 180-degree rotation. We speculate that perhaps before the blossoms open, the plant finds it advantageous to ward off possible pollinators who can only waste their time; later, when pollen and unfertilized seeds are ready, the armature is lowered.

By early August, after the white bracts have withered and been shed, the bunchberry fruits ripen. Each fertile shoot may carry up to about 26 fruits, although commonly far fewer are present, since not all the flowers are successfully pollinated. The orange-to-scarlet fruits are frequently called berries, but technically they are drupes. Each firm,

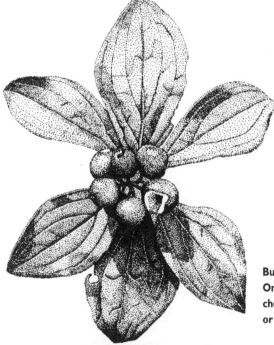

Bunchberry in fruit. One drupe has been chewed by a mouse or vole.

glossy drupe is about a quarter of an inch in diameter and contains a creamy pulp surrounding a single seed. These mealy drupes, not often gathered by people, provide food for birds and forest mammals. In September we've found blue grouse gizzards packed with bunchberry seeds so hard-coated that they may actually need to be abraded or chemically softened in order to germinate.

By the time the attractive fruits have ripened, differential growth has caused the 4 smaller terminal leaves to almost catch up in size with the others. The leaves of bunchberry plants in the forest are evergreen—they stay on the plant throughout winter, even beneath a blanket of snow. Because of their evergreen habit and great abundance, they form an important source of winter food for Sitka black-tailed deer. According to Dr. John Schoen of the Alaska Department of Fish and Game, the leaves of forest bunchberry plants are more nutritious than those growing in muskegs. In addition, many of the leaves of muskeg bunchberries turn red and are shed in the fall.

BLUEBERRIES

Both the early blueberry and the Alaska blueberry are abundant throughout Southeast Alaska. The two are frequently encountered growing together and are quite similar, but attention to a few key characteristics will usually distinguish them.

Both species grow best in clearings in the forest or around forest edges, where light is more abundant, and they are often found together with rusty menziesia and red huckleberry. All 4 shrubs are members of the heather family. Both species of blueberry produce erect perennial stems about 3 to 5 feet in height. Young branchlets have weakly angled sides, and they are conspicuously red or reddish purple in winter. The bark on the young branchlets thickens and turns gray by the second or third year.

In both species the thin leaves of mature plants are deciduous, rather oval, and up to 2½ inches long. In the Alaska blueberry, the branching leaf veins are relatively less prominent when seen from below, and a field lens usually reveals a few glandular hairs along the underside of the midvein. In the early blueberry, the branching leaf veins are more prominent and hairless.

The flowers of these 2 species are quite different, both in form and in time of first appearance. The early blueberry flowers before the leaves begin to expand, in mid- to late April, depending on the length of the preceding winter. This species seems sensitive to a string of several unusually warm days any time after the leaves are shed in the early fall, and it may flower at inappropriate times. On October 15 of one year, we were leading a class of natural history students along a trail near Eagle Beach, just northwest of Juneau, when we came upon several

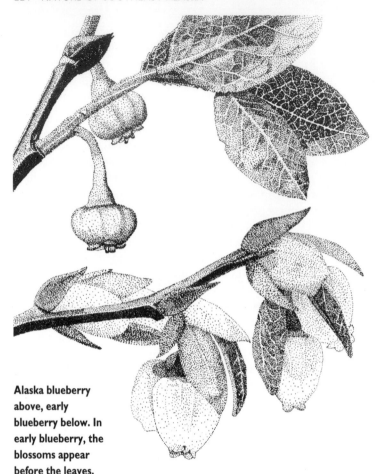

Alaska blueberry above, early blueberry below. In early blueberry, the blossoms appear before the leaves.

bushes which, apparently fooled by a recent warm weather spell, had burst into bloom. "Now, class," we could not resist pointing out, "this is the *early* blueberry!"

The Alaska blueberry usually flowers in late April or early May, when the leaves are already expanded to at least half their final size. The early blueberry is easily forced; cuttings brought indoors in winter and placed in water will produce blossoms in a week, but the Alaska blueberry resists forcing. The difference in flowering time between these and other heather family shrubs reduces competition for pollinators, which are also kept happy by a longer pollinating season.

In both species the blossom is urn-shaped. The urn of the Alaska blueberry is a rich coppery pink. Its slightly squashed shape is broader than it is long, and consequently the pistil usually protrudes just ouside the opening of the urn. In the early blueberry, the urn is pink to almost white and is usually slightly longer than it is broad; hence the pistil is completely hidden from view within the blossom.

The stamens of blueberries are quite intriguing. There are 8 of these bright orange structures in each blossom. The anthers, or pollen sacs, are held upright when the pollen is immature, but as it ripens, the anthers rotate 180 degrees, and fine pores appear, which permit the pollen to be dusted out saltshaker fashion. Such anthers are typical of heathers. We have watched rufous hummingbirds (p. 186) and yellow warblers feed at the blossoms of the early blueberry, so these birds may be cross-pollinators of this species. Other probable pollinators are queen bumblebees, which overwinter and seem to emerge exactly when the early blueberry blossoms open.

The fruits of the 2 blueberry species are also quite distinct. The early blueberry fruits are about half an inch in diameter; they are bluish black with a whitish coating or "bloom" of wild yeasts on the surface. They begin to ripen in July. Alaska blueberries are usually glossy bluish black; they are sometimes called black huckleberries for this reason. They average somewhat larger than those of the early blueberry and are juicier, with a distinctive, almost resinous flavor. Both berries make excellent jams, jellies, and pies, and are often picked and frozen for winter use.

In the harshest winters, Sitka black-tailed deer browse the leafless stems of blueberries. Although not as nutritious as the evergreen leaves of lower-growing plants like bunchberry, the shrubs are easier to find in deep snow, and may take starving deer through the critical period.

APPENDIX

■ ■ ■

COMMON AND SCIENTIFIC NAMES

In consideration of many readers' preferences, we have used only common names in our text whenever possible. For birds and fish, this should create no misunderstandings, since the American Ornithologist's Union (1983, 1985, 1987, 1989) and the American Fisheries Society (1991) have rigorously standardized the common names of those species. Although mammalian common names have not been standardized, they are reasonably consistent throughout North America. We have used MacDonald and Cook (1994) as a source for most mammal common names. For amphibians and reptiles we used Hodge (1976).

Common names for invertebrates, plants, fungi, and lichens are, however, appallingly inconsistent, even among Southeast Alaskan communities! For instance, there are at least 10 different common names for *Fritillaria camschatcensis,* from wild rice to diaper lily. Our authority for common names of vascular plants is Muller (1982). For mosses, since the more technical guides don't even mention common names, we've used Harthill and O'Conner's (1975) friendly guide. For fungi our common names come from Lincoff (1981). For invertebrates we used a combination of Barr and Barr (1983), Kozloff (1983), and Milne and Milne (1980). And for lichens, well—even the friendliest of field guides seem committed to wiping common names out of existence! They do exist, however, and we've dredged them up from a variety of sources.

There have been times, however, when our sincerest attempts to locate common names have failed. For example, there are several unique lichen species lumped under the term "old man's beard." And nobody has thought to give a common name to the moss *Pleuroziopsis ruthenica,* one of our lushest and most beautiful species. In these cases, rather than plucking a name out of the air, we've used the scientific names. We ask that you bear with us and share our commitment to this minimal holding-of-the-line against further name proliferation.

Most birders capitalize the common names of bird species recognized by the American Ornithologist's Union. This practice distinguishes between true species (e.g., Northwestern Crows) and groups of several species (e.g., crows of the world) or generalized statements (e.g., crowlike sense of humor). The convention is useful among birders, and has saved even many professionals the labor of learning scientific names. But for the sake of stylistic consistency, in this book we adhere to the AOU's common names, but do not capitalize them.

MAMMALS

Arctic fox *(Alopex lagopus)*

beaver *(Castor canadensis)*

black bear *(Ursus americanus)*

brown bear *(Ursus arctos)*

bushy-tailed wood rat *(Neotoma cinerea)*

collared pika *(Ochotona collaris)*

Columbian black-tailed deer *(Odocoileus hemionus columbianus)*

Coronation Island vole *(Microtus coronarius)*

Dall porpoise *(Phocoenoides dalli)*

Dall sheep *(Ovis dalli)*

deer or Keen's mouse *(Peromyscus keeni)*

dusky shrew *(Sorex monticolus)*

fin whale *(Balaenoptera physalus)*

Gapper's red-backed vole *(Clethrionomys gapperi)*

gray whale *(Eschrichtius robustus)*

harbor porpoise *(Phocoena phocoena)*

harbor seal *(Phoca vitulina)*

hoary marmot *(Marmota calligata)*

house mouse *(Mus musculus)*

humpback whale *(Megaptera novaeangliae)*

jumping mouse *(Zapus hudsonicus)*

killer whale *(Orcinus orca)*

least weasel *(Mustela nivalis)*

little brown bat *(Myotis lucifugus)*

long-tailed vole *(Microtus longicaudus)*

lynx *(Lynx canadensis)*

marten *(Martes americana)*

masked shrew *(Sorex cinereus)*

meadow vole *(Microtus pennsylvanicus)*

mink *(Mustela vison)*

minke whale *(Balaenoptera acutorostrata)*

moose *(Alces alces)*

mountain goat *(Oreamnos americanus)*

mountain lion *(Puma concolor)*

mule deer *(Odocoileus hemionus)*

muskrat *(Ondatra zibethicus)*

northern bog lemming *(Synaptomys borealis)*

northern flying squirrel *(Glaucomys sabrinus)*

northern fur seal *(Callorhinus ursinus)*

northern red-backed vole *(Clethrionomys rutilus)*

Norway rat *(Rattus norvegicus)*

Pacific pilot whale *(Globicephala macrorhyncha)*

porcupine *(Erethizon dorsatum)*

raccoon *(Procyon lotor)*

red fox *(Vulpes vulpes)*

red squirrel *(Tamiasciurus hudsonicus)*

river otter *(Lontra canadensis)*

Roosevelt elk *(Cervus elaphus)*

sea otter *(Enhydra lutris)*
short-tailed weasel, ermine *(Mustela erminea)*
Sitka black-tailed deer *(Odocoileus hemionus sitchensis)*
Sitka mouse *(Peromyscus sitkensis)*
snowshoe hare *(Lepus americanus)*
sperm whale *(Physeter catodon)*
Steller's sea lion *(Eumetopias jubata)*
tundra vole *(Microtus oeconomus)*
water shrew *(Sorex palustris)*
wolf *(Canis lupus)*
wolverine *(Gulo gulo)*

BIRDS

alder flycatcher *(Empidonax alnorum)*
American bittern *(Botaurus lentiginosus)*
American dipper *(Cinclus mexicanus)*
American golden-plover *(Pluvialis dominica)*
American kestrel *(Falco sparverius)*
American pipit *(Anthus rubescens)*
American robin *(Turdus migratorius)*
ancient murrelet *(Synthliboramphus antiquus)*
Anna's hummingbird *(Calypte anna)*
Arctic tern *(Sterna paradisaea)*
bald eagle *(Haliaeetus leucocephalus)*
barred owl *(Strix varia)*
Barrow's goldeneye *(Bucephala islandica)*
belted kingfisher *(Ceryle alcyon)*
black-backed woodpecker *(Picoides arcticus)*
black-legged kittiwake *(Rissa tridactyla)*
black oystercatcher *(Haematopus bachmani)*
black scoter *(Melanitta nigra)*
black turnstone *(Arenaria melanocephala)*

blue grouse *(Dendragapus obscurus)*
Bohemian waxwing *(Bombycilla garrulus)*
Bonaparte's gull *(Larus philadelphia)*
brown creeper *(Certhia americana)*
bufflehead *(Bucephala albeola)*
Cassin's auklet *(Ptychoramphus aleuticus)*
chestnut-backed chickadee *(Parus rufescens)*
Clark's nutcracker *(Nucifraga columbiana)*
common goldeneye *(Bucephala clangula)*
common merganser *(Mergus merganser)*
common raven *(Corvus corax)*
common redpoll *(Carduelis flammea)*
common snipe *(Gallinago gallinago)*
common yellowthroat *(Geothlypis trichas)*
dark-eyed junco *(Junco hyemalis)*
dunlin *(Calidris alpina)*
fork-tailed storm-petrel *(Oceanodroma furcata)*
golden-crowned kinglet *(Regulus satrapa)*
golden-crowned sparrow *(Zonotrichia atricapilla)*
great blue heron *(Ardea herodias)*
greater yellowlegs *(Tringa melanoleuca)*
great horned owl *(Bubo virginianus)*
green heron *(Butorides striatus)*
green-winged teal *(Anas crecca)*
hairy woodpecker *(Picoides villosus)*
harlequin duck *(Histrionicus histrionicus)*
Harris's sparrow *(Zonotrichia querula)*
hermit thrush *(Catharus guttatus)*

horned lark *(Eremophila alpestris)*

horned puffin *(Fratercula corniculata)*

house sparrow *(Passer domesticus)*

killdeer *(Charadrius vociferus)*

Kittlitz's murrelet *(Brachyramphus brevirostris)*

Lapland longspur *(Calcarius lapponicus)*

Leach's storm-petrel *(Oceanodroma leucorhoa)*

least sandpiper *(Calidris minutilla)*

Lincoln's sparrow *(Melospiza lincolnii)*

long-billed dowitcher *(Limnodromus scolopaceus)*

mallard *(Anas platyrhynchos)*

marbled murrelet *(Brachyramphus marmoratus)*

merlin *(Falco columbarius)*

mountain chickadee *(Parus gambeli)*

northern goshawk *(Accipiter gentilis)*

northern harrier *(Circus cyaneus)*

northern oriole *(Icterus galbula)*

northern pintail *(Anas acuta)*

northern pygmy-owl *(Glaucidium gnoma)*

northern saw-whet owl *(Aegolius acadius)*

northern shrike *(Lanius excubitor)*

northern waterthrush *(Seiurus noveboracensis)*

northwestern crow *(Corvus caurinus)*

oldsquaw *(Clangula hyemalis)*

olive-sided flycatcher *(Contopus borealis)*

orange-crowned warbler *(Vermivora celata)*

Pacific-slope flycatcher *(Empidonax difficilis)*

pectoral sandpiper *(Calidris melanotos)*

pied-billed grebe *(Podilymbus podiceps)*

pine siskin *(Carduelis pinus)*

purple finch *(Carpodacus purpureus)*

red-breasted nuthatch *(Sitta canadensis)*

red-breasted sapsucker *(Sphyrapicus ruber)*

red crossbill *(Loxia curvirostra)*

red-necked phalarope *(Phalaropus lobatus)*

red-tailed hawk *(Buteo jamaicensis)*

red-winged blackbird *(Agelaius phoeniceus)*

rhinoceros auklet *(Cerorhinca monocerata)*

rock ptarmigan *(Lagopus mutus)*

rock sandpiper *(Calidris ptilocnemis)*

rose-breasted grosbeak *(Pheucticus chrysopeplus)*

rosy finch *(Leucosticte arctoa)*

ruby-crowned kinglet *(Regulus calendula)*

ruffed grouse *(Bonasa umbellus)*

rufous hummingbird *(Selaphorus rufus)*

sanderling *(Calidris alba)*

sandhill crane *(Grus canadensis)*

savannah sparrow *(Passerculus sandwichensis)*

semipalmated plover *(Charadrius semipalmatus)*

sharp-shinned hawk *(Accipiter striatus)*

short-eared owl *(Asio flammeus)*

snow bunting *(Plectrophenax nivalis)*

solitary vireo *(Vireo solitarius)*

song sparrow *(Melospiza melodia)*

spotted owl *(Strix occidentalis)*

spotted sandpiper *(Actitis macularia)*

Steller's jay *(Cyanocitta stelleri)*

surfbird *(Aphriza virgata)*

surf scoter *(Melanitta perspicillata)*
swamp sparrow *(Melospiza georgiana)*
Townsend's warbler *(Dendroica townsendi)*
tree swallow *(Tachycineta bicolor)*
tufted puffin *(Fratercula cirrhata)*
tundra swan *(Cygnus columbianus)*
Vancouver Canada goose *(Branta canadensis fulva)*
varied thrush *(Ixoreus naevius)*
Virginia rail *(Rallus limnicola)*
warbling vireo *(Vireo gilvus)*
western grebe *(Aechomorphus occidentalis)*
western sandpiper *(Calidris mauri)*
western screech-owl *(Otus kenni cottii)*
western tanager *(Piranga ludoviciana)*
white-crowned sparrow *(Zonotrichia leucophrys)*
white-tailed ptarmigan *(Lagopus leucurus)*
white-throated sparrow *(Zonotrichia albicollis)*
white-winged scoter *(Melanitta fusca)*
willow ptarmigan *(Lagopus lagopus)*
Wilson's warbler *(Wilsonia pusilla)*
winter wren *(Troglodytes troglodytes)*
yellow-rumped warbler *(Dendroica coronata)*
yellow warbler *(Dendroica petechia)*

REPTILES

garter snake *(Thamnophis sirtalis)*

AMPHIBIANS

boreal toad *(Bufo boreas)*
long-toed salamander *(Ambystoma macrodactylum)*
rough-skinned newt *(Taricha granulosa)*

spotted frog *(Rana pretiosa)*
wood frog *(Rana sylvatica)*

FISH

Alaska skate *(Bathyraja parmifera)*
Aleutian skate *(Bathyraja aleutica)*
American shad *(Alosa sapidissima)*
Arctic charr *(Salvelinus alpinus)*
Arctic grayling *(Thymallus arcticus)*
arrowtooth flounder *(Atheresthes stomias)*
Atlantic salmon *(Salmo salar)*
barreleye *(Macropinna microstoma)*
big skate *(Raja binoculata)*
brook charr *(Salvelinus fontinalis)*
buffalo sculpin *(Enophrys bison)*
burbot *(Lota lota)*
capelin *(Mallotus villosus)*
chinook salmon, king salmon *(Oncorhynchus tshawytscha)*
chum salmon *(Oncorhynchus keta)*
coastrange sculpin *(Cottus aleuticus)*
coho salmon *(Oncorhynchus kisutch)*
cutthroat trout *(Oncorhynchus clarki)*
daggertooth *(Anotopterus pharao)*
Dolly Varden charr *(Salvelinus malma)*
dusky rockfish *(Sebastes ciliatus)*
eulachon *(Thaleichthys pacificus)*
flathead sole *(Hippoglossoides elassodon)*
fourhorn sculpin *(Myoxocephalus quadricornis)*
great sculpin *(Myoxocephalus polyacanthocephalus)*
grunt sculpin *(Rhamphocottus richardsonii)*
kelp greenling *(Hexagrammos decagrammus)*
kokanee *(Oncorhynchus nerka)*
longnose lancetfish *(Alepisaurus ferox)*

longnose sucker *(Catostomus catostomus)*

northern lampfish *(Stenobrachius leucopsarus)*

northern pearleye *(Benthalbella dentata)*

Pacific cod *(Gadus macrocephalus)*

Pacific hake *(Merluccius productus)*

Pacific halibut *(Hippoglossus stenolepis)*

Pacific herring *(Clupea pallasii)*

Pacific ocean perch *(Sebastes alutus)*

Pacific sand lance *(Ammodytes hexapterus)*

Pacific staghorn sculpin *(Leptocottus armatus)*

Pacific tomcod *(Microgadus proximus)*

Pacific viperfish *(Chauliodus macouni)*

pink salmon *(Oncorhynchus gorbuscha)*

prowfish *(Zaprora silenus)*

pygmy whitefish *(Prosopium coulteri)*

rainbow trout *(Oncorhynchus mykiss)*

rock sole *(Lepidopsetta bilineata)*

rougheye rockfish *(Sebastes aleutianus)*

round whitefish *(Prosopium cylindraceum)*

sablefish *(Anoplopoma fimbria)*

salmon shark *(Lamna ditropis)*

silvergray rockfish *(Sebastes brevispinis)*

slimy sculpin *(Cottus cognatus)*

sockeye salmon *(Oncorhynchus nerka)*

spiny dogfish *(Squalus acanthias)*

spinyhead sculpin *(Dasycottus setiger)*

spotted ratfish *(Hydrolagus colliei)*

starry flounder *(Platichthys stellatus)*

steelhead trout *(Oncorhynchus mykiss)*

threespine stickleback *(Gasterosteus aculeatus)*

tubesnout *(Aulorhynchus flavidus)*

walleye pollock *(Theragra chalcogramma)*

white shark *(Carcharodon carcharias)*

wolf-eel *(Anarrhichthys ocellatus)*

yelloweye rockfish *(Sebastes ruberrimus)*

yellowfin sole *(Limanda aspera)*

yellowtail rockfish *(Sebastes flavidus)*

INVERTEBRATES

Arctic natica *(Natica clausa)*

banana slug *(Ariolimax columbiana)*

black fly *(Simulium* spp.)

blue bay mussel *(Mytilus trossulus)*

bluets *(Enallagma* spp.)

boat-backed ground beetle *(Scaphinotus* spp.)

bumblebee *(Bombus* sp.)

butter clam *(Saxidomus giganteus)*

common acorn barnacle *(Balanus glandula)*

Dungeness crab *(Cancer magister)*

file dogwinkle *(Nucella lima)*

geoduck *(Panope generosa)*

golden king crab *(Lithodes aequispina)*

goldenrod spider *(Misumena vatia)*

green burrowing anemone *(Anthopleura artemisia)*

green ribbon worm *(Emplectonema gracile)*

green sea urchin *(Strongylocentrotus droebachiensis)*

heart cockle *(Clinocardium nuttallii)*

ice worm *(Mesenchytraeus* spp.)

intertidal psuedoscorpion *(Halobisium occidentale)*

lacewinged beetle *(Eros* sp.)
little brown barnacle *(Chthamalus dalli)*
moon snail *(Polinices lewisii)*
mottled sea star *(Evasterias troschelii)*
mourning cloak *(Nymphalis antiopa)*
mustard white *(Pieris napi)*
northern rock barnacle *(Semibalanus balanoides)*
northwest neptune *(Neptunea lyrata)*
ochre sea star *(Pisaster ochraceus)*
octopus *(Octopus dofleini)*
painted lady *(Vanessa cardui)*
pink shrimp *(Pandalus borealis)*
pinto abalone *(Haliotis kamtschatkana)*
purple sea urchin *(Strongylocentrotus purpuratus)*
red admiral *(Vanessa atalanta)*
red king crab *(Paralithodes camtschaticus)*
red sea urchin *(Strongylocentrotus franciscanus)*
rock oyster *(Pododesmus cepio)*
rough-mantled sea slug *(Onchidoris bilamellata)*
Sitka darner *(Aeshna sitchensis)*
spoon worm *(Echiurus echiurus alaskensis)*
spot prawn *(Pandalus platyceros)*
steamer clam *(Protothaca staminea)*
sunflower sea star *(Pycnopodia helianthoides)*
tanner crab *(Chionoecetes bairdi)*
thatched barnacle *(Semibalanus cariosus)*
tiger swallowtail *(Papilio glaucus)*
weathervane scallop *(Pecten caurinus)*
wrinkled whelk *(Nucella lamellosa)*

FUNGI AND LICHENS

Black encrusting lichen *(Verrucaria maura)*
chanterelle *(Cantharellus cibarius)*
chicken mushroom *(Laetiporus sulfureus)*
common gel bird's nest *(Nidula candida)*
common laccaria *(Laccaria laccata)*
coral slime *(Ceratiomyxa fruticulosa)*
dog lichen *(Peltigera* spp.)
dye polypore *(Phaeolus schweinitzii)*
Easter lichen *(Stereocaulon* spp.)
false truffle *(Rhizopogon* spp.)
fly agaric *(Amanita muscaria)*
heath lichen *(Icmadophila ericetorum)*
honey mushroom *(Armillaria mellea)*
inflated lichen *(Hypogymnia enteromorpha)*
king bolete *(Boletus edulis)*
lungwort *(Lobaria* spp.)
map lichen *(Rhizocarpon geographicum)*
old man's beard lichen *(Alectoria sarmentosa, Usnea* spp., *Bryoria* spp.)
panther mushroom *(Amanita pantherina)*
pixie cup lichens *(Cladonia pyxidata* and others)
red-belted polypore *(Fomitopsis pinicola)*
reindeer "moss" *(Cladina rangiferina)*
rock tripe *(Umbilicaria* spp.)
scaly tooth *(Hydnum imbricatum)*
scrambled-egg slime *(Fuligo septica)*
suillus *(Suillus tomentosus)*
tawny almond waxy cap *(Hygrophorus bakerensis)*
violet cort *(Cortinarius violaceus)*

western gall rust *(Endocronartium harknessii)*

white-egg bird's nest *(Crucibulum laeve)*

worm lichen *(Thamnolia subuliformis)*

ALGAE

bull kelp *(Nereocystis luetkeana)*

PSP dinoflagellate *(Alexandrium catenella)*

ribbon kelp *(Alaria marginata)*

rockweed *(Fucus distichus)*

sugar kelp *(Laminaria saccharina)*

stonewort *(Chara* sp.*)*

PLANTS

Alaska blueberry *(Vaccinium alaskaense)*

Alaska saxifrage *(Saxifraga ferruginea)*

alpine azalea *(Loiseleuria procumbens)*

alpine bistort *(Polygonum viviparum)*

alpine mitrewort *(Mitella pentandra)*

alpine sweet vetch *(Hedysarum alpinum)*

Arctic cinquefoil *(Potentilla hyparctica)*

Arctic sweet coltsfoot *(Petasites frigidus)*

Arctic willow *(Salix arctica)*

baneberry *(Actaea rubra)*

Barclay willow *(Salix barclayi)*

beach rye *(Elymus mollis)*

beach strawberry *(Fragaria chiloensis)*

bearberry *(Arctostaphylos uva-ursi)*

Beauverd spiraea *(Spiraea beauverdiana)*

bent-leaved angelica *(Angelica genuflexa)*

black cottonwood *(Populus trichocarpa)*

black spruce *(Picea mariana)*

black twinberry *(Lonicera involucrata)*

bog blueberry *(Vaccinium uliginosum)*

bog cranberry *(Vaccinium oxycoccos)*

bog kalmia *(Kalmia polifolia)*

bog rosemary *(Andromeda polifolia)*

buckbean *(Menyanthes trifoliata)*

bunchberry *(Cornus canadensis)*

caltha-leaf avens *(Geum calthifolium)*

chocolate lily *(Fritillaria camschatcensis)*

cloudberry *(Rubus chamaemorus)*

common butterwort *(Pinguicula vulgaris)*

common liverwort *(Marchantia polymorpha)*

common marestail *(Hippuris vulgaris)*

common plantain *(Plantago major)*

Cooley buttercup *(Ranunculus cooleyae)*

copper bush *(Cladothamnus pyrolaeflorus)*

cow parsnip *(Heracleum lanatum)*

creeping spike-rush *(Eleocharis palustris)*

crowberry *(Empetrum nigrum)*

deerberry *(Maianthemum dilatatum)*

deer cabbage *(Fauria crista-galli)*

deer fern *(Blechnum spicant)*

devil's club *(Oplopanax horridum)*

ditchgrass *(Ruppia maritima)*

Douglas fir *(Pseudotsuga menziesii)*

Douglas maple *(Acer glabrum)*

Douglas spiraea *(Spiraea douglasii)*

Drummond mountain avens *(Dryas drummondii)*

dwarf blueberry *(Vaccinium caespitosum)*

dwarf fireweed *(Epilobium latifolium)*

dwarf mistletoe *(Arceuthobium tsugense)*

early blueberry *(Vaccinium ovalifolium)*

eelgrass *(Zostera marina)*

fairy slipper, calypso orchid *(Calypso bulbosa)*

false hellebore *(Veratrum viride)*

fern-leaf goldthread *(Coptis asplenifolia)*

fern moss *(Hylocomium splendens)*

few-flowered sedge *(Carex pauciflora)*

fireweed *(Epilobium angustifolium)*

five-leaf bramble *(Rubus pedatus)*

forget-me-not *(Myosotis scorpioides)*

foxtail barley *(Hordeum jubatum)*

frayed-cap moss *(Rhacomitrium* spp.*)*

giant fountain moss *(Fontinalis antipyretica)*

goatsbeard *(Aruncus sylvester)*

goose-tongue *(Plantago maritima)*

ground-cone *(Boschniakia rossica)*

hair cap moss *(Polytrichum* spp.*)*

hairy butterwort *(Pinguicula villosa)*

highbush cranberry *(Viburnum edule)*

holly-fern *(Polystichum lonchitis)*

Indian paintbrush *(Castilleja* spp.*)*

Indian-pipe *(Monotropa hypopitys)*

Jeffrey shooting star *(Dodecatheon jeffreyi)*

Labrador-tea *(Ledum groenlandicum)*

lady fern *(Athyrium filix-femina)*

large-leaf avens *(Geum macrophyllum)*

licorice fern *(Polypodium glycyrrhiza)*

little shaggy moss *(Rhytidiadelphus loreus)*

long-leaf sundew *(Drosera anglica)*

luetkea *(Luetkea pectinata)*

Lyngbye sedge *(Carex lyngbyei)*

maidenhair fern *(Adiantum pedatum)*

many-flower sedge *(Carex pluriflora)*

marsh cinquefoil *(Potentilla palustris)*

Menzies' rattlesnake plantain *(Goodyera oblongifolia)*

Mertens' cassiope *(Cassiope mertensiana)*

Mertens' coral-root *(Corallorhiza mertensiana)*

monkshood *(Aconitum delphinifolium)*

moss campion *(Silene acaulis)*

mountain cranberry *(Vaccinium vitis-idaea)*

mountain harebell *(Campanula lasiocarpa)*

mountain hemlock *(Tsuga mertensiana)*

mountain marsh-marigold *(Caltha leptosepala)*

mountain sagebrush *(Artemisia norvegica)*

narcissus-flowered anemone *(Anemone narcissiflora)*

Nootka lupine *(Lupinus nootkatensis)*

northern beech-fern *(Thelypteris phegopteris)*

northern burreed *(Sparganium hyperboreum)*

northern horsetail *(Equisetum variegatum)*

oakfern *(Gymnocarpium dryopteris)*

one-sided wintergreen *(Pyrola secunda)*

Pacific alkaligrass *(Puccinellia nutkaensis)*

Pacific red elderberry *(Sambucus racemosa)*
Pacific silver fir *(Abies amabilis)*
Pacific yew *(Taxus brevifolia)*
parsley fern *(Cryptogramma crispa)*
pinesap *(Hypopitys monotropa)*
pondweeds *(Potamogeton* spp.*)*
purple mountain saxifrage *(Saxifraga oppositifolia)*
quillwort *(Isoetes echinospora)*
red alder *(Alnus rubra)*
red huckleberry *(Vaccinium parvifolium)*
round-leaf sundew *(Drosera rotundifolia)*
rusty menziesia *(Menziesia ferruginea)*
salal *(Gaultheria shallon)*
salmonberry *(Rubus spectabilis)*
sea milkwort *(Glaux maritima)*
sheep sorrel *(Rumex acetosella)*
shore pine *(Pinus contorta)*
sibbaldia *(Sibbaldia procumbens)*
Sitka alder *(Alnus sinuata)*
Sitka spruce *(Picea sitchensis)*
Sitka valerian *(Valeriana sitchensis)*
slender bog-orchid *(Habenaria saccata)*
small-fruit bulrush *(Scirpus microcarpus)*
snowberry *(Symphoricarpos albus)*
soapberry *(Shepherdia canadensis)*
speedwell *(Veronica americana)*
spike watermilfoil *(Myriophyllum spicatum)*
spinulose shield-fern *(Dryopteris austriaca)*
spotted gentian *(Gentiana platypetala)*
starry cassiope *(Cassiope stelleriana)*
step moss *(Hylocomium splendens)*
stiff clubmoss *(Lycopodium annotinum)*

stink currant *(Ribes bracteosum)*
swamp gentian *(Gentiana douglasiana)*
swamp horsetail *(Equisetum fluviatile)*
sweet gale *(Myrica gale)*
sword-fern *(Polystichum munitum)*
tall cottongrass *(Eriophorum polystachion)*
tufted hairgrass *(Deschampsia caespitosum)*
water crowfoot *(Ranunculus aquatilis)*
water hemlock *(Cicuta douglasii)*
water sedge *(Carex aquatilis)*
wedge-leaf primrose *(Primula cuneifolia)*
western bracken fern *(Pteridium aquilinum)*
western columbine *(Aquileja formosa)*
western hemlock *(Tsuga heterophylla)*
western red cedar *(Thuja plicata)*
western thimbleberry *(Rubus parviflorus)*
white bog-orchid *(Habenaria dilatata)*
white spruce *(Picea glauca)*
wild iris *(Iris setosa)*
woolly hawkweed *(Hieracium triste)*
yellow cedar *(Chamaecyparis nootkatensis)*
yellow marsh-marigold *(Caltha palustris)*
yellow monkey-flower *(Mimulus guttatus)*
yellow mountain-heather *(Phyllodoce glanduliflora)*
yellow pondlily *(Nuphar polysepalum)*
yellow skunk-cabbage *Lysichitum americanum)*

BIBLIOGRAPHY

■ ■ ■

Alaback, P. B. 1982. Dynamics of understory biomass in Sitka spruce–western hemlock forests of Souteast Alaska. *Ecology* 63(6):1932–48.

———. 1984. Plant succession following logging in the Sitka spruce–western hemlock forests of Southeast Alaska: Implications for management. USDA Forest Service General Technical Report. PNW-173. Pacific Northwest Forest and Range Experiment Station.

Alaska magazine editors. 1982. *Alaska Wild Berry Guide and Cookbook.* Alaska Northwest Books, Seattle.

American Fisheries Society. 1991. Common and scientific names of fishes from the United States and Canada. Special Publication No. 20, 5th ed.

American Ornithologist's Union. 1983. *Check-list of North American Birds.* 6th ed. Allen Press, Lawrence, Kansas.

———. 1985. Thirty-fifth supplement to the American Ornithologist's Union Check-list of North American birds. *Auk.* 102:680–86.

———. 1987. Thirty-sixth supplement to the American Ornithologist's Union Check-list of North American birds. *Auk.* 104:591–96.

———. 1989. Thirty-seventh supplement to the American Ornithologist's Union Check-list of North American birds. *Auk.* 106:532–38.

Angell, T. 1978. *Ravens, Crows, Magpies and Jays.* University of Washington Press, Seattle.

Armstrong, R. H. 1971. Age, food, and migration of sea-run cutthroat trout *Salmo clarki,* at Eva Lake, southeastern Alaska. *Transactions of the American Fisheries Society.* 100(2):302–6.

———. 1995. *Guide to the Birds of Alaska.* 4th ed. Alaska Northwest Books, Seattle.

Armstrong, R. H. and J. E. Morrow. 1980. The Dolly Varden charr, *Salvelinus malma.* In: CHARRS, Salmonid fishes of the genus *Salvelinus. Perspectives in*

Vertebrate Science. 1:99–140.

Arno, S. 1984. *Timberline-mountain and Arctic Forest Frontiers.* The Mountaineers, Seattle.

Barr, L., and N. Barr. 1983. *Under Alaskan Seas, the Shallow Water Maine Invertebrates.* Alaska Northwest Publishing Company, Anchorage.

Beacham, T. D. 1986. Type, quantity and size of food of Pacific salmon, *Oncorhynchus,* in the Strait of Juan de Fuca, British Columbia, Canada. U.S. National Marine Fisheries Service Fish Bulletin. 84(1):77–90.

Behnke, R. J. 1979. Monograph of the native trouts of the genus *Salmo* of western North America. A report funded by USDA Forest Service, Fish and Wildlife Service, Bureau of Land Management.

Bishop, D., R. H. Armstrong, and R. Carstensen. 1987. Environmental analysis of lower Jordan Creek and nearby wetlands in regard to planned airport taxiway extension. A report by Environaid, Juneau.

Brooks, R. C., E. B. Peterson, and V. J. Krajina. 1970. The subalpine mountain hemlock zone. *Ecology of Western North America.* 2:2. University of British Columbia, Vancouver.

Calder, W. A. 1976. Energy crisis of the hummingbird. *Natural History.* 85(3):24–29.

Carefoot, T. 1977 *Pacific Seashores: A Guide to Intertidal Ecology.* University of Washington Press, Seattle.

Carstensen, R. 1996. Southeast Alaska. In: *The Enduring Forests.* The Mountaineers, Seattle.

Clemens, W. A., and G. V. Wilby. 1961. Fishes of the Pacific coast of Canada. Bulletin of the Fisheries Research Board of Canada. No. 68.

Conant, B., J. G. King, J. L. Trapp, and J. I Hodges. 1988. Estimating populations of ducks wintering in Southeast Alaska. In: *Waterfowl in Winter.* University of Minnesota Press, Minneapolis.

Connell, J. H. 1972. Community interactions on marine rocky intertidal shores. *Annual Revue of Ecological Systems.* 3:169–92.

Cowan, I. M., and C. J. Guiguet. 1978. The mammals of British Columbia. British Columbia Provincial Museum. Handbook No. 11.

Craig, P. C., and J. Wells. 1976. Life history notes for a population of slimy sculpin *Cottus cognatus* in an Alaska arctic stream. *Journal of the Fisheries Research Board of Canada.* 33(7):1639–42.

Dauenhauer, N. M., and R. Dauenhauer, eds. 1987. *Haa Shuká, Our Ancestors, Tlingit Oral Narratives.* University of Washington Press, Seattle.

Dickinson, C., and J. Lucas. 1979. *The Encyclopedia of Mushrooms.* G. P. Putnam's Sons, New York.

Drury, W. H. 1981. Ecological studies in the Bering Strait region. Assessment of the Alaskan Continental Shelf, Final Report. Vol. 11. Biological Studies, NOAA-BLM.

D'Vincent, C. 1989. *Voyaging with the Whales.* Oakwell Boulton, Chicago and Toronto.

Emmons, G. T., and F. deLaguna. 1991. *The Tlingit Indians.* University of Washington Press, Seattle.

Eschmeyer, W. N., and E. S. Herald. 1983. *A Field Guide to Pacific Coast Fishes of North America.* Houghton Mifflin Company, Boston.

Foster, M. S., A. P. DeVogelaere, C. Harrold, J. S. Pearse, and A. B. Thum. 1988. Causes of spatial and temporal patterns in rocky intertidal communities of central and northern California. Memoir No. 9 of the California Academy of Sciences, San Francisco.

Franklin, J. F., K. Cromack, W. Denison, A. McKee, C. Maser, J. Sedell, F. Swanson, and G. Juday. 1981. Ecological characteristics of old-growth Douglas fir forests. USDA Forest Service, General Technical Report. PNW-118.

Gabrielson, I. N., and F. C. Lincoln. 1959. *The Birds of Alaska.* The Stackpole Company, Harrisburg, Pennsylvania, and Wildlife Management Institute, Washington, D.C.

Gass, C. L. 1979. Territory regulation, tenure, and migration in rufous hummingbirds. *Canadian Journal of Zoology.* 57:914–23.

Hagen, D. W. 1967. Isolating mechanisms in threespine sticklebacks *(Gasterosteus). Journal of the Fisheries Research Board of Canada.* 24(8):1637–92.

Hainesworth, F. R. 1974. Food quality and foraging efficiency. The efficiency of sugar assimilation by hummingbirds. *Journal of Comparative Physiology.* 88:425–31.

Hale, M. E. 1979. *How to Know the Lichens.* 2d ed. William C. Brown Company, Dubuque, Iowa.

Halfpenny, J. C. 1986. *A Field Guide to Mammal Tracking in Western America.* Johnson Publishing Company, Boulder, Colorado.

Hall, E. R., and K. R. Kelson. 1959. *The Mammals of North America.* Ronald Press Company, New York. 2 v.

Hanley, T. A., C. T. Robbins, and D. E. Salinger. 1989. Forest habitats and the nutritional ecology of Sitka black-tailed deer: A Research Synthesis with Implications for Forest Management. USDA Forest Service General Technical Report. PNW-GTR-230.

Harris, A. S. 1989. Wind in the forests of Southeast Alaska and guides for reducing damage. USDA Forest Service General Technical Report. PNW-GTR-244.

Hart, J. L. 1973. Pacific fishes of Canada. Fisheries Research Board of Canada. Bulletin No. 180.

Harthill, M. P., and I. O'Connor. 1975. *Common Mosses of the Pacific Coast.* Naturegraph Publishers, Healdsburg, California.

Heller, C. A. 1966. Wild edible and poisonous plants of Alaska. Cooperative Extension Service, University of Alaska. No. 28.

Herrero, S. 1985. *Bear Attacks, Their Causes and Avoidance.* Winchester Press, Piscataway, New Jersey.

Heusser, C. J. 1960. *Late Pleistocene Environments of North Pacific North America.* American Geographical Society, New York.

Hicks, S., and W. Shofnos. 1965. Determination of land emergence from sea level observations in southeast Alaska. *Journal of Geophysical Research.* 70(14):3315–20.

Hobson, E. S. 1986. Predation on the Pacific sand lance, *Ammodytes hexapterus* (Pisces: Ammodytidae), during the transition between day and night in southeastern Alaska. *Copeia.* 1:223–26.

Hodge, J. P. 1976. *Reptiles and Amphibians in Alaska, the Yukon and Northwest Territories.* Alaska Northwest Publishing Company, Anchorage.

Holsten, E. H., P. E. Hennon, and R. A. Werner. 1985. Insects and diseases of Alaskan forests. U.S. Forest Service, Alaska Region. Report No. 181.

Hood, D. W., and S. T. Zimmerman, eds. 1986. The Gulf of Alaska: Physical environment and biological resources. U.S. Department of Commerce, NOAA Alaska Office, Springfield, Virginia.

Howe, D. 1984. Bibliography of research and exploration of Glacier Bay, Alaska, 1798 to 1984. U.S. Department of the Interior, National Park Service, Science Publications Office, Atlanta, Georgia.

Hultén, E. 1968. *Flora of Alaska and Neighboring Territories.* Stanford University Press, Palo Alto, California.

Isleib, P., R. H. Armstrong, R. Gordon, and F. Glass. 1987 *Birds of Southeast Alaska: A checklist.* Alaska Natural History Association, U.S. Forest Service Alaska Region, Audubon Society Juneau Chapter, and the State of Alaska Department of Fish and Game.

Ives, J. D., and R. Barry, eds. 1974. *Arctic and Alpine Environments.* Methuen Publishers, London.

Jellis, R. 1977. *Bird Sounds and Their Meaning.* Cornell University Press, Ithaca, New York.

Johnsgard, P. A. 1975. *Waterfowl of North America.* Indiana University Press, Bloomington, Indiana.

Kessler, W. 1979. Bird population responses to clearcutting in the Tongass National Forest of southeast Alaska. USDA Forest Service, Alaska Region. Report No. 71.

Ketchum, R. G., and C. D. Ketchum. 1987. *The Tongass: Alaska's Vanishing Rainforest.* Farrar, Strauss and Giroux, New York.

King, J. G., and K. S. Bollinger. 1986. A catalogue of Alaska's coastal habitats. U.S. Fish and Wildlife Service Report, unpublished.

King, J. G., and D. V. Derksen. 1986. Alaska goose populations: past, present and future. Transactions of the 51st North American Wildlife and Natural Resource Conference. 464–79.

Kirchoff, M. D., and K. W. Pitcher. 1988. Deer pellet-group surveys in Southeast Alaska, 1981–1987. Alaska Department of Fish and Game, Research Final Report, Project W-22-6.

Kozloff, E. N. 1976. *Plants and Animals of the Pacific Northwest: An illustrated guide to the natual history of western Oregon, Washington and British Columbia.* University of Washington Press, Seattle.

———. 1983. *Seashore Life of the Northern Pacific Coast: An illustrated guide to*

Northern California, Oregon, Washington, and British Columbia. University of Washington Press, Seattle.

————. 1987. *Marine Invertebrates of the Pacific Northwest.* University of Washington Press, Seattle.

Krog, H. 1968. The macrolichens of Alaska. Norsk Polarinstitutt. Skrifter Nr. 144. 180 p.

Kvitek, R. G., A. R. DeGange, and M. K. Beitler. 1991. Paralytic shellfish toxins mediate feeding behavior of sea otters. *Limnology and Oceanography.* 36(2):393–404.

Larrison, E. J. 1976. *Mammals of the Northwest: Washington, Oregon, Idaho and British Columbia.* Durham and Downey, Portland, Oregon.

Lawrence, D. B. 1958. Glaciers and vegetation in southeast Alaska. *American Scientist.* 46:89–122.

————. 1979. Primary versus secondary succession at Glacier Bay National Monument. In: R. M. Linn (ed.), Proceedings, First Conference on Scientific Research in the National Parks.

Lebeda, C. S., and J. T. Ratti. 1983. Reproductive biology of Vancouver Canada Geese on Admiralty Island, Alaska. *Journal of Wildlife Management.* 47(2):297–306.

Lincoff, G. 1981. *The Audubon Society Field Guide to North American Mushrooms.* Alfred A. Knopf, New York.

Linsenmaier, W. 1972. *Insects of the World.* McGraw-Hill Book Company, New York.

MacDonald, S. O., and J. A. Cook. 1994. *The Mammals of Southeast Alaska—A Taxonomic Update.* University of Alaska Museum, Fairbanks.

Manville, R., and S. Young. 1965. Distribution of Alaska mammals. Bureau of Sport Fish and Wildlife. Circular No. 211.

Marshall, D. B. 1988. The Marbled Murrelet joins the old-growth forest conflict. *American Birds.* 42(2):202–12.

Martin, C. M., H. S. Zim, and A. L. Nelson. 1951. *American Wildlife and Plants: A guide to wildlife food habits.* Dover Publications, New York.

Maser, C. 1989. *Forest Primeval: The natural history of an ancient forest.* Sierra Club Books, San Francisco.

Maser, C., and J. M. Trappe, technical eds. 1984. The seen and unseen world of the fallen tree. USDA Forest Service General Technical Report. PNW-164.

Mayo, L. R. 1987. Advance of Hubbard Glacier and closure of Russell Fjord, Alaska—Environmental effects and hazards in the Yakutat area. Geologic Studies in Alaska by the U.S. Geological Survey during 1987.

McKenny, M., D. E. Stuntz, and J. F. Ammirati. 1987. *The New Savory Wild Mushroom.* University of Washington Press, Seattle.

McLarney, W. O. 1967. Intrastream movement, feeding habits, and structure of a population of coast range sculpin, *Cottus aleuticus,* in relation to eggs of the pink salmon, *Oncorhynchus gorbuscha,* in Alaska. Ph.D. dissertation, University of Michigan, Ann Arbor.

Meehan, W. R. 1974. Fish habitats. Vol. 4. In: The forest ecosystem of Southeast Alaska. USDA Forest Service General Technical Report. PNW-16.

———. 1974. Wildlife habitats. Vol. 4. In: The forest ecosystem of Southeast Alaska. USDA Forest Service General Technical Report. PNW-16.

Meehan, W. R., T. R. Merrell Jr., and T. A. Hanley, eds. 1984. Fish and wildlife relationships in old-growth forests. Symposium proceedings. American Institute of Fishery Research Biologists and the Wildlife Society Alaska Council on Science and Technology. Bookmasters, Ashland, Ohio.

Merrell, T. R., and K. Koski. 1978. Habitat values of coastal wetlands for Pacific coast salmonids. In: Greeson, P. E., J. R. Clark, and J. E. Clark, eds. Wetland Functions and Values: The State of our Understanding. Proceedings, National Symposium on Wetlands. American Water Resources Association, Minneapolis.

Miller, L. K. 1978. Physiological studies of Arctic animals. *Comparative Biochemical Physiology.* 59A:327–34.

Milne, L., and O. Milne. 1980. *The Audubon Society Field Guide to North American Insects and Spiders.* Alfred A. Knopf, New York.

Milner, A. M., and J. D. Wood. 1988. Proceedings of the second Glacier Bay science symposium. U.S. Department of Interior, Alaska Regional Office, Anchorage.

Mirsky, A., ed. 1966. Soil development and ecological succession in a deglaciated area of Muir Inlet, Alaska. Institute of Polar Studies, Report No. 20. Ohio State University, Columbia, Ohio.

Morrow, J. E. 1980. *The Freshwater Fishes of Alaska.* Alaska Northwest Publishing Company, Anchorage.

Muller, M. C. 1982. A preliminary checklist of the vascular plants in Southeastern Alaska. Wildlife and Fisheries Habitat Management Notes. No. 5. USDA Forest Service Alaska Region Administrative Document No. 112. Juneau.

Murie, O. J. 1954. *A Field Guide to Animal Tracks.* Houghton Mifflin Company, Boston.

Neiland, B. J. 1971. The forest-bog complex of Southeast Alaska. *Vegetatio.* 22:1–64.

Noble, M. G., D. B. Lawrence, and G. P. Streveler. 1984. *Sphagnum* invasion beneath an evergreen forest canopy in Southeastern Alaska. *Bryologist.* 87(2):119–27.

Norse, E. A. 1989. *Ancient Forests of the Pacific Northwest.* Island Press, Washington, D.C.

O'Clair, C. E., and R. M. O'Clair. 1986. Alaskan estuaries. *Alaska Fish and Game.* 18(4):35–37.

O'Clair, R. M., S. C. Lindstrom, and I. R. Brodo. 1996. *Southeast Alaska's Rocky Shores: Seaweeds and Lichens.* Plant Press, Auke Bay, Alaska.

Olgilvie, M. A. 1976. *The Winter Birds: Birds of the Arctic.* Praeger Publishers, New York.

Paige, B. 1979. Birds of Glacier Bay National Monument. A Checklist. Alaska Natural History Association. U.S. National Park Service, Juneau.

Pennak, R. W. 1978. *Fresh-water Invertebrates of the United States.* 2d ed. John Wiley and Sons, New York.

Peterson, I. 1985. On the wings of a dragonfly. *Science News.* 128:90–91.

Phillip, K. W. 1983 [spring]. Butterflies in Alaska? *Alaska Fish Tales and Game Trails.* 12–15.

Pojar, J., and A. MacKinnon. 1994. *Plants of the Pacific Northwest Coast: Washington, Oregon, British Columbia and Alaska.* Lone Pine Publishing, Redmond, Washington.

Price, F. E. 1975. A study of population dynamics in the Dipper, *Cinclus mexicanus.* University of Colorado, Ph.D. thesis in zoology.

Quinlan, S. E. 1981. Winter bird-feeding in Alaska. Alaska Wildlife Watcher's Report. Alaska Department of Fish and Game—nongame wildlife program. 1(1):4p.

Quinlan, S. E., N. Tankersley, and P. D. Arneson. 1983. A guide to wildlife viewing in Alaska. Alaska Department of Fish and Game.

Rearden, J. 1981. *Mammals of Alaska.* Alaska Geographic 8(2). Alaska Northwest Publishing Company, Anchorage.

Reiners, W. A., I. A. Worley, and D. B. Lawrence. 1971. Plant diversity in a chronosequence at Glacier Bay, Alaska. *Ecology.* 52:55–69.

Remmert, H. 1980. *Arctic Animal Ecology.* Springer-Verlag, Berlin, Heidelberg, and New York.

Robuck, O. W. 1985. The common plants of the muskegs of Southeast Alaska. U.S. Forest Service, Pacific Northwest Forest and Range Experiment Station. Miscellaneous publication.

———. 1989. Common alpine plants of Southeast Alaska. U.S. Forest Service, Pacific Northwest Research Station. Miscellaneous publication.

Rogers, G. W. 1960. *Alaska in Transition. The Southeast Region.* Johns Hopkins Press, Baltimore, Maryland.

Ruth, R., and A. Harris. 1979. Management of western hemlock–Sitka spruce forests for timber production. USDA Forest Service General Technical Report. PNW-88.

Saling, A. 1978. The glacier grazers. *Pacific Search.* 12(5):8.

Sandgren, C. D., and M. G. Noble. 1978. A floristic survey of a subalpine meadow at Mt. Wright, Glacier Bay National Monument, Alaska. *Northwest Science.* 52(4):329–36.

Scagel, R. F. 1967. Guide to common seaweeds of British Columbia. B.C. Provincial Musem Handbook No. 27, Victoria, British Columbia.

Schmidt, A., S. Robards, and M. McHugh. 1973. Inventory and cataloging of sport fish and sport fish waters in southeast Alaska. Alaska Department of Fish and Game, Federal Aid in Fish Restoration, Annual Progress Report, 1972–1973. Project F-9-5. 14:1–62.

Schmiege, D. C., A. E. Helmers, and D. M. Bishop. 1974. Water. Vol. 8. In:

The forest ecosystem of southeast Alaska. USDA Forest Service General Technical Report. PNW-28.

Schoen, J. W., and L. Beier. 1985. Brown bear habitat preferences and brown bear logging and mining relationships in southeast Alaska. Federal Aid in Wildlife Restoration Project, Progress Report. Project W-22-3, Job 4.17R. Alaska Department of Fish and Game, Juneau.

Schoen, J. W., M. D. Kirchoff, and M. H. Thomas. 1985. Seasonal distribution and habitat use by Sitka black-tailed deer in southeastern Alaska. Federal Aid in Wildlife Restoration Project, Final Report. Projects W-17-11, W-21-1, W-21-2, W-22-2, W-22-3, and W-22-4, Job 2.6R. Alaska Department of Fish and Game, Juneau.

Schofield, J. J. 1989. *Discovering Wild Plants.* Alaska Northwest Books, Seattle.

Schofield, W. B. 1976. Bryophytes of British Columbia III: habitat and distributional information for selected mosses. *Syesis.* 9:317–54.

Sealy, S. G. 1975. Feeding ecology of the Ancient and Marbled Murrelets near Langara Island, British Columbia, Canada. *Canadian Journal of Zoology.* 53(4):418–33.

Shaw, C. G. III, and E. M. Loopstra. 1991. Development of dwarf mistletoe in sections on inoculated western hemlock trees in Southeast Alaska. *Northwest Science.* 65(1):48–52.

Shelford, V. E. 1963. *The Ecology of North America.* University of Illinois Press, Urbana, Illinois.

Smith, R. B. 1971. Development of dwarf mistletoe *(Arceuthobium)* infections on western hemlock, shore pine, and western larch. *Canadian Journal of Forest Research.* 1:35–42.

Southeast Alaska Conservation Council. 1985. *The Citizens' Guide to the Tongass National Forest: A Handbook for Conservation Activists of Southeast Alaska.* S.E.A.C.C., Juneau.

Stalmaster, M. V. 1987. *The Bald Eagle.* Universe Books, New York.

Stephens, F. R., and R. F. Billings. 1967. Plant communities of a tide-influenced meadow on Chichagof Island, Alaska. *Northwest Science.* 41:178–83.

Stephens, F. R., C. R. Gass, and R. F. Billings. 1970. The muskegs of Southeast Alaska and their diminished extent. *Northwest Science.* 44(2):123–30.

Stokes, D. W. 1979. *A Guide to Bird Behavior.* Vol. I. Little, Brown and Company, Boston.

Streveler, G. 1996. *The Natural History of Gustavus.* Self-published, Gustavus, Alaska.

Streveler, G. P., and B. Paige. 1971. The natural history of Glacier Bay National Monument, Alaska, a survey of past research and suggestions for the future. U.S. National Park Service, Juneau.

Streveler, G. P., and I. A. Worley, eds. 1977. Dixon Harbor biological survey. Final Report on the Summer Phase of 1975 Research. U.S. National Park Service, Juneau.

Streveler, G. P., I. A. Worley, and B. F. Molnia, eds. 1980. Lituya Bay environmental survey. U.S. National Park Service, Juneau.

Tappeiner, J. C., and P. B. Alaback. 1989. Early establishment and vegetative growth of understory species in the western hemlock–Sitka spruce forests of southeast Alaska. *Canadian Journal of Botany.* 67:318–26.

Terres, J. K. 1980. *The Audubon Society Encyclopedia of North American Birds.* Alfred A. Knopf, New York.

Tyrrell, E. Q. 1985. *Hummingbirds: Their Life and Behavior.* Crown Publishers, New York.

Van Horne, B. 1981. Demography of *Peromyscus maniculatus* populations in seral stages of coastal coniferous forest in southeast Alaska. *Canadian Journal of Zoology.* 59:1045–62.

———. 1982. Demography of *Microtis longicaudis* in seral stages of coastal coniferous forest in southeast Alaska. *Canadian Journal of Zoology.* 60:1690–709.

———. 1982. Niches of adult and juvenile deer mice in seral stages of coastal coniferous forest in southeast Alaska. *Ecology.* 63:992–1003.

Viereck, L. A., and E. L. Little Jr. 1972. Alaska trees and shrubs. USDA Forest Service. Agriculture Handbook No. 410.

Vitt, D. II., J. E. Marsh, and R. B. Bovey. 1988. *Mosses, Lichens & Ferns of Northwest North America.* Lone Pine Publishing, Edmonton, Alberta.

Wallmo, O. C., ed. 1981. *Mule and Black-tailed Deer of North America.* University of Nebraska Press, Lincoln, Nebraska.

Wallmo, O. C., and J. W. Schoen, eds. 1979. Sitka black-tailed deer. Proceedings of a conference in Juneau, Alaska. USDA Forest Service Series. No. R10–48.

Weeden, R. B., and L. N. Ellison. 1968. Upland game birds of forest and tundra. Wildlife Booklet Series No. 3. Alaska Department of Fish and Game, Juneau.

Welsh, S. L. 1974. *Anderson's Flora of Alaska and Adjacent Parts of Canada.* Brigham Young University Press, Provo, Utah.

Welty, J. C., and L. Baptista. 1988. *The Life of Birds.* 4th ed. W. B. Saunders Company, Philadelphia.

Westin, L. 1969. The mode of fertilization, parental behavior and time of egg development in fourhorn sculpin, *Myoxocephalus quadricornis.* Report of the Institute of Freshwater Research. Drottningholm. 49:175–82.

Wood, J., M. Gladziszewski, I. A. Worley, and G. Vequist, eds. 1984. Proceedings of the first Glacier Bay science symposium. U.S. Department of the Interior. Science Publications Office, Atlanta, Georgia.

INDEX

• • •

Page numbers in *italics* indicate drawings;
page numbers in **boldface** indicate photographs.

A B O U T   T H E   A U T H O R S

■ ■ ■

Since 1978, Rita M. O'Clair has taught a wide variety of biology courses at the University of Alaska Southeast, Juneau, where she is currently Associate Professor of Biology. She received a Ph.D. in zoology from the University of Washington, Seattle, in 1973. An honorary lifetime member of The Nature Conservancy, she belongs to numerous professional organizations. She has studied and photographed natural habitats around the world.

Bob Armstrong has pursued a career in Alaska as a biologist, naturalist, and nature photographer since 1960. He is the author of the best-selling book *Guide to the Birds of Alaska* and numerous other popular and scientific books and articles on the natural history of the state. From 1960 to 1984, he was a fishery biologist and research supervisor for the Alaska Department of Fish and Game, an assistant leader for the Alaska Cooperative Fishery Research Unit, and Associate Professor of Fisheries at the University of Alaska Fairbanks. Armstrong retired from the State of Alaska in 1984 to pursue broader interests in natural history and nature photography.

Richard Carstensen moved to Southeast Alaska in 1977. He works as a writer, nature illustrator, map maker, wilderness guide, environmental consultant, and instructor for the Discovery Foundation, a nonprofit organization teaching natural history to youth and educators of Southeast Alaska. He divides his time between the backyards of Juneau's schools and the remote wilderness.

Field Guides beautiful enough for browsing

are a specialty of Alaska Northwest Books™. Here is a sample of some of
the books available.

**DISCOVERING WILD PLANTS: ALASKA, WESTERN CANADA, THE
NORTHWEST,** by Janice J. Schofield, illustrated by Richard W. Tyler.
This beautiful book profiles 147 wild plants, with definitive information on
botanical identification, history, harvest, and habitat, as well as recipes. Each
plant is illustrated with color photos and elegant line drawings. Softbound,
368 pages, $38.95, ISBN 0-88240-369-9

GUIDE TO THE BIRDS OF ALASKA, by Robert H. Armstrong.
This comprehensive guide offers detailed information on all 443 species of birds
found in Alaska, with color photos, and a map of the state's biogeographic
regions. This revised edition is the only book exclusively on Alaska's birds.
Softbound, 324 pages, $24.95, ISBN 0-88240-462-8

ALASKA WILD BERRY GUIDE AND COOKBOOK
This book will delight the eye and the palate. Photographs and drawings help
you identify the berries, and the recipes show you how to turn your harvest into
scrumptious treats. A great gift for the whole family. Softbound, 212 pages,
$14.95, ISBN 0-88240-229-3

**ALASKA'S WILDERNESS MEDICINES, HEALTHFUL PLANTS OF THE
FAR NORTH,** by Eleanor G. Viereck, illustrated by Dominique Collet.
Alaska's Wilderness Medicines is a natural history guide to Alaskan and Northwest
plants for health, healing, and first-aid care. More than 50 plant species are
cataloged in detail, including 69 drawings. Softbound, 116 pages, $9.95,
ISBN 0-88240-322-2

Ask for these books at your favorite bookstore, or contact
Alaska Northwest Books™
An imprint of Graphic Arts Center Publishing Company
P.O. Box 10306, Portland, OR 97296-0306
503/226-2402; www.gacpc.com

UPC

51895

6 79536 40488 2